Leviathan Transformed

Series: *Comparative Charting of Social Change*
Series Editor: Simon Langlois

Leviathan Transformed

Seven National States
in the New Century

Edited by
THEODORE CAPLOW

McGill-Queen's University Press
Montreal & Kingston · London · Ithaca

© McGill-Queen's University Press 2001
ISBN 0–7735–2303–0

Legal deposit third quarter 2001
Bibliothèque nationale du Québec

Printed in Canada on acid-free paper

McGill-Queen's University Press acknowledges the
financial support of the Government of Canada through
the Book Publishing Industry Development Program
(BPIDP) for its activities. It also acknowledges the
support of the Canada Council for the Arts for its
publishing program.

Canadian Cataloguing in Publication Data

Main entry under title:
  Leviathan transformed : seven national states in the new
  century
  (Comparative charting of social change)
  Includes bibliographical references.
  ISBN 0–7735–2303–0
  I. Caplow, Theodore   II. Series.

JC311.L49 2001   320.3   C2001–900829–5

Typeset in 10/12 Baskerville by True to Type

Contents

Contributors

Theodore Caplow, Commonwealth Professor of sociology, University of Virginia, Charlottesville.

Juan Manuel Camacho, chief sociologist, Welfare Department, municipality of Madrid.

Salustiano Del Campo, professor of sociology, Universidad Compiutense, Madrid; permanent secretary of the Spanish Royal Academy of Political and Social Sciences.

Nikolai Genov, professor of sociology, Bulgarian Academy of Sciences; vice-President of the International Council of Social Sciences.

Karl Otto Hondrich, professor of sociology, Goethe University, Frankfurt-am-Main.

Simon Langlois, professor of sociology, Laval University, Quebec.

Alberto Martinelli, professor and former dean of Social Sciences, University of Milan; president of the International Sociological Association.

Henri Mendras, professor emeritus, Institut d'Etudes Politiques, Paris; former editor of *The Tocqueville Review/La Revue Tocqueville.*

For by art is created that great LEVIATHAN called a COMMONWEALTH, or STATE (in Latin CIVITAS) which is but an artificial man, though of greater stature and strength than the natural, for whose protection and defense it was intended ...

Among the *infirmities* therefore of a Commonwealth, I will reckon in the first place those that arise from an imperfect institution...

Thomas Hobbes, 1651

There was never any thing by the wit of man so well devised, or so sure established, which in continuance of time hath not been corrupted.

The First Book of Common Prayer, 1549

Introduction

The International Research Group for the Comparative Charting of Social Change, better known as the Comparative Charting Group, was founded at the University of Virginia in 1986 by sociologists and historians from France, West Germany, Quebec, and the United States, who had been studying social trends in their respective countries. These separate studies attracted a fair amount of scholarly and popular attention but did not advance our general understanding of contemporary industrial society as much as they should have, for want of a comparative perspective. Without systematic international comparisons, it is impossible to know whether the trends we discover in national societies are local accidents or features of a larger system.

In the course of time, West Germany became Germany, a research team for all of Canada joined the original team from Quebec and other national teams were added by voluntary adhesion. At the turn of the century, the Comparative Charting Group was composed of small teams of social scientists from each of nine countries: France, Germany, Spain, Italy, Greece, Bulgaria, Russia, Canada, and the United States. Seven of them are represented in this volume.

Each national team has been required to find funding for its own research operations, but a central secretariat has been maintained since the beginning at Laval University in Quebec. Since 1986, programmed meetings have been held at regular intervals, hosted in rotation by the national teams in a variety of delightful places including beach hotels on the French and Italian Rivieras, a ski resort in Utah, the Greek island of Siros, a forest lodge in Quebec, a federalist mansion in Virginia, a conference center in Germany, a winery in Burgundy and central locations in Athens, Madrid, Paris, Berlin and Moscow. The itinerary suggests a degree of frivolity but the meetings have been anything but frivolous. Fifteen substantial volumes reporting the Group's research have issued since 1988, many in a series published by the McGill-Queens University Press; four more volumes in that series are in preparation. Eight other books and numerous papers authored by individual members but based in whole or in part on the Group's collective effort have appeared during the same time. A full list will be found in the Appendix.

Social change is too large a topic to be manageable without further specification. We are specifically interested in the period since 1960, the industrialized or partly industrialized nations and the social structures and institutional patterns that characterize the behavior of mass societies, especially those associated with the family, voluntary associations, work, leisure, education, religion, and government. Our unit of analysis is a trend, i.e. a series of values representing the incidence of some item of social behavior in a given population at points of time in a consecutive sequence. Most of our work is done with numerical series, ending as recently as possible, and covering such matters as family income, household expenditures, employment and unemployment, working conditions, the informal economy, marriage and divorce, household composition, kin networks, housing, migration, educational achievement, criminality, leisure patterns, health care and social movements.

In the scholarly literature, a few trends have received the lion's share of attention. Economists have looked very closely at trends in economic growth, prices and wages. Political scientists have studied twentieth century trends in voting and party affiliation. Demographers have scrutinized trends in fertility and mortality. It is no coincidence that these are the areas of social life which lend themselves most readily to quantification and offer the longest time series. But a description of social change that limited itself to trends in economic development, political participation and population would be incomplete indeed. Even though quantification is initially more difficult in other institutional sectors, many of the difficulties have been overcome in recent years.

The first assignment of each national team in the Comparative Charting Group was to prepare a comprehensive profile of recent social change in its own society, focused on the period from 1960 onward, but with constant reference to earlier tendencies. With the recent completion of the Greek profile, this phase of the work has been completed for all of the participating countries.

Each national profile has been set forth in several hundred pages of text and tables, following a standard outline originally devised by the French team. Thus, for example, the U.S. profile, originally published in 1991, is entitled *Recent Social Trends in the United States 1960–1990*. Its nearly six hundred pages cover 18 major topics and 78 subtopics from "Demographic Trends" to "National Identity" and including a huge volume of material about such diverse topics as childbearing, computerization, political parties, public opinion, social mobility, military forces, vacation patterns, household budgets, crime, and emotional disorders. This vast mosaic of facts and figures is a finely detailed picture of American society in the latter part of the twentieth century but, taken by itself, it lacks the depth that can only be provided by setting it against similarly constructed pictures of other national societies. The construction of national profiles was not an end in itself but a preliminary step towards what we conceive to be the more important work of cross-national comparison.

Such comparisons has been under way since the early nineties with a data set that grows as each national profile is completed.

The first question addressed by the Comparative Charting Group was whether the principal social trends observed in our several countries (at that time, France, Germany, Spain, Canada and the United States) were converging or diverging. The answer suggested by the data was set forth in *Convergence and Divergence*, 1994, and related publications. Most of the numerical trends in these five highly modernized countries are clearly convergent but, because they occur in dissimilar cultural contexts, their consequences are quite diverse. This principle of singularity is the key to cross-national trend analysis.

The next project of the Comparative Charting Group was an inquiry into changing structures of inequality, taking that term in its broadest sense to include economic, class, gender, ethnic and regional forms of inequality and their manifestations in various institutional sectors. The findings of that investigation are too complex to summarize here but support, among other findings, the principle of singularity.

Another interesting research effort, still in its preparatory stage, is the development of a quasi-national profile of social change in the European Union, merging the member nations statistically and analyzing their trends as if they had been a single political unit for the past several decades.

The Leviathan project, our present subject, grew out of a series of discussions, originally initiated by Alberto Martinelli, on the relationship of state and society. It turns out to be a surprisingly difficult topic since (a) neither term has an unequivocal meaning and (b) some of their conventional definitions overlap.

The four-volume Macmillan *Encyclopedia of Sociology* (1992) pays a wordless tribute to this problem by having no entry at all for society; for state it says only "See Nationalism." The older and bolder Macmillan *International Encyclopedia of the Social Sciences* (1968) has entries for both terms.

The article on society refers to "the welter of different and competing meanings of the term." (14, 577). The article on state has this to say:

At one extreme of argument the state is identified with one or more highly specific features, such as organized police powers, defined spatial boundaries, or a formal judiciary. At the other end of the definitional spectrum the state is regarded simply as the institutional aspect of political interaction, no concrete structures are specified, and the state, being coterminous with society, vanishes in universality. (15,149)

Salustiano Del Campo calls attention to the definition of a state originally formulated by Jellinek: a sovereign territorial corporation, its essential elements being sovereignty, land and an organized population. But the definition of a society continues to elude such reduction.

There is no prevailing authority to which we can appeal to remove these ambiguities, but the problem we want to discuss – the relationship of state and society – is real, however slippery the terms. The only way to be sure that we know what we're talking about is to offer our own definitions, good within the covers of this book.

A national society is composed of all the people in given territory in a given interval of time, together with their cultural attitudes and practices, their personal and collective activities, their relationships and interactions, their organizations and associations, their artifacts, their spatial distribution and everything else pertaining to their collective life.

A national state is a particular type of organization that exercises ultimate authority and enjoys a monopoly of legitimate violence within a specific bounded territory by means of written laws, a pyramidal array of officials and bureaus, a judiciary and armed agents. It has an unequivocal collective name, a constitution, criteria for citizenship, a flag, and a national anthem. It coins money, prints postage stamps and issues passports. It authorizes and supervises inferior levels of government within subdivisions of its territory.

In its present form, the national state is a relatively modern invention, usually dated from the Treaty of Westphalia in 1648, although earlier forms flourished in medieval and Renaissance Europe. From Europe, it has since spread to the entire world. Virtually all of our six billion global neighbors are citizens of a state that has all of the features mentioned above. All but a handful of the newest states also have armed forces trained to kill and be killed in their service.

The definition of a national society given above seems to include the state along with other organizations pertaining to a particular society, so that when we talk about national societies in the following chapters we must be understood to be separating from it those features of collective life, like law enforcement, that belong particularly to the state. This is not as clean as we would like but the problem is factual rather than semantic. Some parts of society, as defined above, have only a slight connection to the state or none at all. Some parts are closely connected. Moreover, the degree of the state's involvement in the everyday lives of its people varies dramatically from one country to another.

There is another and perhaps simpler way of looking at the state-society relationship. A state has the defining characteristics of an organization: an unequivocal collective name, a roster of members, a set of named positions with prescribed duties and statuses, procedures for adding and removing members, explicit collective goals, rules for the interaction of positions, a division of labor, prescribed coalitions, a calendar of activities, written or rote records, material equipment, symbolic equipment. A society lacks most of these attributes.

Having explicit goals, the state like any other organization – a commercial enterprise, an athletic team, a military unit – can be evaluated, i.e. its performance can be compared to that of other organizations of the same general type, especially those with which it directly competes. Such evaluation is continuous for commercial enterprises, athletic teams and military units. It is similarly continuous for national states. When an enterprise or an athletic team or a military unit or a state fails to achieve its goals at some minimal level, it must be reorganized, or in extreme cases, absorbed by a stronger entity. In democratic states, periodic elections provide a routine opportunity to evaluate the state's performance. In authoritarian states, the evaluation can be deferred but not permanently avoided.

No such evaluation can be applied to a national society, which has no explicit goals except continued existence, and can not be compared in any objective way with other national societies. Is it better to be French or German? The question is meaningless and even offensive. Is the French state or the German state more effective in governing its national society? That question not only makes sense but can be answered with some degree of objectivity.

Although the public sphere created by the state and the private sphere created by the actions of millions of individuals, families and associations, overlap at many points, they remain distinguishable. A national society exists for no particular purpose; it belongs to the order of nature. A national state is an instrument devised for definite purposes and constantly in need of maintenance and repair.

In this volume of solicited papers, seven social scientists from seven nations attempt to evaluate the current performance of their respective national states, considered as instruments for the achievement of specific goals, with as much objectivity as possible.

We originally proposed to look for a statement of each state's explicit goals in its written constitution. But these statements varied so greatly in form that six of the seven authors eventually decided to use the elegant and straightforward statement of goals found in the preamble to the oldest of these documents – the U.S. Constitution of 1787 – on the ground that precisely the same goals are pursued by every liberal democratic state in the modern world. The seventh paper, by Henri Mendras, uses another time-honored set of goals – Liberty, Equality, Fraternity – to evaluate the performance of the contemporary French state.

The 1787 statement of goals reads thus:

We, the People of the United States, in Order to form a more perfect Union, establish Justice, insure domestic Tranquility, provide for the common Defence, promote the general Welfare, and secure the Blessings of Liberty to ourselves and our Posterity, do ordain and establish this Constitution for the United States of America.

These six categories of performance – union, justice, tranquility, defense, welfare, liberty – served most of us as the framework for evaluating the current performance of the national states of which we are citizens. Proximity in each case entailed some loss of objectivity but provided a more intimate view of the state in action than any foreigner would be likely to have.

In order to maintain the common framework, the authors using the six categories have agreed about what they include:

- *Union*: The stability of the national state, the integrity of its borders and its resistance to partition or secession.
- *Justice*: Civil law, crime and punishment, the redress of injuries and the equitable resolution of disputes. What is referred to in some countries as social justice properly belongs under welfare, but some of the authors reference it here.
- *Tranquility*: The prevention of conspicuously hostile conflicts: of riots, insurrections and violent demonstrations and strikes, culture wars and ethnic hatreds.

- *Defense*: Safety from foreign aggression.
- *Welfare*: Includes both economic management and the provision of human services. The usual objects of economic management are rising GDP per capita, rising average earnings, low inflation, low unemployment, favorable trade balances, the abolition of poverty and the reduction of inequality. Human services include health care, education, child care, pensions, and the various forms of public assistance.
- *Liberty*: The whole sphere of human rights, including freedom of speech, movement, and religion; free elections; equality before the law: due process; and the absence of discrimination against minorities, women, and immigrants.

These categories are not watertight; they overlap to some extent but the overlaps have been noted and taken into account in the several chapters without prejudice to the general scheme. Each of these chapters gives particular attention to the less satisfactory aspects of that state's performance. Each author has attempted to determine which criteria of performance are not currently satisfied and what consequences follow? Since the contributors have read each other's chapters in draft, there are frequent cross-references, especially among the west European contributors with respect to the implications of membership in the European Union for their respective states. In a final chapter, the editor take the opportunity to compare these specimens of Leviathan and to hazard some predictions about the future of the species.

Weak State/Strong Society

ALBERTO MARTINELLI

THREE PRELIMINARY COMMENTS

The first preliminary remark concerns the complex meaning of the word state. On the one hand, a democratic state is a community of citizens ("we, the people" as in the U.S. Constitution), and on the other, it is a set of governing institutions and of elected representative bodies. The very title of our volume "Leviathan Transformed" makes reference to the latter meaning. While I will not neglect the notion of the state as community, in this essay I will try to evaluate mostly the performance of the state as government, focusing on the basic conceptual pair: state-civil society. The time span covered is the second half of the twentieth century.

The second preliminary remark is that evaluating state performance is not a simple task because the scope of state functions has progressively widened since the nineteenth century's "liberal interlude" that stemmed from the development of the self-regulating market. State functions have advanced from the traditional roles of guaranteeing internal order and external defense to heavy involvement in the economy and in the society through the implementation of a wide array of economic and social policies. Although functions have not grown in a linear way, but through phases of relative widening and shrinking (we witness now in several countries a selective retreat of the state), in the long run and on the whole, state tasks have become more complex and diverse, and state bureaucracies have grown larger and more intrusive.

The third preliminary remark concerns the ongoing process of European integration. The six criteria of performance drawn from the U.S. constitution but applicable to other liberal democratic states, that are used as sub-headings of most of the following chapters, should be framed in the context of the European Union. The Italian state, as well as other European states, has already agreed not only to coordinate decisions with the other fourteen member states of the European Union in major areas such as agricultural and industrial policies, but to transfer, together with ten of them, decision-making power to the supranational level in the key area of monetary policy through the recent constitution of the European central bank and the introduction of a unified European currency. The process of European integration changes the criteria for evaluating the performance of the national state by the six criteria, and particularly as concerns the criterion of union. The transfer of portions of state sovereignty by the Italian state to supranational European institutions, and the weaker national identity of most Italians, rather than being considered elements of poor performance in maintaining union at the level of the Italian nation state, can be considered a facilitating factor in the pursuit of the goal of European union which is a declared legitimate goal of the Italian government and of a majority of the Italian people.

THE ITALIAN CONSTITUTION

The first constitution of the Italian nation state was the Statuto Albertino granted by Carlo Alberto in 1848 on the wave of democratic reforms in Europe to his kingdom of Piedmont, and later extended to all of Italy after the independence war of 1859–60. The Statuto provided for a constitutional monarchy and a parliamentary democracy. It recognized fundamental rights of citizens. But it was authoritarian with respect to the powers of the head of the state and it did not prevent the fascist dictatorship in the period between the two world wars.

At the end of the second world war, the democratic parties that had fought in the resistance movement against Nazi Germany and against the fascist government in the center and the north of the country agreed on a popular referendum to decide the form of the state and to draft a new constitution. The supporters of the new republic, who were much stronger in the northern regions, won by two million votes over the defenders of the monarchy. The new king, Umberto II, who had just succeeded to the throne in a last attempt to save the monarchy, left the country, and the first republican president, Enrico de Nicola, was elected.

The outcome of the eighteen months of work by the Constituent Assembly elected in June 1946 was a reasonable compromise among the three major political subcultures of post-war Italy: catholic, marxist and liberal. The values and institutions of free enterprise were affirmed, along with solidarity and equality of opportunity. Confirmation of the privileged status of the Catholic Church went hand in hand with recognition of the central value of work and of the representative organizations of the workers' movement. In the first twelve articles stating the fundamental principles and in the forty-two following articles specifying citizens' rights and duties, all of the basic rights and civil liberties that had been either limited or completely denied by the fascist regime – such as personal freedom, inviolability of the home, freedom of movement, free and secret elections, freedom of speech, association and religious beliefs – were solemnly affirmed and guaranteed.

In the 85 articles of the second part dedicated to the constitutional fabric, the basic democratic principles of representative government, the rule of law, and the division of powers were laid down according to a model of a parliamentary democracy with an independent judiciary, limited administrative decentralization, and a strong role for political parties. It has been said that the constitution was overweighted in democratic guarantees at the expense of governmental effectiveness, but there were reasons for this choice by the constituent fathers. First, the recent experience of authoritarianism led to a stress on constitutional rights and democratic controls. Second, given the uncertain outcome of future elections, each major party was more concerned with guaranteeing and emphasizing the role of the opposition rather than creating the conditions for effective policy making. Yet, despite this imbalance between democratic guarantees and governmental effectiveness and despite the fact that some vital provisions such as regional decentralization were either not implemented at all or implemented only after many years, the constitution was an important achievement, which facilitated a smooth transition to democracy and fostered national unity through the "patriotism of the constitution."

UNION

Under this subheading we discuss the questions of stability of the state, the integrity of its borders and its resistance to partition or secession, as well as the more general question of the integration of the national community.

At the end of the Second World War, and eighty-five years after its birth as a unified nation-state, Italy was a deeply divided country.

Nation-building had been difficult because of the century-long fragmentation into a multitude of regions and towns. Political élites had
failed to integrate the masses through a democratic state and economic élites had failed to integrate workers through a developed
market economy, with the result of sharp economic inequalities, profound social cleavages, and a polarized political culture. And there was
the legacy of the recent civil war.

First, Italy had an heterogeneous genetic code. At the birth of the
Italian nation-state, less than a century before, the country was divided
into five major political entities and several smaller ones. Along with
this fragmentation, there was the traditional cultural diversity of the
"thousands of steeples". Taking language as a major indicator of this
diversity, it is worth recalling that until the Second World War, Italian
was mainly a written language for educated élites and that until
the 1940s the majority of the population spoke other minor languages
or dialects. Even today, there are 13 minor languages and 12 dialects
in use; in spite of the homogenizing effects of compulsory education
and television, 14 percent of the people speak only a minor language
or dialect, while 60 percent know one. Cultural diversity has historically been both a strength and a weakness for the country: a major
source of local pride and a rich breeding ground for great art and
craftmanship on the one hand, but also the source of widespread rival-
ries that weakened the country and exposed it to foreign domination.

Second, the civil war had sharpened political and ideological cleavages, the most important of which was the division between the majority of the people who either did not support the fascist regime or
rejected it when it became clear that it was responsible for the national
tragedy (including about 100,000 partisans who fought in the Resistance Movement) and the minority of more or less disguised fascists.
The anti-fascist majority was itself divided between catholic and non
catholic, conservative and progressive, liberal and marxist, socialist
and communist. And there was another cleavage between the monarchists and the republicans, who blamed the king for accepting Mussolini's dictatorship and for agreeing to the war.

Equally deep and visible were the economic and social rifts between
north and south and between the cities and the countryside. As
recently as 1954, according to the Parliamentary Inquiry on Poverty,
85 percent of poor families lived in the southern regions, and per
capita income was 3.5 times higher in Piedmont than in Calabria.
Italian society was sharply stratified: there were great differences in
income levels, living conditions, cultural values, life styles, and consumption patterns between bourgeois and blue-collars workers, peasants and clerks, artisans and state employees.

The result of all these cleavages was a deeply divided nation and a population with a weak national identity. The very idea of "nation" itself had been distorted by the fascist regime. Patriotic nationalism had been transformed into Mussolini's aggressive chauvinism; there was a large gap between the official intention to create the triumphs of imperial Rome and the reality of an irresponsible ruling élite which shamefully abdicated in the dramatic summer of 1943, when the entire state organization collapsed. The monarchy was also a discredited institution, since it had favored Mussolini's dictatorship and proved unable to lead the country in troubled times or to restore its prestige.

The situation at the end of the war was so dire that one may well wonder why the country did not break up, either along political-ideological lines (through a continuation of the civil war), or along regional lines (by the growth of independent movements such as Sicilian separatism). To answer this question, one must consider the combined effect of several factors.

The division of the world among the three winning powers at Yalta put Italy in the Western sphere of influence, set clear boundaries to the range of political options, and encouraged political realism among the Italian leftist parties, which did not want to engage in an armed struggle and repeat the tragic experience of the Greek civil war.

Traditional institutions, such as the extended family, the church, and the local community, also played a major role in holding the country together. The family and the parish were core institutions in a country where most people still lived in the countryside and small towns. Their joint influence increased during the war years, when, in times of hardship and sorrow, after state authority collapsed and anomic relations spread, they appeared to many people as the only safe havens.

The Catholic Church had maintained a degree of autonomy under fascism. With the compromise reached between church and state under Mussolini's 1929 concordat (the Patti Lateranensi), catholic institutions were officially recognized and the catholic religion became a compulsory subject in schools, and fascism gained more legitimacy among the catholic masses. In the free climate of post war democracy, and by virtue of the 1948 Constitution, which confirmed the 1929 concordat, the Catholic Church was free to establish a powerful network of para-catholic organisations and to increase its influence in various sectors of society under the parent organization of Catholic Action.

But the cornerstone of national union was the constitutional pact – signed by all the anti-fascist political forces – that broke away from the authoritarian past and laid the foundations of the new democratic Italian state. The resistance movement and the national-unity governments contributed to foster mutual trust and respect among the newly born (or reborn) democratic political parties, and to legitimize them as the major emerging social actors. Building on the strong ties and feelings of solidarity developed in the common struggle, anti-fascist parties of various ideological leanings – the Christian Democrats, the Communists, the Socialists, and the smaller but influential Partito d'Azione – represented major political subcultures; they showed a remarkable spirit of co-operation in the drafting of the new constitution. Although they competed fiercely with each other, they accepted the new democratic values and practices and organized the consensus necessary for economic recovery and political stabilization.

Political parties were thus the major actors in fostering political union and social integration. They were legitimized by their role in the struggle against fascism and found fertile ground for vigorous growth in the new democratic setting. The three largest parties proved very effective in organizing mass consensus through ideological indoctrination, the action of powerful party organizations, and the influence exerted by strong collective movements and their allied associations, such as the peasant movement, workers' unions, employers' associations, small farmers' associations, women's and youth associations.

The political parties' strength was due to both international and domestic factors. In the all-out Cold War battle between alternative ideologies and conflicting models of man and society, political participation in parties was high and intense. Political parties were the protagonists of the new Italy and were able to fill the void left by the collapse of fascist institutions and the failure of traditional élites.

A generation of capable and dedicated political leaders and militants contrived to enhance the parties' prestige and form new collective identities. Many people drew a sense of common purpose from the huge tasks of reconstructing the country and building the institutions of the new democracy. After more than a decade of hard work, entrepreneurial ingenuity, fierce disputes, hardship, and sacrifice, the transition to a united democratic nation was essentially achieved, together with industrialization.

But the unified democratic nation was directed by a huge, centralized, weak and relatively inefficient state. Article 5 of the Constitution states that "the Republic, one and indivisible, recognizes and promotes local autonomies; implements in state services the widest possible administrative decentralization; inspires the principles and methods of its laws by the principles of autonomy and decentralization."

The 20 articles of Title 5 in the second part of the Constitution are specifically aimed at defining the prerogatives of regions, provinces, and city councils. The main reason for choosing a centralized state model was that, given the deep cleavages of the country, most constituents did not dare to choose a federal model, but tried to compensate to some extent by wide administrative decentralization.

Actually this decentralization did not occur. It took twenty-two years to create the regional governments and then in a form which made them very dependent on the national government for financial resources. The Report of the 1997 Parliamentary Commission to reform the Constitution proposed a strong decentralization (which was incorrectly presented as federalism). But the Report failed. After that failure, the chances of reform lie in the laws presented by the Prodi government and voted in 1997 by the Parliament which try to implement as much administrative development to regional and local governments as is possible within the present constitution. Given the fact that the state, huge, centralized, weak and relatively inefficient, could not contribute much to strengthening feeling of national union, social cohesion was guaranteed by other actors.

Political parties, the church and the family were the major integrative institutions of contemporary Italian society; they superseded a weak state and made its strengthening more difficult. Parties were the source of strong identities, which often came before the national identity. Religious faith helped to create common bonds among Italians, but it often implied a loyalty to the church that superceded the rights and duties of citizenship. And although the family constitutes the basic cell of the social fabric, family obligations were often so engaging and deeply felt that they interfered with a serious commitment to the larger society.

National union is better maintained wherever an active and resilient civil society exists. But if non-state institutions such as parties, families and churches, are very strong sources of identity, the state as a national community is threatened, and its capability to maintain union is weakened. Today, fifty years after the enactment of the new constitution, Italy is a more united country in terms of language, beliefs and practices, styles of life and patterns of consumption. But if major political and cultural cleavages have been overcome, the economic and social ones have not.

The relatively weak state is at least partially responsible for the persistence of cleavages which, in their turn, contribute to keep the state weak. The persistent economic and social cleavages between different areas of the country and the high tax burden, together with the new problems of an increasingly multi-ethnic society (stemming from large immigration flows from underdeveloped countries), have fueled a political protest movement, the Northern League. The League, which at first demanded a federal state, today calls for the secession of the northern regions. The real threat of secession is very low. The vote for the Northern League is declining and is limited to small and middle-sized towns and to the countryside in the sub-alpine region, with little support in the major urban areas. Only a minority of its voters take secession seriously and the League's leadership no longer talks about it.

Yet the League is a symptom of the state's inability to achieve real national unity. It conveys, although in extreme form, the widespread sentiment among northern Italians that the state is huge and centralized, but weak and inefficient; that the costs and benefits of the state budget are unevenly distributed among regions (Lombardy, by far the most affluent region, gets back only a fraction of what it pays in taxes); that the costs of government and of the political class far exceed the value of their performance.

Alongside the traditional Southern question, a Northern question has arisen in recent years which is complimentary. Whereas many southerners denounce the lack of employment opportunities, the poor quality of state services, the inefficiency of the state bureaucracy, many northerners complain about high taxes, lack of basic infrastructures, Mafia controlled organized crime, and the government's misuse of public resources in aid programs for the poorer regions. Those political attitudes arise from the different social structures of different regions of the country. They cannot be traced to a simplified north-south cleavage. Many people in the South depend on the state for their living either as state employees or as welfare recipients, while in the North as well as in the "Third Italy" of the newly industrialized eastern regions there is a much higher percentage of self-employed persons with a self-made mentality, unwilling to recognize the role of public institutions in their own success. In the Italian Northeast the gap between a booming economy and a dynamic society, on the one hand, and a lack of effective government, on the other, is particularly evident.

If we consider the cleavages of Italian society at the end of World War II, the present degree of union rates rather high. If we consider the persistent economic and social divisions, the weak sense of national identity, and the secessionist tendencies, we may settle somewhere in the middle, with the proviso that the whole question of union must be framed in the larger context of European supra-national integration, where "negative" elements such as a weak national identity can become "positive" potentialities for overcoming nationalistic resistance to a unified Europe.

JUSTICE

Justice is a basic value of social life and can be understood two ways: as justice before the law, and as social justice. I will discuss it here in the former sense, while the latter will be covered in the section on welfare.

The confidence of the people at large in the judiciary (as well as in the other law enforcement agencies) and in the fairness of the judicial system has increased in Italy in recent years. The main reason is the initiative taken by some public prosecutors, first in Milan and then in other Italian cities, against political corruption – the so called "clean hands" investigations. These investigations have, at least to some extent, conveyed the impression that citizens are really equal before the law and that powerful people can be prosecuted and even punished.

Yet, in despite this widespread sentiment, the Italian state's capacity to "establish justice" and enforce the law cannot be considered satisfactory, for a variety of reasons. First of all, Italy has a huge, excessive number of laws which make the regulation of behavior an intricate matter open to abuse. Second, the structure of law enforcement agencies is excessively complex; there are three degrees of judgement both in criminal and in civil law – under the Supreme Court level – and judgements are made effective only after the second degree; in the judiciary there is no distinction of roles between public prosecutors and judges; the hundreds of thousands of police officers are divided into three major corps (Polizia, Carabinieri and Guardia di Finanza) often competing with each other and lacking coordination.

Third, the judicial process takes too long – with the exception of labor disputes which according to a special law must be decided quickly. The process is in many cases too expensive, so that the differential ability of citizens to pay legal fees amounts to de facto discrimination – again with the exception of labor disputes and to some extent of family cases. Although the oversupply of lawyers has kept the price of legal services in check, legal fees are generally too high because of the length of the process and of applicable taxes.

Fourth, although according to Article 24 of the Constitution, all can act in court in order to defend their rights and legitimate interests, Article 112 states that public prosecutors must take legal action for any criminal offense, with the result that law enforcement is in fact often subject to the arbitrary initiative of a given prosecutor.

Fifth, law enforcement shows big differences in space and in time: the probability of being arrested and sentenced for a given crime varies greatly from one region of the country to another; and the degree of law enforcement in specific areas, for instance, political corruption, varies greatly from time to time according to the climate of public opinion, the strength of political parties, the culture of judges and prosecutors, and the linkages of the judicial elite with the business and political elites.

Current political debate in Italy has focused on the relation between the judiciary and the other two branches of government, rather than on the necessary reforms to make the establishment of justice more effective and fair. The former question is certainly important, but the latter is more so.

On the basis of Montesqiueu's famous tripartition of powers and recalling the subordination of the judiciary to Mussolini's dictatorial power during the fascist regime, the democratic Italian Constitution establishes the complete independence of the judiciary. According to Article 104, the judiciary is an autonomous order independent of any other type of power. It governs itself through a constitutional body, the Consiglio superiore della magistratura, chaired by the President of the Republic, in which two-thirds of the members are elected by all the ordinary magistrates and the other third by Parliament from among law professors and experienced lawyers. The members of the judiciary are nominated in public national competitions based on credentials and examinations; their careers are regulated by their self-governing body; public prosecutors and judges in different courts belong to the same order with the same status, stipend, and career patterns, and differ only in terms of their actual functions.

The constitutional debate focuses on the separation of careers between public prosecutors and judges, and on the respective roles of the minister of justice and of the magistrates' self-governing body in defining the tasks, careers and performances of the members of the judiciary. The position of those aiming at changing the Constitution – who want to reduce the independence of the judiciary and to introduce separate careers for public prosecutors and judges – was weakened by the fact that their most aggressive spokesman, the political leader of the center-right coalition, was himself under investigation and already sentenced for political corruption. The defenders of the present Constitution – most of them belonging to the center-left coalition – were attacked on the ground that they wanted to defend the status quo since most magistrates are ideologically close to themselves and treat them more leniently in the political corruption investigations. The unresolved question of the degree of independence to be granted to the judiciary was the major cause of the failure of the 1997 Parliamentary Commission on Constitutional Reform. A popular referendum on the separation of functions between public prosecutors and judges took place in May 2000.

The constitutional role of the juduciary is only one of the causes of the unsatisfactory performance of the Italian state in the establishment of justice. For the average citizen the central questions are not the degree of independence of the judiciary from the executive branch of government but the length of trials, the cost of legal services, the effectiveness of law enforcement in the pursuit of criminal offences, and, in general, the fairness of the judicial system.

For all those reasons, the nation's performance on justice must be evaluated as poor, in spite of recent achievements in fighting political corruption.

TRANQUILITY

In defining the framework of our comparative analysis, we agreed that the criterion of domestic tranquility implies:

- that acute internal conflicts, such as riots, insurrections, and violent demonstrations, are prevented;
- that the safety of persons and property can be guaranteed;
- that private and public transactions are conducted with civility, and that citizens are mutually respectful.

Conflict is an intrinsic component of social relations, which can have positive effects in market competition in the democratic polity, as a safety valve for accumulated tensions and as a way to express legitimate claims. But for society to be possible, conflict must be regulated and held in check. Conflict regulation is one of the main tasks of a well-performing state.

Riots, insurrections and violent demonstrations

In contrast to previous times – especially to the years after the first and the second world wars – there are today no organized movements or parties of any consequence on either the extreme right or the extreme left of the political spectrum, that seek to overthrow Italy's democratic form of government. In spite of complaints about the performance of state institutions and declining confidence in political parties, the values, attitudes, and rules of the game of political democracy have been internalized by the vast majority of Italians.

The present tranquility is in sharp contrast to the successive waves of violent conflicts and demonstrations that took place in the half century after the end of the Second World War. First, there was the spillover of the civil war in the months following the defeat of fascism;

then, in the late 1940s and in the 1950s, there were the demonstrations of landless peasants in the South demanding land reform, and the protests of factory workers in the North asking for higher wages and better working conditions – both of which were violently repressed by anti-riot police.

In 1960, mass demonstrations erupted in Northern Italy in reaction to the formation of the Tambroni government which had the support of the neo-fascist party, mostly in Genoa, where that party wanted to organize its congress, and in Reggio Emilia where demonstrators were killed by the police. Tambroni resigned and the door was opened for center-left governments. With the mass strikes of the economic boom years in the early 1960s, labor disputes started to change significantly. Unions grew stronger, more autonomous, and more concerned with specific union demands than with general political strategies while the new center-left governments adopted less violent forms of prevention and control, and passed reformist labor laws.

At the end of the 1960s, a new wave of collective protest erupted in Italy. As in many other Western countries, students protested against authoritarian tendencies in the school, the family, and the society in general, as well as against the Vietnam War and the foreign policies of the U.S. and its allied Western governments. Youth protest was common to the western world. It was a generational revolt, anti-authoritarian, and highly symbolic. The major features of the Italian student movement, as compared with the American one, were its ideological character and its linkage with workers' radicalism. Whereas American students' protest stressed the moral incoherence between declared principles and political practices, the Italian protest was framed in ideological terms and fragmented into marxist and leftist sects.

In Italy, a workers' movement developed alongside the students' one. It erupted in the so-called "hot autumn" of 1969 and continued in the early 1970s. It was stirred by student protests but it had its own logic. It resulted from the alliance of two different types of industrial workers: the more skilled, unionized and politically indoctrinated workers of the North and the younger, former peasant, recently immigrated workers of the South, who were not accustomed to industrial work and suffered from the hardships of newcomers in large industrial cities.

The state response was flexible, but also weak and incoherent. It avoided illiberal over-reactions, but the weak coalition governments were unable to implement adequate reforms either in educational or labor policies. Under the influence of radical protests, Parliament passed legislation in education such as the law which liberalized access to higher education (without implementing badly needed reforms of the academic institutions involved) and in labor relations with the so-called statute of workers which, along with the recognition of basic workers' rights, introduced heavy constraints on entrepreneurial activity.

Law enforcement agencies reacted with violent repression in a few instances, but more often with insufficient firmness in defending democratic legality.

What was worse, the government was unable to prevent segments of the secret services from involvement in mass murder attacks with bombs in banks, train stations and public squares while right wing terrorist groups in the so-called "strategy of tension", tried to provoke a coup d'état for the purpose of restoring order. Those attacks fostered the counter violence of left wing terrorist groups like the "Red Brigades" which kidnapped and murdered key managers, state officers, and intellectuals, in an escalation of violence that culminated in 1978 in the kidnapping and murder of Aldo Moro, the leader of the Christian Democrats. Terrorism continued until the mid 1980s and then ebbed away, leaving behind a legacy of blood, destroyed lives, and shattered ideologies. The recent murder of an advisor of the D'Alema government by self-proclaimed heirs of the Red Brigades raised fears of a resurgence of terrorism, but the group seems totally isolated. On the whole, democratic institutions and democratic sentiments survived these assaults.

Today, riots, insurrections and violent demonstrations have almost disappeared. The Northern League often uses a violent language of secession and struggle for independence from Rome, but its leadership is very careful in controlling militants' behavior. Radical fringes of the youth movement sometimes occupy empty buildings and brawl with police, but with limited violence. Students sometimes occupy schools, but enjoy the benign neglect of teachers, parents and public opinion.

Public safety

A continuous rise in crime occurred in recent decades. It has been ascribed to rapid and intense economic growth and related social transformations. And it is now more and more influenced by globalization, as in the case of international drug traffic, prostitution, and car theft. In the 1991–95 period, the number of reported crimes for which the judiciary enacted a penal sanction increased by 30 percent over the previous five years. Even higher increases occurred for voluntary murders (42.2 percent), the production and sales of drugs (37.6 percent), and thefts (33 percent).

In 1995 the total number of persons charged was 565,366, of whom 25,683 were youth under 18. The general crime rate was around 10,000 delicts per 1,000,000 inhabitants. The total number of people convicted in 1995 was 204,481. The total number of inmates in national prisons in 1995 was 47,759, of whom about 60 percent were there because of a court's sentence, and the others were awaiting judgement and restricted because they were either dangerous to others or expected to destroy evidence. Although the number of inmates has not increased significantly in recent years, several prisons in large cities are overcrowded.

In assessing criminal behavior, two major distinctions should be made, between big organized crime and small crime, and between regions and social groups with high criminal density and regions and groups with low criminal density. As far as the first distinction is concerned, the organized crime of "mafia," "camorra" and "drangheta" has been a long lasting problem of Italian society. These organizations, based in the south and rooted at first in the social relations of the countryside, have progressively extended into urban areas and into other regions of the country. Their spread was facilitated by increased economic and social links such as migration, but also by a very unwise law that interned "mafiosi" in distant villages and small towns that did not have significant criminal activity. The intended purpose was to separate criminals from their environment, but the unintended consequence was to introduce their activities into new areas.

The various mafias were able to exploit opportunities stemming from economic growth and patronage politics. They run successful criminal businesses, from public works contracts to the control of the drug trade, from kidnapping to the control of prostitution. And they have developed ties with segments of the party system that rely on patronage politics to organize consensus, and on political corruption to obtain extra resources in the competition for political power. Mafias have also been successful in building multinational criminal organizations and developing strong ties with other countries' delinquent associations, as the Sicilian mafia did with the Italo-American mafia, mostly for drug dealing, and the "Santa corona unita" of Puglia did with Albanians and Eastern Mediterranean criminal associations in the transportation of illegal immigrants.

In recent years there has been an escalation in the state's fight against big crime. More determined judiciary and police action at first provoked a mafia reaction that cost the lives of several state officials, among them General Dalla Chiesa, "prefetto" of Palermo, and the two most prominent public prosecutors, Falcone and Borsellino. Then the tide changed. An outraged public created a climate more favorable to effective state repression of mafia activities. A new law granting reduced sentences for "mafiosi" willing to cooperate with judiciary investigations helped to break the conspiracy of silence within the organization. Several big bosses of the criminal organizations were caught and sentenced to long prison terms. More human and financial resources were invested in the fight against crime. As a result, mafias have been greatly weakened, although by no means eliminated.

While big organized crime has been successfully attacked, small crime is on the rise. Thefts by deviant youngsters, drug addicts, and non-integrated immigrants are on a continuous rise. People feel less safe in their daily lives, although great differences exist between sectors and areas.

Large cities show much higher crime rates than the rest of the country, 6.4 times higher for robberies, 3.6 times higher for the production and sale of drugs, 3.1 times higher for thefts, according to 1996 data. We can supplement these objective data with an appropriate subjective indicator such as the perception of risk for public safety. According to a recent survey (Istat, 1997–98), 29 percent of Italians do not feel safe walking alone when dark in the streets of their own neighborhood. Women feel more insecure than men (40 percent vs. 17 percent), and young women feel the most insecure of all (50 percent for those 14 to 17 years old, and 45 percent for those 18 to 24 years old). The region with the most fear is Naples, where 42 percent of the people feel unsafe when walking alone in the dark, 27 percent when going back to the car, and 16 percent even when they are alone at home in the evening. Significant percentages report having had a direct experience of crime: 19 percent of the people interviewed report having witnessed drug users, 10 percent drug pushers, 13 percent prostitutes at work, and 34 percent acts of vandalism against public property. Moreover, 54 percent of families have some sort of protection for their homes, such as alarm systems, armored doors, window bars, and safety boxes, with higher percentages – between 60 and 70 percent – in the wealthiest regions (Lombardy, Piedmont, Emilia and the region of Rome).

Finally, 42 percent of the people think that police forces cannot control criminal behaviour in their living areas, with higher percentages in the metropolitan areas (52 percent). Public safety is thus a rather unevenly distributed common good. Alongside the well known social problems of metropolitan areas there are "happy islands", mostly in small and medium cities of the central and northern regions where criminal activity is low due to greater social cohesion and community control.

Civility and mutual respect

Much of the answer to this question depends on how we define civility and mutual respect, and which indicators we select for measuring them. If we define them as tolerance – a major dimension of social life in multicultural societies – we witness significant improvements in Italian society in recent decades, and we have to acknowledge that state institutions, such as public schools and public television, have contributed to it. Tolerance for different political views and opinions has increased, and ideological polarization has diminished. Both religious fundamentalism and anti-clericalism have decreased. Deviant sexual behavior is increasingly accepted.

If, on the other hand, we consider other basic expressions of civility and mutual respect such as caring for public places and the natural environment, abiding by the norms of car driving, engaging in rational and civic political debate, we must assign low scores. Civic ethics are not widespread. Strong particular loyalties leave little space for a common identity. Too many Italians still consider what is public – such as parks, beaches, natural parks – a resource to be exploited, rather than a common good to be preserved.

State institutions do little to change these uncivic behaviors. In the 6th to 8th grade of compulsory school a course in Civic Education is taught, but it is generally boring and largely irrelevant. Even when the school tries to teach youngsters to respect formal and informal norms of behavior in public places, the bad examples given in daily life by their parents and other adults often undo that instruction. Car driving is a typical example in this respect. Italy has one of the worst records in Europe with respect to vehicular accidents and the trend is on the rise.

A special case for evaluating civility and mutual respect is the attitude toward foreign immigrants. In the last 25 years Italy has shifted from a labor exporting to a labor importing country. According to the most reliable statistical estimates, at the end of 1997 there were 928,000 foreigners with legal permits of entry, most of them from underdeveloped countries outside the Europian Union (an estimated 250,000 to 300,000 irregular immigrants must be added to these regular entries).

In contrast to the post-war decades, this immigration takes place at a time when European developed countries are suffering from structural unemployment. Migrations are caused more by push factors-such as demographic overcrowding, economic hardship, discrimination against minorities and the repression of political dissent – than by pull factors, like an expanding labor market. The predominance of push factors in many immigrants' decisions to migrate provokes problems of social and cultural integration.

As a newcomer among countries of immigration, Italy trails other developed countries in the necessary laws, policies, and administrative structures, although the gap is narrowing. On the other hand, Italy enjoys the latecomer advantage of learning from others' achievements and shortcomings, while the recollection of their own emigrant experiences make many Italians more tolerant than others. Some institutions, especially schools, show a remarkable ability to integrate, and episodes of xenophobia have been rather rare. But problems tend to become more severe and tensions more widespread with the increasing number of immigrants, especially clandestine and criminal immigrants.

DEFENSE

Defense has been a major concern for Italy, but not a major role for the Italian state in recent years. During the cold war years and in the general confrontation between the two superpowers, Italy held a strategic position; it was a "frontier region" at the center of the Southern flank of NATO. But it was the opinion of the US and NATO that the major responsibility for the defense of this strategic position could not be left to the Italian armed forces.

The Italian army had deteriorated under fascism, losing the prestige it had gained during the national independence wars (the Risorgimento) and in the victorious first world war. First, the colonial war against Ethiopia led to Italy' s international isolation in the 1930s. Then its military collapse in the second world war destroyed the social prestige and the self-confidence of the army. Top military commanders were not solely responsible for the defeat, they shared the blame of the collapse with Mussolini, the civilian leadership of the fascist regime, the king and the royal court. The army as an institution took several decades to recover and only regained prestige when it persuaded Italians that it shared their basic democratic and peace-oriented values.

In the last fifty years the Italian state has "solved" its defense problems by becoming part of NATO, which is the strongest military league in history. The few professional elite corps of the Italian army are well-integrated into the NATO organization. Compulsory military service has been progressively reduced in length and the number of young men who choose some kind of community service in place of military service is growing. Support for a professional army among the population at large is also growing.

The tendency to transfer the defense problem to a supranational level is a constant of post-war Italian foreign policy. What is new is a greater willingness to cooperate in peace-keeping initiatives under the aegis of NATO and of the United Nations, as Italy is now doing with peace-keeping missions in several countries in the world. This is in accordance with Article 11 of the Italian Constitution which states that "Italy repudiates war as a means of offense to the freedom of other people and as a way of solving international controversies."

With the collapse of the Soviet Union, there is no longer "the enemy," but there are multiple local conflicts that are potentially explosive and have consequences for the country. Hence, there are partially conflicting attitudes in the political class and in public opinion.

On the one hand, there is a growing awareness that Italy is an economic giant and a military dwarf and that the end of bipolarism in international relations opens new political and military responsibilities in world affairs for Italy and the other large European states as the Gulf War and the conflicts in the former Yugoslavia made clear. On the other hand, the scope and the cost of these new responsibilities, and the risks involved, foster the tendency to delegate the defense function to a supranational level, in the direction either of greater integration and coordination in NATO or the development of a common defense policy by the European Union, or both (although the two are not fully compatible).

Italy's involvement as a NATO member in the Kosovo war elevated the defense issue to the top of the political agenda for the first time in many years. The Italian center-left coalition government, headed by D'Alema, leader of the post-communist party, has loyally complied with NATO decisions. This attitude – approved by the centre-right opposition in Parliament – has increased the international legitimacy of the government, but has created tensions within the majority coalition, and between it and the leftist oppositions both of the neo-communists and of the Northern League. Government parties, most of all the Greens, paid an electoral price, losing votes in the 1999 elections for the European Parliament. Public opinion was divided, with the majority supporting the military intervention and significant minorities questioning it on various grounds.

WELFARE

According to Article 3 of the Italian Constitution, "All citizens have equal social dignity and are equal before the law, without any distinction of sex, race, language, religion, political opinions, personal and social conditions. It is the task of the Republic to remove the economic and social obstacles which de facto limit the liberty and the equality of citizens and hinder the full development of the person and the effective participation of all workers to the economic, social and political organization of the country."

Has the Italian Republic removed the economic and social obstacles which de facto limit the liberty and the equality of citizens and hinder their full development? Has progress been made in granting greater equality of opportunities for Italian citizens? In order to answer these questions we have to briefly assess the modernization of Italian society in recent decades and the implementation of the government's welfare policies.

Economic performance and income levels

In the half century since World War II, Italy achieved remarkable economic growth and a thorough societal transformation. Economic growth in the 1950s and 1960s was rapid, intense and uneven. It was stimulated by a set of different and complementary factors: on the supply side, an explosion of entrepreneurial energies that had been held in check during the fascist period; an abundant hard working and technically skilled labor force earning lower wages than those of foreign competitors; and subsequent waves of technological innovation and organizational rationalization; on the demand side, expanding exports of competitive Italian goods in a reconstructed international market and greater domestic demand due to rising wages and mass consumption. Economic growth was supported, at first, by postwar reconstruction, U.S. financial aid, and government recovery policies as well as by growth of the domestic housing market, the infrastructure, and markets for basic consumer goods; and, later, after the signing of the Treaty of Rome in 1958, by the long, postwar expansion of the international economy, the high competitiveness of Italian exports, and the growing integration of the Italian economy into the Western European market. Italy's gross domestic product grew at the average rate of 5.5 percent between 1951 and 1958; in the "boom years," between 1958 and 1963, at the average rate of 6.3 percent a year; and after the short 1964 recession, again at an average rate of more than 6 percent until the oil crisis. Productivity became an implicit core value. Over this period, inflation rates remained low, and in 1961 the Italian lira won the Economist prize for the most stable currency. A growing domestic market for mass industrial products was formed; imports and exports as a proportion of the GDP exceeded 15 percent. Fixed capital investments were about 25 percent, growing at an average rate of 14 percent a year. The average annual increase in electricity consumption during the 1960s was 8.4 percent. Unemployment was down to a minimal 3 percent in 1962.

Italy's industrial structure consisted – and a large extent still consists today – of a few large oligopolistic firms, both private and state-owned, in energy, steel, chemicals, automobile, electronics, and telecommunications together with a multitude of small firms, some dependent on the large ones for their orders, but others playing an increasingly independent and aggressive competitive role in both domestic and foreign markets.

Since the early 1970s growth rates have been lower and inflation higher than before, more so than in other Western countries. Deep processes of economic restructuring occurred, with favorable effects for the new small firms of the northeastern regions, while several large state-owned firms and some private ones fell into crisis. Italy maintained its position among the economically advanced countries of the world, but a major macroeconomic problem came to the fore, the state debt, which reached in the 1990s a staggering 140 percent of the GNP.

Mass consumption is now a distinctive feature of Italian society. The widespread experience of rising income levels and more comfortable lifestyles, the concrete opportunity to obtain the symbols of affluent society (cars, television sets, domestic appliances, mass produced clothing, computers) fostered a consensus in favor of the market economy and helped legitimize the values and institutions of Western democracy and of the governing elites that upheld them. A "virtuous circle" between accumulation, mass consumption and political consensus was installed. Since the post-war recovery there has been an unstoppable growth of mass consumption. In 1997, the average monthly expenditure for the five main expense categories was 21 percent for food, 7 percent for clothing, 31 percent for housing, 18 percent for transportation, and 6 percent for leisure.

Today, consumption patterns are becoming homogeneous, insofar as most Italians have access to the same set of goods and services, although differentiated by age, sex, social class and family composition. The revolution in consumption fostered both individualism and familism. The role of the family as the basic consumption unit has been enhanced. Cars, television, and computers contributed to forms of leisure centered on the nuclear family.

The remarkable performance of the Italian economy and the impressive increase in the incomes and consumption levels of most Italians reduced basic differences in the lifestyles of different classes; but did not prevent the persistence of social inequalities and of relative poverty for a minority of the population. Absolute poverty has almost disappeared in Italy, although there are social groups at risk – the so called "new poor," such as lonely elderly people, unemployed uneducated young, and single parent families. In 1996, 10 percent of Italian families were below the international standard of poverty – which defines as poor a family of two components whose consumption is either equal or below the per capita consumption level. The percentage of poor families is correlated with age and level of education (it goes up to 29 percent for persons older than 65 with no educational degree), with occupational status (it goes up to 33 percent for those seeking work), and with the area of the country (more than 70 percent of poor families live in the Mezzogiorno). The social group at risk of poverty includes a further 7 percent. There has been some improvement in recent years, since in 1990 the percentage of poor families was 12 percent, and the percentage of families just above the poverty line was 9 percent. The gap between North and South, however, is smaller when subjective indicators are taken into account. The Mezzogiorno, with 34 percent of Italian families, has more than 70 percent of families below the poverty line (but only 51 percent of those perceive themselves as poor).

In comparative terms, according to the 1994 data of the Eurostat panel of European families, Italy occupied an intermediate position with an index number of 106, below Denmark (53), Germany and Belgium (76) at one extreme and above Portugal (171), Greece (141) and Great Britain (135), at the other.

In spite of the huge state debt, and of persistent relative poverty, the performance of the Italian economy has been remarkable. But we should not forget that in this volume we discuss the performance of the state, and not of the society as a whole. If we focus on state performance we see a picture of lights and shadows. Both the state's achievements and its shortcomings are clear. On the one hand, state economic policies have favored the steady growth of the GNP, a rise in average earnings, favorable trade balances. On the other hand, traditional north-south cleavages have persisted, unemployment rates are high, especially among southern youngsters, there have been recurrent inflationary crises, and a staggering public debt was incurred in the 1970s and 1980s. Significant improvements have been made by the government since 1992: inflation has been tamed, the public debt is diminishing, although very slowly, and some government monopolies such as those in telecommunications and energy have been abolished. These improvements allowed Italy to enter the European monetary union. The recent experience of advanced countries shows that high rates of economic growth and employment and redistributive policies are highly compatible. The value of social justice and the related policies of job security and welfare are upheld in Italy, according to the continental European model of the social market economy, but implementation involves an 11 percent unemployment rate and a cleavage between tenured workers and those who work in the black economy.

Welfare policies

From the historical experience of western European countries we can draw two major ideal types of welfare system (or solidarity model): the universalistic model (as exemplified in the Swedish case), where all citizens are entitled to welfare services, and the occupational model of social insurance (as exemplified in the German case), where coverage is granted to separate categories of citizens identified by occupational status. In the light of this typology, the Italian welfare system can be characterized as mixed. After the introduction of the national health system in 1978, it became mixed, but with the predominance of the occupational model, and it can be defined by the formula: health for all citizens, pensions for all workers.

In comparison with other European Union countries, Italy's social expenditure is above average for pensions and below average for health and education and especially for scientific research. I will therefore focus on the social security system as the major problem which governments must resolve in order to reduce the public debt and assure intergenerational justice.

Pensions are by far the most important type of family income support by the state. The social security system remains a huge labyrinth. Formerly limited to dependent workers, since the 1960s it has progressively taken in the various categories of autonomous workers and raised pension levels. In recent decades the cost of social security as a percentage of GNP has grown faster than total state expenditures. The ratio between contributions and benefits for the seven major social security funds (including those of dependent workers, public employees, farmers, artisans, and workers active in the trade sector) was level until 1964 and then became increasingly unbalanced.

The increase of social security expenditures is partly related to demographic and economic changes common to other Western countries, and partly related to political decisions specific to the Italian situation. Among the former, there are the lengthening of life expectancy and the fall of birth rates, which increased the retirement age population and modified the ratio between financial resources and benefits in a pension system operating according to the pay-as-you-go rule. There are also the steady rates of unemployment which now affect European economies even in the upswing phase of the economic cycle, and the growth of precarious jobs in the "post-industrial" society, which, together with the specific persistence in Italy of various forms of informal and "black" economy, reduce the amount of contributions paid by workers and entrepreneurs for social security.

Together with these general causes, other more specific factors which resulted from state policies were at work in Italy. The most important was the already mentioned extension of coverage to previously excluded categories of autonomous workers, which between the 1950s and the end of the1970s, accounted for about three fourths of the increase in expenditures for retirement pensions. Italian governments have traditionally relied on the extension of social security to an increasing number of beneficiaries, on the granting of such privileges as reduced retirement ages for public employees, and on tolerating large numbers of disability pensions in backward areas (many of which were disguised unemployment benefits) as tools of consensus formation.

The result has been a huge and growing deficit worsened by the very limited role of private insurance and by various capitalization schemes. The Italian social security system is not only costly, it is also rather inefficient and unjust. It has been plagued by lack of coordination, unequal distribution of burdens and benefits for different social categories, and privileges for special groups.

The seriousness of the financial deficit and the predicted worsening of the situation because of an aging population finally induced the government to act. In 1995 a reform was passed, with the consent of trade unions and employers' associations, which introduces significant changes in the calculus of the pensions and retirement ages, favors capitalization schemes alongside the pay-as-you-go system, and sharpens the distinction between social security and social assistance. The law is a turning point in social security policy, but it envisages a very slow implementation. It will not take full effect until 2015. Expenditures on pensions in Italy are still well above the European Union average, while total welfare costs are slightly below.

The other major welfare state policy is health care. The Italian health care system has long been fragmented along occupational lines. It was initially financed through health insurance schemes, with different contributions for different categories. It developed steadily, and progressively extended its coverage to autonomous workers. Then, in 1978 a law was passed which introduced the national health service, granting health coverage to all citizens. The reform was made possible by political cooperation among the major government and opposition parties, the perceived interest of many categories to join a unique community of risk sustained by the state, and generally favorable public opinion. The law envisaged a reorganization and rationalization of health services, greater responsibility for regional and local governments, a policy of preventive care and health education, an appreciation of professional competence and autonomy, and a reduction of regional inequalities in the provision of health services. While major university hospitals remained at the core of the system, its organizational base was the "local health unit," a new institutional device for managing health services.

The establishment of the national health system improved a situation characterized by a vast and confused network of health insurances. But the ambitious goals of the law ran against the increasing state budget deficit, to which it contributed by raising the cost of hospital care and hospital equipment and doctors' fees, and by greater consumption of expensive pharmaceutical products. The implementation of the reform was also hampered by the inherent contradictions between centralized financial control and decentralized operations, and by growing conflicts of interests among the main actors – doctors and other health care workers, actual and potential patients, public and private health institutions, pharmaceutical and health industry firms, taxpayers, national and local bureaucrats. In general terms, it can be said that Italy came to a system of universal welfare without the bureaucratic capability to act effectively according to universalist principles and to resist particularistic pressures.

In the 1980s, governments introduced cost-control devices, such as vouchers for given services and drugs, and ceilings on certain types of expenditures, with partial success. Then, in 1992, a new law transformed the local health units into legally autonomous agencies with their own budgets and their own management, accountable both for the effectiveness and quality of the services they provide and for economic results and organizational efficiency. Administrative boards, usually controlled by political parties, were eliminated. Wage incentives related to the productivity of health workers, and criteria for measuring performance in the treatment of different pathologies were introduced, as a base for determining the amount of financial contributions. The situation has bettered, but the whole picture is still one of lights and shadows: oversupply of doctors, regional inequalities in the cost-effectiveness of health care, on the one hand, and good quality care and centers of excellence in clinical medicine, on the other.

In welfare the overall performance of Italian society is good. The functioning of the welfare state is much less satisfactory.

LIBERTY

After World War II, the new Italian democracy wanted to affirm the liberties that had been either limited or denied for more than two decades by an authoritarian regime. Fascism had impeded free speech, free elections and the political organization of opposition movements; had restricted movement across the country; had violated the principles of due process and of equality before the law by submitting the judiciary to fascist political control and by establishing a "special tribunal" for repressing anti-fascist opinions and action; worst of all, it had discriminated against the Jewish minority with the infamous racial laws.

The new Italian Constitution, both in its "fundamental principles"and in Part I on the "rights and duties of citizens", dismantled the whole authoritarian fabric of fascism, and established principles aimed at protecting the citizen from the power of the state and at defending minorities from the power of majorities, on the model of established liberal democracies. In the four sections dedicated to civil, socio-ethical, economic, and political relations, both the negative liberties from the constraints and abuses of authoritarian power – the "liberties of the modern" according to the famous definition by Benjamin Constant – and the "positive liberties" of opinion, speech, press, teaching and research, political association, voting, and political action within the rule of law, are solemnly affirmed, as are economic and labor rights.

Contemporary Italy is a free society to a degree never approached in the past. This outcome is a result of the ideas and actions of successive generations. The first generation rejected fascism and restored and strengthened civil and political liberties in the new democratic constitution. The second generation, which reached adulthood in the 1950s and 1960s, was the main actor in the successful struggle against economic underdevelopment and social need. As I remarked earlier, the most important development of Italian society in the post-war period, along with the consolidation of a democratic polity, was the "virtuous cycle" among accumulation, mass consumption, and political consensus, which for the first time in Italian history broke the old equilibrium between low wages and low consumption on which the relations of social classes had been based.

In the years of the "economic miracle," the widespread experience of rising income levels and more comfortable lifestyles, the concrete opportunity to be part of an affluent society, induced the Italian people to abandon the dream of unachievable political grandeur and to discover unimaginable opportunities for success in productive activities. Old problems and sufferings were perceived and dealt with in their real dimensions. For the first time, the ideals of modern Western democracy commanded a wide consensus, not only as a belief of cosmopolitan elites but also as an ideal shared by the masses; and Italy effectively entered the community of Western nations

The combined effect of political democracy and a market economy undermined hierarchical mechanisms of social control (dogmatic religious teachings, paternalistic management in firms, centralized party structures, authoritarian state bureaucracies) and fostered social integration by means of collective bargaining (primarily, but not only, in labor relations) and of compromises among multiple free options. Meanwhile, the influence of television and of closer relations with other developed countries limited the constraints of parochial attitudes.

The third generation, that of those involved in the collective movements of the late 1960s and 1970s – mainly students, women, and young workers – were the key actors in the revolt against authoritarianism in the school, in the family, and in the workplace. Most of those who were young in that period, not only the militant minorities of collective movements, developed a generational culture with deeply anti-authoritarian values and sentiments. To freedom from political dictatorship and freedom from economic want they added freedom from paternalistic rule and traditional authorities.

The most striking changes took place in the condition of women who liberated themselves from their centuries-old subordination to male power – father, husband, boss, priest. In the 1970s, major reforms were approved in family law, affirming gender equality and permitting divorce and abortion, while attempts to repeal them through referenda were defeated by large majorities. Women in growing numbers entered the labor market, gaining greater personal autonomy through economic independence. Gender inequality in education was abolished.

Very significant changes took place in the relations between parents and children as well. Children now enjoy much greater freedom that in the past, and the experience of severe discipline and authoritarian parental attitudes seems gone forever.

In contemporary Italy, both individual liberty and collective liberty are strong. Personal choice is the key principle for action in the market, in the polity, and in every sphere of life. Structural constraints, such as inequalities in income and wealth, in education, in the family's social capital, and differences of gender and age, still exist, but they do not overrule the fundamental principle of individual choice.

Young southerners have much higher unemployment rates that their peers in the rest of the country, but they no longer emigrate as their parents and grandparents did in the past; on the contrary, their regions attract significant numbers of foreign immigrants who accept the jobs that local people choose not to do.

Young women still have to face the problem of their double responsibility at work and in the family, but they can choose much more than in the past to postpone marriage and childbirth; they may still run into more difficulties than males in getting access to – and making careers in – certain jobs, but are catching up fast.

Radical students may find it difficult to achieve what they consider better and more egalitarian education, but they have the full chance to express their views.

State institutions have become more concerned with the issue of freedom, and the Italian people have become more tolerant than in the past. This is not to say that problems do not exist. Two issues are becoming increasingly relevant in Italian society. The first concerns religious freedom. For decades Catholicism has been the state religion of Italy. Article 7 of the Constitution states that "the state and the Catholic Church are both independent and sovereign, each in its own order. Their relations are regulated by the Patti Lateranensi" (1929 concordat). Article 8 states that "all religious confessions are equally free before the law." And Article 19 says that "all have the right to freely profess their religion in every form, individually and collectively, and to spread it." The Catholic Church enjoys a privileged status, according to the 1929 concordat, which was confirmed and updated in the 1980s. It is a complex institution playing multiple roles. "Church" means different things: the very extended network of parishes and the Vatican bureaucracy, the religious orders and the web of catholic associations active in daily life, catholic doctrine with its impact on individual experience. However, Italian society has become in recent decades increasingly secularized. Religious teachings are less relevant than in the past in influencing moral values and codes of social behavior, except for the community of true believers.

Moreover, still more recently, Italy is becoming a multi-ethnic, multicultural, and multi-religious society. The Italian government has, in recent years, signed official agreements with Protestants, Jewish, and Buddhist institutions. The traditional cleavage between Catholic values and secular ones has been reduced in recent decades, although is still relevant in such issues as abortion. It is being replaced by the issues of coexistence between believers of different faiths.

The second question concerns the very meaning of liberty. A major sociological problem of contemporary Italy is not the lack of personal freedom, but rather a restricted and selfish interpretation of freedom as the right to do whatever seems useful or pleasant for the selfish individual, with little sense of civic duty and little willingness to exert responsible leadership in public affairs.

CONCLUSION

The performance of the Italian state with respect to the six major purposes is on the whole mediocre. The performance of Italian society as a whole can be judged more satisfactory, in terms of economic competitiveness, social innovation, flexible adaptation to globalization, better living conditions, the resilience of key institutions such as the family, and social cohesion.

The Italian experience is a case of uneven but successful modernization, which shows that the state is not the *primum mobile* of development and modernization. Social relations and cultural attitudes changed profoundly in Italy, in spite of the limited effectiveness of deliberate reform policies and the low efficiency of state institutions (Martinelli, Chiesi, Stefanizzi, *Social Trends in Italy, 1960–1995* [Montreal: McGill-Queens, 1999]).

The rapid growth of the economy and the impressive transformation of civil society were not accompanied by adequate institutional changes and government reforms or by a parallel modernization of education, culture, legislation, and public administration. There is rich empirical evidence on the malfunctioning of public services in certain regions of the country, the inefficiency of large sectors of the state bureaucracy, the overproduction of laws, the low level of respect for the law shown by many citizens, and the weakness of civic culture in certain regions. In the last decade the gap has been reduced, government performance has bettered, but unequal modernization is still present, mostly in areas of the country like the northeast where economic growth and social change have been rapid and intense.

In Italian modernization, civil society has been more important than the state, and the strategies of individual actors have often proved more effective than the strategies of collective actors. The main reasons for this are a fragmented party system, which made it difficult to form strong and stable governments; the chronic backwardness of the Italian civil service; and the intricacies of the legal system, which delayed or made impossible the effective implementation of needed reforms. The backwardness of the state went hand in hand with a limited legitimation of state authority not only among rebellious minorities, but also in large areas of the Mezzogiorno where "amoral familism" and criminal organizations such as the Mafia and the Camorra compete with the state for people's loyalty.

The Italian state is weak in the double sense of its weak legitimation among segments of the population and its fragmented administration, with little communication among its different branches, and incoherent policies. In post war Italy, the state bureaucracy was the sector in which there was the most continuity with the preceding authoritarian regime. In 1973, 95 percent of top bureaucrats had been hired before 1943 (Putnam, 1993) and many of them had problems identifying with a democratic state and accepting the values and practices of representative democracy. In the next decades, generational turnover in the bureaucracy and democratic culture in the society changed authoritarian attitudes, but other features conspired against efficient and effective administration.

The civil service is still composed mostly of bureaucrats either from the Rome region where a strong centralistic culture prevails, or from southern areas with high unemployment rates, where a state job is the only opportunity available. Recruitment of top officials does not take place through specialized schools and has often been influenced by party allegiance. Careers are made on the basis of seniority rather than merit; the civil service is divided into departments and there are limited opportunities for officials to move from one department to another (Cassese, 1982). The educational background of most bureaucrats remains law school and the predominant attitude is still the rigid application of norms and procedures with no concern for outcomes. The strict division of bureaucratic roles tends to fragment the decision-making process and delay decisions through frequent use of veto power.

Bureaucratic culture is generally not very open to innovation, but conservative attitudes are stronger in the Italian bureaucracy than in most others. Indicators of the lack of efficiency and effectiveness of Italian bureaucracy are the number of laws that are not implemented and the *residui passivi*, i.e., the financial resources allocated for given purposes that return to the state treasury because they are not spent in time. Typical examples of the latter are subsidies granted to the southern regions and the limited use of European Community credits for agricultural modernization and the development of underdeveloped areas. Instances of effective performance and administrative efficiency do exist, as in the several universities, the central bank, some of the newly created public authorities, and various departments of the national and local governments. But the general performance is below the average of other developed countries.

Lack of implementation of reform laws, however, is an even more serious problem. Even among reform-oriented governments, such as the centre-left governments of the 1960s, the 'national solidarity' gov-

ernments of the late 1970s, and the reform-oriented governments of
the 1990s, policy implementation has been difficult, not only because
of conflicts among the various components of the governing coalitions, but mostly because of the limited efficiency and effectiveness of
the state bureaucracy.

Such inefficiency and ineffectiveness helps to explain why, in Italian
democracy, leftist forces always had a difficult time implementing their
strategies of change. While the political right relies upon the spontaneous forces of the market, requiring only limited government direction, the political left tends to think that society can be redesigned by
reform policies that require an effective state apparatus. The less efficient the government, the more difficulty it has playing this role. This
may help to explain why in Italy we tend to have governments with
rightist policies and leftist rhetoric.

The gap between socio-economic transformation and political-insti-
tutional innovation was one of the major factors accounting for the
political turmoil of the 1990s, the judiciary's investigation of political
corruption and the attempt to introduce institutional reforms. The
recent governments, since 1992, have had a better record than previous ones, mostly in the area of budget control. Curbing inflation,
getting the public debt under control, and joining the first group of
European countries in the Monetary Union was a notable achievement, as was the weakening of criminal organizations and the liberalization of important sectors of the economy. But new versions of old
problems such as the "southern question" are still present.

A reform of the state in the direction of federalism and a reform of
the governmental structure aiming to increase the stability and the
effectiveness of the executive seem necessary to better the performance of the Italian Leviathan. The increasing scope and complexity
of problems in the global world require the devolution of portions of
national sovereignty both to the supranational level of the European
Union, as a true political entity, and to the sub-national level of
regional and local authorities. Leviathan has to become larger and
smaller at the same time according to the nature of the problems to
be solved and the type of policy involved.

The German State in Comparative Perspective in the Year 2000

KARL OTTO HONDRICH

1 GENERAL REMARKS

"Einigkeit und Recht und Freiheit fuer das deutsche Vaterland ..." Unity, Justice, and Liberty (Freedom) – those are the guidelines the German national anthem puts forward to the striving of "all of us." We are supposed to strive for it "as brothers" – not on our own "as individuals." The text of the anthem was written in 1841. It reminds us of the core values of the French Revolution: *liberté, égalité, fraternité*. And the same extended value set – with the exception of brotherhood – appears in the founding document of the United States of America: It evokes a more perfect union, justice, domestic tranquility, common defense, general welfare, and the blessings of liberty.

It is amazing that those basic value orientations did not lose their meaning – and changed it very little – during two centuries of extremely strong societal dynamics. It is no less remarkable that a growing number of very different societies, putting different emphasis on one value or the other, nevertheless would subscribe to all of them. By taking the American value set as a point of departure for comparative analysis, we do not run into serious problems of validity. From that point of departure, we will argue, in the course of our analysis, that some values, for instance "justice," have somewhat different meanings in the German context.

Values – and political goals – are culturally defined expressions of what Emile Durkheim called collective feelings or *conscience collective*. Collective feelings – in democracies even more than in authoritarian states – do not only determine what a politically organized collectivity is expected to strive for. Collective feelings are also the final standards for judging the performance of a political system. The political system must satisfy them.

Thus, the sociologist, looking for criteria to evaluate the performance of a political society, needs a certain conception of societal well being as defined by collective feelings. This conception can only be a diffuse and not a clear-cut one, for the following reasons:

- there are internal conflicts of values (and value-realizations) within collective feelings: for example, the maximum realization of justice may have extremely high costs in liberty.
- the boundaries of the state do not necessarily coincide with the framework of collective feelings that may operate within a smaller framework or extend to a larger one. This is particularly true for the ongoing process of European unification, where the value of unity is to be realized both on the national and on the European level.

Those considerations make it clear that a "good policy" in a "good society" may imply not only value realization on the national level, but an appropriate achievement of political goals within a larger context. But what is "appropriate"? Again Durkheim might help. His idea of defining societal normality as an average degree of value realization by comparing different societies (on approximately the same level of social development) is not only a good basis for comparative research. It also invites us to base criteria of evaluation on empirical grounds.

Unfortunately, neither the average nor a higher or lower degree of value realization is a definitive measure of the performance of one Leviathan as compared to others. It is not the activity of Leviathan – the political system – alone that determines the "state of the nation." There are other factors, including especially the international and the historical position of a national society and its particular cultural heritage. They may have a stronger influence on the pattern of value realization than the political system. The fact that every national society has developed its own pattern of value realization – and that the different patterns may be seen in a competitive struggle – helps us to understand that there is no universal "best pattern" for all societies.

Thus, the purpose of this paper is not to evaluate German society and its political system with respect to some measure of societal or political excellence, but to describe the "German pattern" of value realization, loosely comparing it to those of other western societies.

2 UNION

Almost all European states, even those that achieved political unity earlier than the 19th century, are still struggling with the problem of unity. There is, most recently, the disintegration of the Soviet empire, of Yugloslavia, and of Czechoslovakia. There are violent separatist movements in Spain, Great Britain, even in France. Italy, which has hardly managed to integrate its German speaking alpine province, recently experienced a – not very efficient but noisy – declaration of independence by its Northern region. Belgium has problems with bi-lingualism. And even Switzerland, the stronghold of stability securely integrated by common interests and history, endures a permanent rivalry between its German majority and its proud Roman minorities.

In this context, the unification of Germany in 1989/90 looks like an exception – a movement against a trend. It involved the territorial extension of the Federal Republic by about 30 percent, increasing the population from 65 to 82 million. Although the eastern part of the earlier German Reich, which became part of Poland after the war, is not included (the term unification is preferable to re-unification), that does not constitute a problem of national unity in German politics today. The loss of part of its earlier territory is accepted, by much of the German public, as the price that Germany had to pay for not recognizing and resisting the criminal character of national socialist policies. Those Germans who were expelled from their homes in East Prussia and Silesia do not think that it is a just price. Nevertheless, they know that the Polish people who took their places were victims of expulsion themselves, and that aggression started from the German side. Meanwhile, the German expellees and their children are firmly integrated elsewhere in Germany. There is neither a moral nor an economic basis for further revision of borderlines. As far as territorial extension is concerned, the "German question," after centuries of war and internal conflict, finally seems to be settled.

It is ironic that this settlement came about at a moment when no one really expected it; when most people, particularly in the Federal Republic, had accepted the idea that the future of Germany would not be with the nation-state but with the integration of western Europe and that the enlarged nation-state did not result from any particular effort by the Germans themselves but from the failure of state socialism and Soviet imperialism. Thus, the Germans enjoyed a national triumph without really wanting it. West German opinion polls during the previous decades had shown a steady fading away of national feelings while East Germans had undergone an intensive schooling in "socialist internationalism"; nevertheless, they had little to lose and much to gain by joining their "brothers and sisters" in the West within the framework of an enlarged Federal Republic. And thus it happened: in a bold stroke, Chancellor Kohl, bringing to bear his good relationship with the Soviet leader Michail Gorbachev, took over the German Democratic Republic and made it a part of the Federal Republic of Germany. No new political institutions were created by this unification. The state and the institutions in the East dissolved. The western institutions remained as they were and expanded into the East. It was a takeover of the East by the West.

As the surveys show, the majority of the people in the East liked it that way. On the other hand, both eastern and western intellectuals were disappointed. For a moment they had dreamt of combining the best elements of liberal democracy and socialist planning in a rationally negotiated new society. But on the eastern side, there was nothing substantial to negotiate. The political elite of the old regime had no remaining support and the new elite of the movement that overthrew the old regime had no political experience.

The process might have been less hasty and less reckless. The imposition of western currency and market forces on the eastern economy without any shock-absorbers destroyed most of its industry. This resulted in a high level of unemployment that has been only slightly reduced in recent years. What industry remained or recovered was taken over by investors from the West. The investigation of crime and corruption in the old regime's huge secret service was conducted by western judges and reported by western journalists. The people of the former German Democratic Republic, although better off with respect to wealth and freedom in the extended Federal Republic, experienced, and still experience, relative deprivation in other ways; they have higher rates of unemployment; lower wages; much less economic capital; less political influence; fewer scientific, educational, judicial, and other elite positions. They have reason to feel economically, politically, and morally dominated by their western countrymen.

Thus, the achievement of national unity was followed by the growing awareness of an inner division between the western and eastern parts of the country. But this inner division has a somewhat nebulous character; it is more a mood than a cultural divide. Cultural values in West and East Germany nowadays show a high degree of similarity despite the fact that there were two different states with competing value systems for four decades. The only small difference is that East Germans put more emphasis on equality, and less on freedom, than West Germans.

What inner division there is, refers to differences of everyday experience and of life-styles and to differences in wealth and influence. There is no political sentiment for the re-separation of the two parts of the country. Very few people in either part want to turn the wheel back completely, but more than 20 percent of East Germans say they would welcome some kind of socialism "under certain conditions."

3 JUSTICE

Another division, nearly a decade after the unification of Germany, might well be described in terms of justice. Both sides feel that the outcome of the unification process is not entirely just and that the other side demands too much. As seen from the West, people in the East demanding equality of wages and social services are asking more than they deserve. As seen by people in the East, their lower level of performance and wealth is not their fault but the result of the partition of Germany after the war. Since Germans have a collective responsibility for that event, it would be just, in this perspective, for the lucky West to pay for the unlucky East. Although there is an enormous and continuing annual flow of funds from West to East, the "gap of injustice" remains a deep one: 53 percent in East Germany – as against 28 percent in the West – feel that the system of society in the Federal Republic is "not just." The percentage of those in the East who think that the system as it is is worth defending declined from 46 to 41 between 1991 and 1995; in the West it declined too, from 77 to 66 – but on a level considerably higher (Noelle-Neumann, Köcher 1997, 645).

Justice is a basic value of social life. Since Aristotle, it has implied that everyone receive from society what he or she deserves. Individuals should be rewarded or punished according to what they contribute to, or take from, the collectivity, as collectively judged. An individual supporting collective feelings should be rewarded correspondingly. An individual violating the collective feelings should be punished according to the degree of violation. The principle of equity, better known as reciprocity, is the regulative mechanism for the realization of justice.

There are three problems with the realization of justice. First, there is a considerable degree of ignorance or very selective knowledge about positive or negative contributions to the collectivity; many crimes are never discovered; many entrepreneurial, scientific and professional achievements are difficult to attribute to individual persons. Second, the mass psychology of the collectivity may induce extreme and exaggerated reactions both to positive achievements and to violations of the moral order. Thus, the effort to be just may lead to extreme inequality, even inhumanity. The third problem is that justice as reciprocity, realized uncompromisingly and without regard to consequences, runs into conflict with other basic values, particularly with equality.

In Europe, equality seems to be much more valued than in the American context with its emphasis on liberty and individuality. These differences express themselves in different conceptions of the state. Europeans have fused the value of equality with their value of justice. The result of this fusion is the concept of social justice. People should not receive what they deserve under strict reciprocity (represented, particularly, by the market) but should receive less or more. Strong and successful performers should get less than their entitlement under strict reciprocity; weak and deviant performers should get more. What matters is the outcome. Social justice is (re)distributive justice – a corrective to justice as reciprocity. It assumes an a priori collectivity that delegates part of its regulative function to the reciprocity principle (i.e., to the market) and corrects the outcome in the name of equality and solidarity. Justice *tout court* starts with the assumption of the priori autonomy of individuals, who form a collectivity and develop collective feelings as a result of social exchange .

The tension between justice and social justice exists in the economy, particularly with regard to the distribution of income and wealth. It dominates the legal system, with regard to crime and punishment, too. Those members of a society who do not take part in the production of income and wealth or who perform very badly, are treated harshly under the rule of justice but more leniently under the aegis of social justice. Likewise, those members of society who do not share the collective feelings or who strongly deviate from collective norms have more to hope from social justice than from ordinary justice.

Interestingly enough, in both fields of justice there seem to be characteristic differences between America and Europe. In the United States, more than in Europe, there is a belief that justice in the distribution of income and wealth is best served by the rule of the reciprocity principle in free markets. Corrections of the outcome in favor of the most disadvantaged sectors of the population may be necessary, but they are not conceived in terms of justice but rather as necessary social engineering.

On the other side of the Atlantic, when the problem of justice arises in public debate, it is seldom related to the legal system, but generally refers to economic outcomes. In Germany, the concept of social justice has been considerably modified by changes in political power. In the first decades of the Federal Republic, the concept was associated with social democrats and trade unionists promoting redistributive reform policies. Today, the concept has become completely defensive: social justice is evoked against the pressure of global markets and the polities of economic liberalization and deregulation.

As a matter of fact, as will be shown later, the earlier emphasis on social justice had very little effect on the distributive system. As the numbers show (see Section 6) there has been amazing stability in the distribution of income and poverty throughout the history of the Federal Republic.

The way the welfare system has been successfully defended against all attempts to diminish its services and to diminish the tax burden in favor of the affluent strata indicates a high degree of acceptance of the status quo as socially just.

When we turn to the problem of justice before the law, we may usefully distinguish three types of injustice:

- the legal norms themselves are seen as unjust, defining behavior as more or less criminal than the collective feelings do; in the first case we may speak of "authoritarian injustice," the second case may be labeled "liberal injustice";
- the norms, although regarded as just, do not lead to sentences that satisfy the collective feelings of justice; injustice is produced by the procedures of the legal system itself, which may be authoritarian, liberal or arbitrary/irregular;
- legal penalties, although regarded as just, are imposed more severely or less severely than the norms anticipated or that the collective feelings support.

In Europe, in the last half century, there seems to have been a drift from authoritarian to liberal injustice before the law. This tendency was particularly pronounced in Germany. The new states, both the Federal Republic and the German Democratic Republic, started their judicial life with the depressing experience of the enormously authoritarian and arbitrary injustice of the Nazi regime. The double task of building a new judicial system for the future and punishing the crimes of the past led to considerable ambivalence.

On the one hand, there was a collective feeling that authoritarian injustice was represented both in the harsh procedures of the new state socialism in the East and in the restoration of the traditional judicial system in the West, the latter reinforced as a type of "class justice" by the re-emerging capitalist structures. The restoration was sharply criticized by intellectuals; we do not know whether the general public held the same opinion. At the same time, the system was held by the same critics to be too indulgent towards criminals and towards Nazi collaborators.

During the next decades, particularly in the 1960s and 1970s, with the growing affluence of the Federal Republic, there was a steady liberalization of legal norms (cf. section 7). Within the legal system, there was a tendency towards more permissiveness and lighter punishments. Those tendencies were fostered by liberal interpretations of the functions of trial, sentencing and punishment. The Durkheimian idea that judicial processes and punishment have the function of satisfying collective feelings was replaced by the idea that the judicial system must reintegrate the offender. Justice should not reciprocate the violation of collective feelings, but should protect society against the offender and the offender against collective feelings. The offender, in his or her minority status as an outsider and victim of society, must be supported, like other socially disadvantaged minorities, against the unfiltered sentiments of justice aroused in the majority. Thus, the mitigation of punishment and the efforts to reintegrate the outsider can be seen as measures of social justice, bridging the gap of inequality between the criminal and the law-abiding majority.

There are signs now that the tendency towards more and more liberal justice leads to allegations of liberal injustice by the liberals themselves. This has to do with changing images of offenders and victims. To the degree that the offender is no longer visualized as really poor and weak or as an anti-authoritarian youth, as the rubric of class justice would have it, but as a white collar criminal, an agent of organized crime, an abusive husband or father or a young neo-nazi torching an asylum for foreign refugees, liberals join those who feel that the judicial system is too indulgent to do justice to violated collective feelings.

The opinion that, generally speaking, the German judicial system is too permissive to produce justice is not manifested yet in public discussion. But there seems to be a beginning (Böhlk 1997). The police, complaining that they are left alone to fight crime, try to alert the public to their viewpoint. The association of German Crime Agents (*Bund Deutscher Kriminalbeamter*) published a study in 1997 purporting to show that 75 percent of all offenders referred to the courts by the police are dismissed and that of the remainder only 18 percent are fined and only 7 percent sentenced to confinement. Between 1982 and 1992 the state attorneys (*Staatsanwaltschaften*) received 39 percent more complaints but produced only 4 percent more accusations. To blame the indulgence of state attorneys and judges, the criminal police provocatively calls it "*Gesetzesungehorsam der Justiz*" (non-compliance to the law by the judicial system) (Böhle 1997).

The impression of growing liberal injustice in Germany may be particularly interesting if compared to the U.S. According to American observers, the American judicial system produces more authoritarian injustice (the criminalization of relatively harmless drugs, very high incarceration rates, and a strong bias against blacks and hispanics). American legal norms are clearly less liberal than their German counterparts and American public opinion is vastly more punitive, presumably because the German system, wary of collective feelings of injustice, invokes social justice in favor of the offender.

Also it may be that all societies need a "leading crime" for public discussion. It mobilizes and attracts collective feelings of indignation from different strata and cultural contexts. It creates integration by indignation. Drug dealing seems to be the leading crime in the U.S. and even, to a lesser extent, in Germany. It permits the exercise of heavy sanctions against classic minorities. The ongoing de facto discrimination against those minorities is labeled in universalistic and idealistic terms as a "fight against crime."

Altogether, justice before the law seems to be more of a problem for discussion in America than in Germany. The predominance of procedural concerns, regardless of the outcome, is more pronounced in the United States than in Germany; the same is true for the proliferation of litigation and of bureaucracy; the tort liability system, charging big and wealthy organizations to pay for individual negligence or malfeasance, is almost unknown in Germany. Nevertheless, there have been dramatic complaints from within the judicial system and from the minister of justice himself that the system will break down under a growing burden of prosecution and litigation. One answer to the problem is: more liberalism. In some overburdened courts, defendants are sometimes released without trial, as judges in Hessen did not long ago, with drug dealers, to demonstrate that they were overworked. Nonetheless, there is, in Germany, a tradition of trusting the legal and judicial system, somewhat balanced by scepticism about their actual workings.

4 TRANQUILITY

The value of tranquility, in Germany today, carries a strange ambivalence. "Ruhe ist die erste Buergerpflicht" – tranquility as the first duty of the subject was the normative guideline of the traditional Obrigkeitsstaat. Tranquility as a value cannot be evoked today without ironical nostalgia. It recalls 19th century authoritarianism as well as the more recent authoritarianism of the German Democratic Republic (1949 to 1989). It is not only outmoded but also morally compromised by Nazi totalitarianism which perverted and enforced traditional values of tranquility and order. Nevertheless "Ruhe und Ordnung" (tranquility and order) as a political goal sounds, to German ears, less authoritarian than "law and order"; that American formula is widely used in German political discourse to characterize a right-wing, punitive philosophy of dealing with deviant behavior.

Taking into account that even those values that have wide cross-cultural acceptance carry particular cultural connotations that vary among national societies, the value of domestic tranquility implies:

- that riots and insurrections are prevented,
- that persons and property are safe,
- that private and public transactions are conducted with civility,
- that citizens are mutually respectful.

Riots and insurrections

After the war, German society found itself in a paradoxical situation. On the one hand, after a period of distressful restlessness and arbitrary rule, there was a strong need for tranquility and peace. On the other hand, the failure of the old totalitarian order called for new political structures legitimizing conflict and opposition.

Fortunately, German society was not left alone with this paradox. It was solved by an unintended division of labor. The occupation powers provided a framework of tranquility. German political elites, interest groups, and intellectuals filled it with conflict. In West Germany, conflicts followed the pattern of Western democracies; in the East, internal conflict was more or less suppressed and diverted into conflict against the "class enemy" on the other side of the iron curtain.

In the East, internal tranquility was controlled in a double way: by a new authoritarian state and its extensive security service (Staatssicherheitsdienst); and by the Russian occupying forces. Only twice, at the beginning and at the end of its forty-year history, was the tranquility of the German Democratic Republic disturbed by mass movements. In 1953, a strike of construction workers spontaneously turned into mass demonstrations against the political system. Russian tanks suppressed the upheaval with bloodshed. In 1989, the so-called "Monday demonstrations" in Leipzig and other places expressed collective desires for freedom and unity. This time, the Russians did not interfere but retired instead, bringing to an end the East German state that had not been able to develop a legitimacy of its own.

As to West Germany, three times in its history the Federal Republic experienced waves of political unrest of a highly symbolic character. At the end of the 1960s, students protested against authoritarian tendencies within democratic systems as well as against the anti-socialist positions of the western democracies within the international arena. The wave of student protests swept through most of the western democracies and Japan. In a way, it integrated the youth of the developed world.

A decade later, the youth movement had split into two branches: On the one hand, feminist, peace, and ecological organizations recruited large numbers of people; their mass demonstrations were impressive and peaceful. On the other hand, small bands of young people engaged in terrorist activities against capitalism, consumerism and the state. In the seventies, more than thirty members of the political, judicial, and political elites, together with their guards, were taken hostages or killed in Germany as representatives of "the system." About the same number of young terrorists lost their lives. Terrorism lost its popular support (substantial among youth) in the famous "German Autumn" of 1977, when a Lufthansa jet was hijacked and liberated, and four leading terrorists committed suicide in jail.

More than ten years later, there was another wave of violent aggression – this time against immigrants taking advantage of their constitutional right to political asylum. Burning out people from Asia, Turkey and Africa became a fad. This kind of violence had a nationalist background but it lacked a political organization and ideology. Seen in the context of unification, it was a reaction to the policy of "open borders." The coincidence, in 1989, of opening the border between West and East Germany, of repatriating millions of people of German origin from eastern Europe and of accepting an unexpected number of political refugees at the same time placed great strain on the nation's integrative capacities. When new restrictions were placed on the right to asylum the number of immigrants decreased, and violent acts against foreigners fell back to an earlier level.

Confronting each episode of rioting and unconventional political behavior, the political class displayed considerable irritation, helplessness and over-reaction. Nevertheless, in the long run, it proved sufficiently responsive, incorporating the young revolutionaries into its institutions and adding to those institutions a Green party which takes pride in representing ideological minorities and which entered the federal government for the first time in 1998. Against terrorism, the political system mobilized the investigative and suppressive resources of the state and won the support of an overwhelming majority. Thus, ironically enough, terrorism turned out to strengthen the legitimacy of the state. In a more conventional way, the legitimacy of the political system gained from democratic changes of government and from the adjustment of policies to new circumstances.

Public Safety

Between 1980 and 1989, the general crime rate more than doubled, from 3000 to 7000 reported delicts per 100,000 of the population. At the beginning of the 1990s it rose again, reaching a peak of 8000 in 1993, since when it has slightly declined. For murder and attempted murder, the figures show approximate stability during the past 16 years – around 4.3 per 100 000 of the population – with a peak in 1993. Other violent crimes like burglary and assault went on increasing through the 1990s, as did the sexual abuse of children. Sexual violence, by contrast, has very slowly declined.

It is evident that the rise of crime rates in the early 1990s was influenced by three factors: first, the unification of Germany and resulting disappointments; second, the immigration of young people taking advantage of the liberal asylum law or of the government's policy of repatriating people of German origin from the former USSR, Poland, and other east European countries; and third, the rising criminality of children, adolescents, and young adults.

There is a long-standing dispute between those sociologists who take crime rates and changes in crime rates as indicators of a quasi-natural reality to be explained by other factors, and those who take crime rates as social constructions which are made and explained by collective definition. The dispute does not need to be settled here. In either view, deviant behavior and crime are part of social reality. By drawing special attention to East Germans, to immigrants, and to young people and their increasing crime rates, the collective conscience informs itself about the neuralgic points of social integration. Young people from the East and young immigrants do not become criminals because they lack social integration. On the contrary, they lack integration because they are defined as marginal. Such definitions are not made arbitrarily. They mark the limits to integration, not in the sense that minority groups do not want integration but in the sense that the collective conscience has limited flexibility.

Germany as an aging society with well-established mechanisms of economic and cultural integration would have few problems of social control were it not for the integration of newcomers from outside and from younger generations. There are no problems with foreign people from the "guest worker" generation; their crime rate is as low as that of the native Germans. Neither are there integration problems with young people qualified for apprenticeships. With the general unemployment rate above 10 percent, youth unemployment has been around 5 percent – much lower than in France and the U.S. The problem group, as indicated by criminal statistics, consists of young people, most of them from poorer countries, including young ethnic Germans ("Aussiedler"), who lack the cultural qualifications for an apprenticeship. For them, the promise of open borders is not fulfilled. The additional promise of full citizenship cannot provide them with jobs and cultural qualifications as real prerequisites for social integration. Their hopes become frustrations, and frustrations may result in criminal acts.

The majority of the population is not really threatened by "open border criminality" and youth criminality. Criminality is largely confined to its ethnic and age group milieus. Nevertheless, most Germans, and the elderly in particular, although not victims of crime, are convinced of ever rising crime rates and remain apprehensive. Is their view of reality "wrong," as some social scientists would claim? It may rather be the other way around. Social scientists are mistaken if they think that people take notice only of those social facts that touch them individually. There is a collective reality as well. As social beings and as participants of *conscience collective* people notice changes in their collective frameworks. They feel responsible not only for their individual lives but also for their collective life. Even without being individually victimized and without knowing that statistically one of three criminal acts is committed by a foreigner, they know that open borders have changed their collective life. If they give the "fight against crime" a prominent place in the hierarchy of political goals, it does not mean that they feel personally threatened but that they want to live, as collective beings, in a collectivity with low crime rates.

Civility and Mutual Respect

More than any other of these topics, civility and mutual respect can be studied by anybody in everyday life. For those traveling abroad, this can easily be done in a comparative perspective. As compared to service societies like the U.S. and Japan, Germany is far behind in friendly behavior in public places and in client and customer service. Compared to a basically egalitarian society like the U.S., Germans in office or privileged by education often show remarkable disregard for the intelligence, opinions, and needs of the "simple people." In education itself, teachers and professors put much emphasis on "die Sache", show little devotion to the student, and neglect the formation of social and political competence. In communication, there is a disregard for "form" and an emphasis on "content," which makes for the harsh and unpleasant character of many intellectual discussions.

On the other hand, values like politeness and tolerance that supposedly were declining during the 1960s and 1970s, are on their way back and compete strongly with the values of personal strength and power.

5 DEFENSE

After the war, both the Federal Republic and the German Democratic Republic started with no capability of self-defense. When the first soldiers were recruited in the mid 1950s, each state became firmly integrated within its respective military bloc. Until 1990, neither part of Germany had any military independence and even today, Germany, as a member of the NATO and without access to nuclear weapons, is completely reliant on its allies, particularly the U.S., in the military sphere.

Strange as it may seem, powerlessness and dependency in matters of defense matched both the feelings of guilt in the German *conscience collective* and German interests. As military latecomers, both Germanys, East and West, could concentrate on economic and moral reconstruction, cultivate new images of peacefulness, and avoid any responsibility for maintaining international order by political and military means. Under the shield of the NATO alliance and the U.S., West Germany could develop a respectable peace movement. In a situation of collective powerlessness, it demanded even less power. But eventually, the re-establishment of economic and political power in Germany began to restore moral and military power. Nobody could help it.

Following the collapse of the Communist empire and German reunification in 1989, there were almost revolutionary changes in the defense constellation: The military forces of both Germanys, amounting to 700,000 soldiers, were unified and reduced to 330,000 – a reduction of forces that no peace movement had envisaged. Without a local enemy, the defense function had to be redirected towards very different problems of securing order in distant places. When such places were identified outside the national and NATO territory, the defense function takes on an offensive character. Perhaps most important, the new constellation provokes anxiety and insecurity within and outside the army.

As a result we see two seemingly contradictory tendencies. On the one hand, there is awareness of a sudden political and military responsibility for European, and even world, affairs. The Gulf War and the Balkan wars made this clear and developed a new consensus in favor of a volunteer army. On the other hand, in view of its new and risky military responsibilities, German inclination towards integration into

NATO becomes even stronger. NATO is seen as a refuge – not so much from Russia but from all the problems of disorder and insecurity in the world. Defense, from a German perspective, is the one state function that definitely must be transferred from the state to a supranational entity. It is the part of Leviathan that Leviathan must abandon.

6 WELFARE

Three aspects of the economic and social welfare of a national society may be distinguished. The aspect of growth implies a) a continuous rise in Gross Domestic Product (GDP) per capita, b) a continuous rise in average earnings, c) rising productivity or efficiency of the economy, d) favorable trade balances, e) low inflation, f) low unemployment, g) growing human capital, and h) progressive improvement in human services, especially education and health care. The aspect of distribution implies particularly the reduction of inequality of wealth, income, education, and life chances. The aspect of security implies security of employment and rising protection against the risks of unemployment, sickness, and old age.

Economic growth, after a long post-war period of high rates and a second period, after the mid seventies, of lower and fluctuating rates, has stabilized at lower rates since the beginning of the nineties, i. e. since unification. In five decades, gross domestic product per capita increased five-fold, from DM 11000 in 1950 (in constant 1997 DM) to DM 49000 in 1997. The consistency of the trend is striking. A continuous increase of wealth of this magnitude is unprecedented in history. By contrast, the American GDP per capita barely doubled from 1960 to 1995.

Economic growth in Germany has been accompanied by high and rising rates of productivity per labor hour, growing capital stock, a continuously high surplus of exports over imports, low inflation, and high rates of unemployment (around 11 percent). There seems to be a "German pattern" of moderate and continuous economic progress on all indicators except for employment. Relatively high and steady unemployment seems to be the price of today's continued moderate growth.

To explain the "German pattern," it is worth looking at it in comparative perspective. The core differences from the "American pattern" lie in the development of capital stock and in the productivity of work. In 1970, the U.S. and Germany had about the same capital stock per labor hour. By the mid nineties, the German figure was about 50 percent greater (Kommission für Zukunftsfragen, 1997, 62ff.) The different input of economic and human capital expresses itself in productivity. Productivity per labor hour increased by 25 percent in the U.S. during this period, but by 220 percent in Germany. In 1994, to produce a value of 100 Deutschmarks, the German economy needed a labor input of 1.72 hours as compared to 1.85 hours in the U.S. and 2.51 hours in Japan (Kommission für Zukunftsfragen 1997, 64).

Thus, the outstanding feature of the German economy is its high and still rising labor productivity. It involved the reduction of work time, intensive training, rigorous standards, and high wages, all of which are incentives to entrepreneurs to substitute capital for labor, thus further stimulating the increase of productivity. It involves the habit of good workmanship, vocational education, scientific orientation, and the collaboration of technically minded managers with technically oriented craftsmen. And it likewise involves an increasing risk of unemployment for those who cannot meet the performance standards of a "productivity economy." Thus, unemployment in East Germany went up sharply after unification when a highly unproductive economy had to be adapted to the productivity standards of the West. As a consequence, the German unemployment rate exceeded the average of the European Union during the 1990s.

Individual dissatisfaction and social disintegration are the expected consequences of unemployment. But, strangely enough, high unemployment in Germany has not been marked by any signs of social disintegration. Throughout all macro-changes in rates of employment and growth, satisfaction with "one's own economic situation" has been steadily high; about 80 percent of the population report themselves as satisfied. On the other hand, satisfaction with the "general economic situation" oscillates with economic developments and their public discussion. It was low at the beginning of the 1980s, rose in the early 1990s, and fell again after 1993 (Hondrich 1997 and Mielke 1998). Regarding their own situations, people are consistently satisfied. Expressing the conscience collective, they are less easily satisfied and dissatisfaction with the economic situation has been recently rising, more so in the East than in the West.

Despite continuously high unemployment and dissatisfaction with the economic system, the stability of German society today is unmistakable. An explanation for this stability – perhaps "overstabilization"– may be found in distributive processes and security. Although the "German pattern" does not protect against unemployment, it has a built-in system of social security that assures that people excluded from the active economy do not fall into extreme poverty or lose their social ties. The security systems for old age, sickness, and unemployment date back to Bismarck's innovations more than a century ago. They are often criticized today as outmoded and costly. Indeed, the rate of social security contributions has steadily increased and, in recent years has exceeded the average for the European Union. The reasons for this trend are a) the greater life expectancy of the elderly; b) the reduction of the retirement age; c) later entry of the young into the labor force; d) costlier medical treatment; and e) the high unemployment occasioned by the effort to bring East German productivity into line with West German standards. Undeniably, those factors do increase the cost of the social security system. But they cannot be attributed either to mismanagement or to faulty design, but rather to the successful realization of such goals as better medical treatment, increased longevity, improved vocational preparation, national unification, higher productivity, more qualified young workers, the early retirement of unqualified older workers, and the abandonment of outmoded industrial facilities in the East.

In effect, the growing burden on social security systems is nothing else but the reverse of the medal of an economy which is oriented, in the first place, towards increasing productivity. Security systems, far from paralyzing the economy, are essential elements of a productivity-oriented society. Any sweeping reform of the social security system, as sometimes proposed in Germany today, would entail not only a loss of social justice, but also a reduction in potential productivity.

On the other hand, it is quite clear that within the system of social security there has to be some flexibility to deal with increasing costs by economizing and by redistributing contributions as well as benefits. The announcement of such measures always provokes criticism and resistance and it remains to be seen whether the corporatist regime of the German Leviathan is efficient enough to impose necessary sacrifices on the interest groups involved. So far, the renunciations asked of the poor by conservative-liberal governments as well as the contributions asked of the rich by leftist governments have not changed the long-term picture of social justice and wealth. Unlike the United States and the United Kingdom, Germany did not experience an increase of income inequality between 1962 and 1995 (Glatzer and Hauser, 1999). There is increasing poverty in Germany, but less than in the US or in France.

7 LIBERTY

Liberties or freedoms are supposed to protect the citizen against the power of the state – and to protect minorities against the power of majorities. By doing so, liberties fulfill regulative functions for state and society. The free expression of opposition to ruling policies serves to control the ruling class. The free expression of disagreement with majority values points to alternative value orientations and stimulates collective feelings.

By dissenting from ruling policies and collective feelings, the practice of liberties leads into what may be called "the liberal paradox": it demands approval for policies and collective feelings with which it disagrees. The paradox may be solved by appealing to a more general consensus on the value of tolerance or freedom. But this is only a theoretical solution. Practically speaking, freedom always has limits that are approached when:

- the rights of others individuals are injured,
- collective feelings are offended by minority values,
- the liberal state is challenged in the name of liberalism.

This rather abstract formulation has to be filled out by definitions of particular situations and by practical decisions about what will or will not be tolerated by the state. Agents of the state seem to be free to make such decisions. But sociologically speaking, their decision-making is limited by cultural heritage and by collective feelings.

After World War II, West German democracy was confronted with a major freedom paradox: on the one hand, it should be free – i.e. completely different from Nazi totalitarianism and earlier Wilhelminian authoritarianism; on the other hand, its freedom needed special safeguards against falling back into patterns of the past. Oddly enough, the rejected patterns were not only totalitarian and authoritarian but also democratic. The Weimar Republic (1918–1933) was so weak a democracy that it was considered partly responsible for its own failure. Thus, the new constitution of freedom had no positive model in its own society; it defined itself *ex negativo*. Not continuity, but discontinuity was its device. The same was true for East Germany: its "socialist society" and "people's democracy" had no roots in German cultural tradition. Under such conditions, the limits to freedom are narrow since liberties seem to lead back into the old structures. To an authoritarian regime like that of the German Democratic Republic, this was less of a problem since it did not promise freedom. It is different for regimes with a freedom program. They must cope with the liberal paradox: to install liberties, they have to restrain them; to create something new, they have to rely on old patterns of authority.

How did the new German democracy, Western style, deal with this paradox? It was helped by three social facts:

- the Allied powers occupied the country and stayed there, as NATO partners, until 1989. Their sheer presence provided a protective framework. The Federal Republic was not left alone to guarantee the new liberties. It could grant them with minimum risk.

- The German *conscience collective*, officially and unofficially, was deeply depressed and ashamed. It acknowledged guilt for Nazi totalitarianism, war and holocaust. Although some German intellectuals complained that there were not enough feelings of shame and guilt, it may be asked whether modern history knows of any other military and moral defeat that was accepted to the same degree. After World War II – in contrast to the aftermath of World War I – there were no collective feelings of revanche or revenge.
- Instead, there was an inclination to do better. The new liberties would not be used to return to the old structures. The confrontation with the illiberal Soviet regime and its German satellite provided a warning, strengthening the adherence to western liberties and the readiness to defend them.

Political Freedom

Out of this socio-political and moral constellation, developed the concept of "Wehrhafte Demokratie" – of a democracy prepared to defend itself. It implied several restrictions on political freedom. Parliament is not free to vote the government out of office unless the opposition presents a majority for a new government; this "vote of constructive distrust" (*konstruktives Mißtrauensvotum*) reflects a lesson learned from the Weimar Republic, where extreme political parties felt free to overthrow governments without replacing them by new majorities. The new arrangement is designed to force the opposition into responsible majorities. Political parties that do not gain the support of at least 5 percent of the electorate are in general not represented in Parliament. Communist and parties of the extreme right were outlawed in the 1950s and 1960s. People belonging to those parties or otherwise considered as not firmly committed to the constitution were not acceptable as public servants. This practice was attacked, particularly by Marxist intellectuals, as "*Berufsverbot.*" It was and is illegal to express opinions which do harm to the memory of the victims of the holocaust. People who publicly claim the holocaust did not take place ("*Auschwitz-Lüge*"; the lie of Auschwitz) are sentenced.

The bundle of rights that constitute due process are not often considered to be endangered in Germany. Nevertheless, in cases of terrorist attacks against the constitutional order, culminating in 1977, there were accusations that the captured terrorists were denied those basic rights. It is difficult to decide from this vantage point whether that was so. But it is quite likely that the German judicial and political

system, always remembering how the Weimar democracy was over-
thrown by the national socialists, would withdraw basic freedom rights
rather than tolerate organized activity against its constitutional order.
The threshold of tolerance may be lower than in other western
democracies.

Religious Freedom

As to religious freedom, the overwhelming majority of Germans share
the opinion that there are no restrictions on it in the Federal Republic and that all religious minorities, be they Islamic, Scientologists or
other denominations including atheists, are allowed to exercise their
religion or lack of religion freely. Nevertheless, some religious minorities see it quite differently. They complain about restrictions or even
allege persecution. In relation to the traditional rights of Christian
churches, Islamic communities perceive discrimination. They do not
participate in the system whereby the public tax system collects a
"church tax" (8 or 9 percent of the income tax) for the account of the
churches. In addition, Islamic communities are confronted with local
opposition to the muezzin's call to prayer while the ringing of church
bells is rarely contested. Recently, in the "crucifix case," a (non
Islamic) German family sued the state of Bavaria, arguing that the
Christian symbol of the crucifix, traditionally present in Bavarian
schools, affronted the religious feelings of their daughter. The highest
Federal court, in an approach to French and American judicial
laicism, ordered the state of Bavaria to remove the crucifix. After an
outburst of collective feelings, the state of Bavaria enacted a special law
to preserve the tradition of crucifixes in classrooms.

   In another recent episode, leading German politicians joined representatives of the majority churches in attacking the Scientology
church as a disguised business enterprise that exploits and abuses its
members. Several courts accepted this position and withdrew recognition of Scientology as a religion. In some states, intelligence services
were ordered to investigate possible violations of constitutional law by
the Scientologists. Those measures were largely approved by the
German public. In reaction, the American Scientology church characterized Germany as a Nazi state and a German member requested
political asylum in the U.S. Indeed, Germany was mentioned in a
Human Rights report of the U.S. State Department as one of the countries persecuting religious minorities. The case makes it clear that patterns of religious freedom differ from country to country. In Germany,
its basis is a strong institutionalized connection of the Protestant and
Catholic churches with the state. Churches and state share important

societal functions like welfare and education. The churches reinforce the moral foundation of the state, and the state, in return, guarantees the solvency of the churches. All other religious communities, be they Christian or non Christian, are latecomers and outsiders with respect to this well established pattern. They enjoy freedom but not equality. The two majority churches have the privileges of being symbolically represented in everyday life (ringing the bells, showing the crucifix) and of being financed through the state. When other religious communities ask for the same privileges, does this mean that they request liberty, equality of chances, or a change in the national culture?

In France, the cultural pattern of religious freedom is different. French laicism means that the state cut all connections with the Catholic church and that it does not support any religion or tolerate religious symbols in public institutions, particularly schools. In this respect, there is equality among religious groups, but no liberty or tolerance towards religious expression in public institutions.

In the United States, there never was any control of the state over religious communities. Nevertheless, the ideal of complete neutrality of the state towards religion is contradicted by the ritual bases of American political life, with curious results. "Thus, while both houses of Congress have salaried chaplains and open their sessions with prayer, public schools are not permitted to sponsor prayer in any form" (Caplow, 208, this volume). Religious freedom was constitutive for the new society from the very beginning. A great number of religious denominations, all taking care of their own recruitment and finances, compete for adherents. What is normal to American society looks strange and "sectarian" to Germans. The business activities, aggressive recruitment and opaque practices of a church like Scientology are incompatible with the German understanding of religion. Features which are basic to the American pattern of religious freedom are considered dangerous to individual freedom in Germany.

Liberties and open borders

The problem of intolerance is not particularly vexatious in today's Germany. However, issues about immigration have stimulated political discussion and stirred up collective feelings during the last decades. It should not be forgotten that the unification of Germany meant a very unusual increase in liberties for the seventeen million people of the former German Democratic Republic. In addition, opening the borders offered access to a democratic polity to more than two million political and war refugees as well as to repatriates of German descent coming from former communist countries.

The complete freedom of movement granted to all citizens of the member states of the European Community and to family members of guest workers up to the age of 16 has had the same effect: more liberties and more social rights for more people coming from outside. There is a present tendency, in democratic societies, to extend constitutional rights beyond the territory of the state. Human rights belong to all humankind. What happens to a state that follows this principle? At the very least, a conflict between residents and newcomers. Can a state really abandon all preferential action in favor of its own citizens? Can a state guarantee the freedom to immigrate?

It is not clear what this really means in terms of social and economic costs and benefits. For a society whose fertility rates have fallen far below the reproductive level, the benefits may prevail in the long run. In the short run, the strains on employment, education and welfare systems are considerable. The problems are aggravated by the "egalitarian" self-image of a society that feels obliged to guarantee a certain welfare level to whomever enters its territory (in contrast to "individualistic" societies like the U.S. which tolerate more inequality of treatment). To guarantee the stipulated welfare level for citizens and newcomers alike, it eventually becomes necessarily to restrict entry. This is what has happened in Germany during recent years. It took the form of progressive restrictions to the liberal asylum law. The sequence may be interpreted in terms of "social physics": an unusual increase in access to the society leads to conflicts and restrictions within the society and turns outward to impose limits on access.

There was a substantial increase of de facto immigration from the late 1980s to the mid 1990s. During the same time there was a visible increase in crime, partly attributable to the incoming foreigners and ethnic Germans, most of them young, active and ambitious but without the means to satisfy their expectations in legal ways (Pfeiffer 1998). At the same time, "hostility towards foreigners," as reported in criminal statistics, rose dramatically during the early 1990s and decreased after rights to asylum were restricted. Strangely enough, the rise and decline in violent acts against foreigners ("*Ausländerfeindlichkeit*") is not reflected in the survey data, which show a slow but continuous rise in sympathy and acceptance towards immigrants. The apparent contradiction is probably due to the fact that hostility by only a small number of people, increased against the rising number of newcomers at the same time as sympathy was growing for foreigners, especially already settled "guest workers".

Still, requirements for naturalization, traditionally based on *ius sanguinis*, are higher in Germany than in the classical immigration countries. In this respect the freedom of newcomers is restricted. Nevertheless, there is a growing movement to enlarge their rights and to permit them and especially their children to become German citizens. One of the first steps of the new "leftist" government, at the end of 1998, was to facilitate the naturalization of persons born or long resident in the Federal Republic. This process is going on with new laws facilitating immigration, particularly with respect to highly qualified persons. Thus, Germany is gaining a self-conception more similar to classical immigration countries such as the US and Canada.

8   GRADING LEVIATHAN

As to the value of union (unity), many countries, particularly in Eastern Europe, have achieved national unity during the past decade; among them the Baltic states, Slovenia, Croatia, Slovakia and the Czech Republic. All of them did so by separating from larger empires or states. We may label this process "unity by fission." Germany is the only country in the West – and perhaps in the world – which achieved "unity by fusion" during the same interval. Seen from a national perspective, this must be considered a success (although some "real nationalists," pointing to the loss of pre-war territories in the East, might call it a failure). A positive evaluation of German unification is supported by the observation that it had no perceptible adverse effect on the process of European unification. On the contrary, political parties throughout the European Union, more or less afraid of the potential power of a German Leviathan, agree on the necessity of confining the enlarged state within the framework of the European Union and NATO. Thus, the value of national union is put into perspective by the competing value of transnational union. Incidentally, it is not clear to whom or what the credit for German unification should go – to a particular constellation in world politics, to Gorbachev, to chancellor Kohl?

German politicians certainly seized the opportunity – without working very hard for it. We may award this an "A," although the relative deprivation of the East German people with respect to their fellow citizens in the West has led to a long-lasting resentment which might well be interpreted as a sign of inner disunity. A more sensitive policy of national solidarity might have done better. And the same politics of unity that initially deserved an "A" probably did not deserve more than a "C" or a "D" during the following years.

The notion of Justice, in central Europe, is applied both in the socio-economic field and in the legal system. On the one hand, it refers to the distribution of wealth and income; in this respect, people speak of social justice. On the other hand, as justice before the law, it refers to the distribution of penalties for violations of laws. As to social justice, the West German system of *"Soziale Marktwirtschaft"* (social market economy) with its particular mix of market elements and corporatist negotiation has led to fairly stable and widely accepted distributive patterns (see Welfare); in a long term perspective, more than half of the population approve of it as "just," the remainder are divided between those who would like a more favorable tilt either towards the poor or towards the middle class.

After unification, the relative deprivation of the Eastern part with respect to social justice led to regional resentments. The same was true of justice before the law. The fact that West German law was simply extended to the whole of Germany and that judges and lawyers from the West went East contributed to the impression held by many East Germans that they suffered a special kind of "conqueror's justice." "We were looking for justice, but we got the rule of law." This famous paradoxical saying of a civil rights fighter in the East describes a widespread attitude. Apart from this special situation, Germans continue to trust in the rule of law. While opinion polls show decreasing trust in judicial institutions during the past fifteen years, this is in line with a loss of trust in all public institutions; political institutions in particular suffered a greater lost of trust during the same interval. Sentiments of injustice before the law are seemingly due to two long-term trends: the liberalization of punishment norms (see liberty) and the growing burden of civil and criminal litigation. Thus, injustice is seen less as the result of a systemic fault but rather as an overload of the judicial system. As to justice, the German state deserves at least a "C" and perhaps even a "B."

The value of tranquility, always highly esteemed in German history, was challenged three times in recent history: at the end of the sixties by the student rebellion, ten years later by a wave of terrorism against economic and political institutions and their representatives, and again ten years later by the huge "Monday demonstrations" against the socialist regime in East Germany. After unification, there was a wave of incendiarism against immigrants seeking asylum. Those riots had a largely symbolic character. Leviathan, although irritated and overreacting, managed to organize and unite a majority against violent minorities and to transform rebellion into legitimacy. As to public safety, rising crime rates accompanied the economic and social progress of West Germany until the beginning of the 1980s, remained stable for a decade and then rose again, mostly in the form of juvenile criminality, a trend clearly connected with the opening of borders and with unification. The state reacted by tightening control of the borders and by incarcerating the young offenders; 80 percent of those incarcerated come from abroad. Was there too much or too little state activity to ensure tranquility? It is difficult to say. Obviously, there is a conflict between the value of tranquility on the one hand and open borders on the other. In this dilemma, Leviathan can not satisfy all interests. It must settle for a "C."

As to defense, Germany has played a restricted and unspectacular part within the framework of NATO. Due to its role as military aggressor in World War II and to its reputation as a seedbed of militarism, it was and is extremely reluctant to participate in collective peacekeeping efforts. German defense policy traces a fine line between the roles of free rider and full military partner. So far, there has been little occasion for evaluating the defense function of the German Leviathan. With respect to defense and perhaps other functions, a partial loss of national sovereignty has different implications from one country to another. What is not accepted in the US or in France, is greatly appreciated in Germany.

Similarly in welfare, national societies follow different national patterns. All of them subscribe to the value of economic growth. But on their way to that goal, they enlist additional values which appear in culturally specific constellations. German culture, which traditionally emphasized the value of productive work, has brought about an export-oriented economy with productivity as a tacit core value: rising productivity goes together with international competitiveness, high salaries for skilled and expert work and unemployment for those who do not meet the standards of productive excellence (in the 1950s and 1960s, there was practically no unemployment). This is the German pattern today. It guarantees high wages to a diminishing labor force of highly skilled people working with modern equipment. Less qualified and elderly people are protected by the security systems of the welfare state – not so much as Leviathan but as the *Sozialstaat*, dating back to Bismarck.

On the other side of the Atlantic, both Leviathan and the *Sozialstaat* are absent from the American tradition. The U.S. pattern of a "service society," oriented towards profit more than towards productivity, reduces costs by reducing salaries. De facto (and not necessarily by intention) it gives preference to high employment at the expense of productivity. The German system, although performing poorly with regard to full employment, maintains higher rates of productivity, provides more adequate support for the unemployed – and has preserved a long term stability in distributive social justice. Although at this writing (1999) the American system has a higher rate of economic growth, German economic growth has been higher over the past four decades. Now, which system deserves the higher grade in "welfare"? Should we award a "B" to the U.S. and a "C" to Germany or vice versa? Is it not a matter of taste to prefer one system or the other? And are our preferences not coined by habits of culture anyway? Finally, is it Leviathan or the more embracing national culture that deserves to be praised or blamed ?

Behind those considerations, there is the problem of conflicting values. Within the value of welfare, there are conflicting requirements that cannot be fully satisfied at the same time. Maximum productivity and full employment do not go together in the long run. The same is true for liberties on the one hand and values like security, social justice, and unity on the other.

The more liberties for deviant minorities, the less security for the majority. As people who follow the norms, we may feel threatened by a growing number of those who use the freedom not to do so. Even if we do not feel endangered individually, we are made to feel insecure as collective beings who notice that the norms we share are losing their binding force. If we try to be tolerant, we lose some of the reward for obeying the norms. We feel that it is unjust for deviant individuals and groups to be treated in the same way as conforming ones. Finally, the value of distributive justice within a group is lessened by the freedom of outsiders to enter the group if those entering take part in the distribution without having contributed before. This conflict may become acute when immigrants, whether foreigners or ethnic Germans, are perceived as taking unfair advantage of the welfare state. The conflict may be mitigated by economic growth and high employment but under conditions of relatively high unemployment, as in Germany today, the conflict is resolved by restricting immigration.

Should we consider this restriction and others previously mentioned as indicating a deficient performance of the state with respect to liberties? Or are those restrictions necessary to ensure a kind of equilibrium between minorities – be they political and religious dissenters or immigrants – and the majority who share a *conscience collective* that provides the basic socio-cultural pattern of the society? Liberties may be part of that pattern but majorities never accept unlimited liberties because they are viewed as dangerous to core values. Be the danger real or imaginary, the highest grade for liberty should not go to the political system that offers the highest degree of freedom, but to the system that grants the appropriate degree of freedom, i.e. that which makes it possible for majorities and minorities to accept each other fully.

In the final instance, it is the citizens themselves who evaluate Leviathan a) as a type of democratic political system and b) as to its fulfillment of democratic values. Those two aspects – legitimacy and performance – of the political system are not always easy to distinguish. Political sociologists (Fuchs et al. 1995; Fuchs 1998; Fuchs and Klingemann 1998) have argued that, contrary to a popular view of a legitimacy crisis, the performance of the state in West Germany during more than four decades has gained it strong and stable support. The legitimization of democracy in Germany has occurred in the context of other successful democracies confronted by unsuccessful socialist regimes. Thus, in western Europe, satisfaction with democracy remained high and stable until the beginning of the 1990s (Fuchs et al. 1995). In West Germany, it was particularly high and reached more than 80 percent in 1990. It has since declined dramatically but still remains above the 50 percent level. Satisfaction with democracy is considerably lower in East Germany.

The loss of support for democracy during the past decade is clearly due to the unification of Germany. West Germans, and East Germans even more, became aware that the expectations stimulated by this extraordinary event were not met by the performance of Leviathan; in particular, East Germans were disappointed in their aspirations for social justice.

On the other hand, the insecurities of the nineties cannot be attributed to unification alone. In the larger context of globalization, Germans have lost some of their confidence in the problem-solving capacities of the state. Confidence in all institutions has suffered, but political institutions like government and parliament more so than churches, trade unions, or the military. Declining trust in institutions does not necessarily indicate that those institutions did, or will do, a bad job. It may as well indicate an anxiety that national institutions will not be able to solve problems generated by world-wide competition. Ironically, the rhetoric of globalization may undermine the confidence in democracy that it is supposed to strengthen.

Despite the declining trust in traditional institutions in general and declining satisfaction with the performance of the democratic state in particular, Germans, in their large majority, continue to believe that "the democracy we have in the Federal Republic is the best form of government." This may be taken as a clear sign of the legitimacy of democratic Leviathan. Only the East Germans, with a less libertarian and more paternalistic image of the state, remain somewhat unconvinced. It remains to be seen if they will change their minds, which would entitle Leviathan to better grades.

REFERENCES

Böhlk, Joachim. "*Verbrechen lohnt sich wieder*,": *Frankfurter Allgemeine Zeitung*, 8 November 1997.
Bundeskriminalamt. *Polizeiliche Kriminalstatistik 1996*. Wiesbaden 1997.
Fuchs, Dieter. "The Political Culture of Unified Germany," paper FS III 98–204, Wissenschaftszentrum Berlin für Sozialforschung, Research Unit, Institutions and Social Change, 1998.

Fuchs, Dieter, and Hans-Dieter Klingemann. National Community, Political Culture, and Support for Democracy in Central and Eastern Europe. Draft submission to the joint project between the Forward Studies Unit, European Commission, and the Robert Schuman Centre, European University Institute, Florence, on the Long-Term Implications of EU Enlargement: The Nature of the New Border. Florence, 17–18 Sept. 1998.

Fuchs, Dieter, Giovanna Guidorossi, and Palle Svensson. "Support for the Democratic System." In Klingemann, Hans-Dieter, and Dieter Fuchs, eds. *Citizens and the State*, 323–53. Oxford: Oxford University Press, 1995.

Glatzer, Wolfgang, Karl Otto Hondrich, Heinz-Herbert Noll, Karin Stiehr and Barbara Wörndl, *Recent Social Trends in West Germany 1960–1990*. Frankfurt am Main, Montreal: Campus, McGill-Queen's University Press, 1992.

Glatzer, Wolfgang, and Richard Hauser. "The Distribution of Income and Wealth in European and North-American Societies," in Lemel, Yannik, and Heinz Herbert Noll, eds., *Changing Structures of Inequalities*. Montreal: McGill-Queen's University Press, 2001.

Hondrich, Karl Otto. "Standorte in der Standortdebatte," in "Merkur." *Deutsche Zeitschrift für europäisches Denken* 1 (1997): 52–8.

Institut für Wirtschaft und Gesellschaft (IWG). *Germany in Europe in 20 charts*. Bonn: IWG, 1998.

Klingemann, Hans-Dieter. "Mapping Political Support in the 1990s: A Global Analysis," paper FS III 98–202, Wissenschaftszentrum Berlin für Sozialforschung, Research Unit, Institutions and Social Change, 1998.

Kommission für Zukunftsfragen der Freistaaten Bayern und Sachsen, Erwerbstätigkeit und Arbeitslosigkeit in Deutschland. Bonn, December 1997.

Mielke, Ralf. "Individuelle Orientierung versus kollektive Orientierung am Beispiel der Einschätzung wirtschaftlicher Lagen." Thesis, University of Frankfurt, 1998.

Noelle-Neumann, Elisabeth, and Renate Köcher, eds. *Allensbacher Jahrbuch der Demoskopie 1993 – 1997*. München-Allensbach am Bodensee: K.G. Saur Verlag 1997.

Pfeiffer, Christian. "Juvenile Crime and Violence in Europe." *Crime and Justice* 23, 1998.

Six Aspects of the Spanish State

SALUSTIANO DEL CAMPO AND
JUAN MANUEL CAMACHO

1 INTRODUCTION

The current Spanish Constitution is only twenty years old. It was adopted by Congress and the Senate on 31 October 1978 and ratified by referendum on 6 December of the same year. Since Spain had had no less than twelve constitutions since 1808, the persistence of this Constitution is encouraging. It followed Franco's dictatorship and abolished the seven Basic Laws with which he governed, enacted between 1936 and 1975.

Its first article states that "Spain is a social and democratic State ruled by law and promoting liberty, justice, equality and political pluralism as the uppermost values of its legal system." It aimed to bring Spain into line politically with the industrialized countries in a process that was concluded in 1986 when Spain became part of the European Community, now the European Union.

Its first article mentions two of the criteria of the effectiveness of democratic systems that are used in this work: liberty and justice. The other four are included either in the Preamble or in the Preliminary Title. Article 2 refers to the union thus: "The Constitution is based on the indisoluble unity of the Spanish nation, the common and indivisible country of all Spaniards, and recognizes and guarantees the right to autonomy and solidarity for all of the peoples and regions that compose it." Defense is referred to in Article 8 which states that the mission of the Armed Forces is to "guarantee the sovereignty and independence of Spain, defend its territorial integrity and its Constitution."

With respect to tranquility and welfare, the Preamble specifies that the Spanish Nation proclaims its will to "guarantee democratic coexistence pursuant to the Constitution and the laws in keeping with a just economic and social order (and) promote cultural and economic progress in order to insure a decent quality of life for all."

From its beginning, the 1978 Constitution enjoyed the favor of practically the entire Spanish people. The social modernization and economic development of the the two preceding decades opened the way for the peaceful political transition so widely praised internationally. Since then, its implementation has revealed a few defects that do not diminish the achievement that this has been the longest and truest democratic period that Spain has enjoyed.

The following pages deal with what has occurred in the fields chosen for our comparative study in some detail and with a reasonable collection of empirical data and the epilogue underlines some conclusions of the analysis.

2   UNION

The 1978 Constitution defines Spain as a social and democratic State subject to the rule of law in the form of a parliamentary monarchy recognizing and guaranteeing the right to autonomy for the nationalities and regions that compose it as well as the solidarity among them. It brought political stability and laid the foundations for the development of democratic institutions. The overriding need to construct a State comparable to those of western Europe and to design a regulatory scheme for the future, agreed by consensus and capable of overcoming the old conflicts among Spaniards, made the political transition from an authoritarian regime to a democratic one possible in a brief period that concluded in 1978, three years after the death of Francisco Franco, the former head of state. During this period, the representatives of the Spanish people, freely elected in 1977, tackled great national issues. Included among these issues, according to Adolfo Suarez, the first President of the transition government, were the organization of a modern social and democratic state subject to the rule of law, the form of the state, its non-denominational character and self-government for component nationalities and regions.

Constructing a legal framework for coexistence was not the Constitution's only challenge. It also had to modify the political, social and economic structures that existed in Spain prior to 1975. As Suarez stated, "It was necessary to substitute the centralist state with a state of autonomies; to pass from a strongly controlled economy to a stage where liberalization was an essential part of our integration into the free world; to modify the system of social relations, to organize a more efficient independent judiciary; to modernize the armed forces, to organize a new education system and, in short, to make liberty, equality and solidarity the most significant human and political values of Spanish society as a whole."[1]

The changes and transformations occurred with unwonted speed. Spanish society was ready for the modernization it had been demanding for some time. However, this was not the case with some of the institutions that had constituted the backbone of the old regime. These have been transforming gradually at the vegetative rate of generational replacement. Thus the new generations have been more willing and able to take on the adaptation of certain structures.

The Spanish Constitution's main challenge was the creation of a plurinational state able to make a place for certain regions and recognize their singularity. The territorial organization of the state, provided for under Title VIII of the Constitutional Charter, includes 17 autonomous communities, 50 provinces and 8,048 municipalities, in addition to the autonomous cities of Ceuta and Melilla. The creation of the autonomous communities generated three administrative levels: state, autonomic and local. The legal framework for the operation of the different communities is in their respective statutes.

Our Constitution establishes a model based on the concept of decentralization that includes the right to autonomy and self-government for the Spanish regions and whose aim is to overcome the centralist and unitary concept of Spain still latent in our society today. The Constitution of 1978 endeavored to resolve the conflict between the two models with the use of the terms "nation," "nationalities" and "regions,"[2] although this confrontation is still alive, maintained by the nationalist parties whose credibility and existence depend upon it. The federalist conception has been gaining followers since 1976, and has maintained a stable level of support since 1985. The faction claiming independence for the so-called historic territories is a solid minority.

On the other hand, the Spanish Constitution's recognition of the existence of cultural nationalities within the Spanish state entails the consideration of whether Spain is a nation of nations, and forms the new duality between Spanish identity and cultural identity. Even so, the Constitution separates the condition of being a Spaniard from other identification. According to Lamo de Espinosa, the Constitution emphasizes the political identity of all Spaniards making this separate from the different cultural identities.[3]

With the exception of Catalonia and the Basque Country whose respective statutes were adopted very early, the other autonomies were launched between 1981 and 1983. The autonomic map has been completed recently with the adoption of special statutes for the autonomous cities of Ceuta and Mellilla, in North Africa. In short, the institutions regulating the self-government of the various autonomies have their basis in the Constitution.

At present, the autonomous governments have wide powers in the most diverse matters and manage large budgets. The regional budgets together amounted in 1998 to a third of the national budget. The transfer of powers from the state to the autonomies has entailed, in many cases, significant budgetary increases. Since 1986, the majority of regional governments have seen their budgets multiplied by an average factor of 7. Aragón was the autonomous community with the greatest budget growth, while La Rioja and Catalonia had the least. In the case of Catalonia and the Basque Country, the budget increases have been more restrained due, mostly, to the fact that they started with some very ample powers and generous transfers. As a result, adapting their budgets to their new responsibilities called for less increase than in other autonomous communities.

This state structure, however, generates a delicate balance between the different territories and a separatist tendency that challenges the existence of a Spanish identity. The territories of the so-called historic nationalities are assuming important powers that until recently belonged to the state and the permanent conflict between the state and one or another autonomous community shows that the State of Autonomies, as set up in the Constitution, is not the final solution for the "peripheral nationalisms."

The process of exclusive identification is supported by the existence of significant objective differences not only in culture or language, but also in the economic and educative processes that have brought complementary elements to the shaping of a true group consciousness.

Even though language and culture are the cornerstone on which the differentiation sought by the inhabitants of these territories rests, it is certain that Spaniards' perception of the developmental divergence between the regions is based on the opinion that there is discriminatory treatment by the central government.

It was hoped that the creation of the autonomies would reduce interregional inequalities as one of its positive results. However, this possible effect has not been perceived by the Spaniards. In 1992, the majority of the public believed that the autonomies had increased or, in any event, had not lessened the existing interregional differences, and in 1996 they perceived a great disparity between the different regions with respect to prosperity and wealth and 30 percent believed that these had increased since the creation of the autonomous communities.[4]

The regions that make up the Spanish territory have, in the last century, had an unequal evolution that the important social, cultural and economic changes of the past 30 years have not been able to mitigate. Beyond some territories' demand for separate identities, a noticeable rift has developed between the regions of the center and of the periphery. Socioeconomic indicators show the divergences among regions. Thus, the populations of the Balearic Islands and the Canaries increased 7 percent between the 1991 Census and the Municipal Register of 1996, and regions such as Andalusia and Murcia more than 4 percent. On the other hand, there were regions, such as Castille and León and Asturias and, to a lesser extent, Aragón and the Basque Country, with net losses of population.

The growth or loss of population is explained by the migratory flows from less fortunate zones to those with higher and more stable levels of income and well-being. Such is the case of the Balearic Islands, that have, at present, a disposable family income 32 percent higher than the average Spanish family income, and, at the same time, one of the lowest unemployment and poverty indexes in Spain, whereas the regions of Andalusia, Murcia and Extremadura have 30 percent less disposable family income than the nation as a whole and 60 percent less than the inhabitants of the Balearics and the highest rates of unemployment and poverty in Spain.

The objective indicators of territorial inequality coincide with the Spaniards' perception of a growing imbalance that explains their eagerness to find remedial mechanisms. The majority of our fellow citizens believe that there is more inequality now than ten years ago, although they would not renounce the autonomic model. For the most part, the autonomies receive strong support. The regional differences in well-being and wealth are the main causes of dissatisfaction.

The majority of Spaniards believe there is a tendency for inequalities and the gap separating poor and rich regions to increase. Convergence among the autonomies has not occurred. The richest, with exceptions, continue to gain relative weight in the economy and distance themselves from the average. It is true that the growth of the most backward regions has been faster and more intense than that of the more prosperous ones, but there still remains a long road to travel before any uniformity can be achieved.

These inequalities between regions are due, according to the majority of Spaniards, to history; they attribute "relative poverty and lesser development simply to a slower pace that, as such, can be corrected more or less easily. Then, the existence of inequalities is blamed on differential investment," directed towards more developed regions with better perspectives for profit. But the reason most named by Spaniards for this situation of relative inequality is that "the State favoured some regions (thanks to which they prospered) and abandoned others (to become poorer and less developed.)."[5]

This last perception has a strong subjective component based on the general impression that there is favorable treatment of certain autonomies to the detriment of others, related to their position of privilege, power and influence in the nation's government. Of course, the perception of unequal treatment is less acute when the reference is to one's own community. Not surprisingly, it is the autonomous communities with the highest levels of income that perceive the least discriminatory treatment. To these can be added those that have strong popular backing, or a strong regional government.

Underlying all this is the need to redefine the State of Autonomies, since it was created at a time when the newness of the debate and the pressure to provide ourselves with a constitutional framework obscured fundamental problems, in particular, the necessity for national institutions to guarantee the same rights and benefits for all citizens, whatever their origin, language or cultural identity.

Nevertheless, the presence of the autonomies has imposed itself on Spaniards, especially in those regions where there was little local consciousness. The phenomena of interregional inequality have consolidated with time and have shaped a growing resistance to the opposition to a Spanish national identity. However, the possible negative effects on Spanish unity that might be attributed to the autonomies are rejected by the majority. Thus, 55 percent of Spaniards reject the claim that the autonomies contribute to the disintegration of Spain, and this absolute majority is maintained in all the autonomous communities, whatever the ideological position of the respondent, although it is true that those on the left and right show considerable differences.[6]

In the historic nationalities and in the emerging ones, such as Andalusia, a non-exclusive national identity has been gaining strength and the proportions of those with more localist sentiments remains stable with the passage of time. The fact that our Constitution recognizes the existence of differentiated historic nationalities has not stopped the regional political parties from demanding higher levels of power and influence for their regions in pursuit of what they call "shared sovereignty." It is precisely the Constitution that guarantees coexistence among territories, whatever their histories. Repeating the words of Alain Touraine, "... either we recognize the difference and respect the rules that guarantee coexistence or we assert the belief in values that lead us to reject those who do not share them."[7] The variable desire for more self-government by those territories with historic, cultural or economic particularities expresses the more or less integrated character of their societies and whether or not they perceive the Spanish state as a threat to their cultural survival. Only the Basque Country, Catalonia, Galicia, Navarra and, more recently, the Canaries, have regional parties with strong implantation and popular support. However, the regional impulse has emerged in other areas with no differentiated traditional identity, such as Andalusia, La Rioja, Aragón or Asturias (even in Castille there is a Castille Nationalist Party). But we can't forget – as one of the fathers of the Constitution pointed out – "that the Constitution, when distinguishing nationalities and regions, recognizes Catalonia and the Basque Country and Galicia as nationalities while other parts of Spain, also with deep historic roots, had abandoned their differences in the construction of the concept of Spain. It also recognized regional differences of language, culture and law. What it did not recognize was a right to be separate or to receive preferred treatment."[8] The appearance of regionalist parties in communities that historically had none was a reaction against the regions that had achieved high levels of self-government, prosperity and well-being by using, at times, pressure that springs from their regionalism and that flaunt a persistent inconsiderateness with respect to the concept of Spain and those who believe in it.

Language continues to be one of the most powerful features of regional identity in our country. Catalonia as well as the Basque Country and Galicia have used language as differentiating features in opposition to Spanishness, beyond its use as an instrument of communication. In the words of Javier Marías, "language or languages, it often seem to be forgotten, are first of all a means, a tool, an instrument, a vehicle of transmission at the service of what we want to transmit. Today, in many places, they are treated as if they were the thing itself, the essential, the sacred, that which defines and determines the rest."[9]

Under the Spanish constitution, Spanish is the official language of Spain but "the other Spanish languages will also be official in their respective autonomous communities." This recognition of the different languages has generated difficulties of cultural adaptation and has strengthened the identities other than Spanish in the territories that have their own languages. Five of the seventeen autonomous communities with 40 percent of the total population have a language other than Spanish and in a sixth, Navarra, the coofficiality of the local language is established for part of the territory. Aside from these languages, there are others with less extensive use and of less importance. Among these are Bable in Asturias, Aragonese that is still spoken in some counties of Huesca, and Aranese of the Aran Valley in Catalonia, a Gascon dialect of Langue d'oc.

The case of Euskara, or Basque, is, perhaps, the most symptomatic use of a language as a regional symbol. Around it, or them, since it is a group of languages that have been artificially unified in order to strengthen the cultural identity of their speakers, a powerful mechanism has been constructed for social discrimination and a revindicative sentiment has been woven that perverts the essence of the language. The myth of the origins of the Basques and their culture as unrelated to the other peoples that form Spain is scientifically questionable.[10] However, the use of Euskara and other local languages is related to their worth as a vehicle of communication beyond cultural frontiers and regional identities.

Only in Galicia and the Balearic Islands does a majority of the population consider the community language their mother tongue. They were more isolated and have been more reluctant to accept external influences. The everyday use of the language and the low levels of emigration from other regions have historically conditioned a more pronounced survival than in other regions that have their own language where, although collective commitment may be greater, a very important part of the population has its origin in other Spanish territories, as is the case in Catalonia.

Despite all this, Spanish society has no real linguistic conflicts aside from partisan interpretations. Opinions on linguistic policies are not polarized around extreme positions but primarily seek understanding between those who speak one language and another.

One way of learning about the levels of language skills in each of the territories that has its own language is through the linguistic censuses that some territories have conducted since 1975, using the Register of Inhabitants and the Population Census. However, the data refers to language knowledge and not to its effective use. The use of a language in everyday activities and the need to express oneself in it determine its vitality. Thus, 16 percent of the population in Euskadi and 10 percent in Navarra have Basque, or Euskara, as a mother tongue, while in Euskadi more than 30 percent of those who speak Spanish as a mother tongue, and 14 percent of the population in Navarra, speak, read or understand Basque. Thus, nearly 40 percent of the population in the Basque Country have a more or less extensive knowledge of Euskara, but that is not to say they use it outside of a small circle.

The peripheral regionalisms emphasize their resistance, especially in the case of the Basque Country, to the threat they perceive in that which is Spanish. The Basque industrial society of the 19th century needed immigrant workers to fill the numerous jobs generated by heavy industry. Immigrants from other Spanish regions brought lifestyles and cultural patterns that collided head-on with the Basque society's traditions and were considered a threat to the traditional culture (a threat that was overestimated by the traditional Basque middle class from which the PNV sprang). The idea that Spanish immigrants – and by extension, all things Spanish – were responsible for the Basque people's oppression has survived to the present day. Juan Olabarria Agra explains anomalies in the Basque country as "victimist falsification of recent history: the civil war is not interpreted as a fascist aggression against democracy but as a Spanish aggression against the Basque Country and its natural representatives."[11]

The persistent belief in this historical oppression has lead the regional parties to insist on special interpretations of history in order to support some supposedly inalterable regional values. Those Basque historians and intellectuals who dare to diverge from the official regionalist vision of history, claim that it is necessary to put an end to the myth in order to arrive at an objective interpretation of the historical trajectory of the Iberian peoples.[12]

The diversity of regions and ways of acting and expressing oneself have generated a set of simplified mental images of other people – those who are not like ourselves. Although many of these images are based on stereotypes, there is no doubt that they condition attitudes. The stereotype, like other forms of social categorization, serves as a frame of reference when processing information and as a basis for judgments and inferences. However, we cannot talk about stereotypes without taking into consideration the role of the group in which they are created and the group functions to which they respond.[13] In our country, stereotypes have buttressed local identities against the exterior and, in some cases, regional identity has become rooted in them as in no other country in the world. It is the local sphere that attracts our interest to the detriment of the national and international spheres.[14]

The image of Spaniards held abroad is composed of stereotypes that come from particular regions, or by the sum of these. Regional diversity favors a varied image of Spain, in spite of the appropriation of certain unique local stereotypes as Spanish.

In the same way that the movement of people from one region to another within Spain has contributed to the clash of different cultural realities and has been used as an excuse to strengthen regional identities, we must consider the important migratory flows from other countries.

The growing number of immigrants has generated a number of problems that are aggravated by the unenthusiastic and long-standing policy of the Spanish government on this issue, as well as by popular attitudes of rejection. Until recently, the small contingent of immigrants did not arouse much resistance. In the last ten years, however, violent incidents have occurred. The murder of a Dominican immigrant in 1992 was the first sign that there might be a wave of reactions against immigrants. Such incidents have been repeated and we have lost hope that they might be isolated thoughtless acts. Opposition to the presence of foreigners in Spain has spread. The results of a recent investigation by Professor Calvo Buezas alerts us to an impulse towards ethnic identification as a reaction to universalization and globalization.[15] This study,[16] a survey of a sample of 6000 students from elementary to advanced levels in Spanish educational institutions, shows the high percentage of students who believe that there are already enough foreigners in Spain and that further entries should be prevented. A large component of xenophobia can be seen in the considerable percentage of Spanish students who would expel the gypsies from Spain (27 percent), in the 24 percent who would expel the Moors, in the 15 percent who would expel the Jews and the 13 percent who would do the same with blacks and Indians. Only one in four Spanish citizens would choose a solution that did not limit the number of immigrants and would facilitate their incorporation into our society. Expulsion as an option, however, has less support. The majority of Spaniards have been moving towards a third option along the lines indicated by the Law of Rights and Liberties of Foreigners of July 1985. This law established an immigration policy centered on the control of migratory flows and oriented to Spain's position on an exterior border of the European Community. The regulations established under that law made it much more difficult to comply with the requirements for becoming a legal immigrant. This precarious situation, and the confusion that ensued, led to the mass entry of illegal immigrants. In 1991, a process of legalization of foreigners began that was repeated in 1996.[17] The adoption of quotas for entry, applied either in fact or by legal regulation, is the preferred option of the great majority of Spaniards. The *numerus clausus* has the most followers (49 percent). On the other hand, 18 percent of the survey respondents would refuse everyone who wanted to enter the country, whatever their motivation, ethnic origin or nationality. That figure has been increasing since 1992, although more respondents (53 percent) would not discriminate against any immigrant because of his origin. A marked proportion (almost 20 percent) feels that preference should be given to Latin Americans, who should not have any impediment placed on entry. Other ethnic, racial and national groups do not receive sufficient support to single them out. There is a new element conditioning these debates. Regionalisms and the model of shared sovereignty that they advocate, as the regional parties of Galicia, the Basque Country and Catalonia indicated in the "Declaration of Barcelona," incorporate the aim of European integration. They seek the recognition and strengthening of their identity at a time when national borders are dissolving or weakening. Spain has participated actively in the European Union since its incorporation in 1986, as well as in the debates whose object it was to widen the interests of the Union. Spaniards' eagerness to be European is not recent and Spain's historical trajectory cannot be understood in isolation from the European continent.[18] Europe has become the main reference of our future. The Spanish nation has been socially and economically transformed within a brief period of time and, once the political transition was completed, it achieved a privileged position in the European Union. Entry into the Union was made possible by the insistence of the Spanish democratic governments, by the unexpected "workers' Europeanization," and by the conviction of political leaders that it was the solution to Spain's problems. This is shown by some of the surveys of the Center for Sociological Investigation after its foundation in 1964, and more recently, by the INCIPE reports of 1991, 1992, 1995 and 1998, according to which economic goals take second place to social and political integration in Europe. The disappearance of the barriers separating the European peoples is one of the continent's greatest aspirations, since otherwise, the construction of a political order runs the risk of bogging down in technical regulations that do not create a true European identity. To this we can add the difficulties of defining the interior borders claimed by local and regional movements who see in Europe a source of liberation from a Spanish national identity that they accept only reluctantly. The willingness of Spaniards to contribute to the new organization of the Old Continent is seen in the results of numerous opinion surveys. Spaniards want their country in Europe's first line, laying aside once and for all a collective identity that has sometimes bordered on caricature.

3   TRANQUILITY

Strikes

The most important form of labor dispute is unquestionably the strike – a collective stoppage of work in order to bring about certain decisions or change the attitudes of those who contract, pay and receive the product of said work: employers and private or public enterprises.[19]

Strikes have various motivations, most commonly to pressure employers to negotiate. A strike can also be a protest against some specific problem or an expression of solidarity with other workers on strike. Although there are other forms of labor disputes (boycotts, work to rule, etc.), the strike constitutes the principal form and has been an essential tactic of the workers' movement since its beginnings.

A strike requires a degree of cohesion and collective action that implies a certain degree of organization. A conflict becomes institutionalized when it tends to resolve itself in the same way every time it occurs. Collective bargaining is the principal means of resolving socio-labor disputes in industrialized societies, but not the only one. The role of unions in Spain is affected by the short time in which they have been able to act freely. The legalization of the unions and the first free union elections (1978) marked the beginning of a massive affiliation of men and women to the trade unions.[20] The unions sought the strong support of the working class in order to strengthen themselves as channels for the grievances of workers and to overcome the lack of an associational tradition in our society and the passivity of workers accustomed to a vertical model of industrial relations.

In 1978,[21] as a result of this first surge of affiliation, 57 percent of employees in the industrial sector belonged to a trade union. Two years later, in 1980, affiliation had dropped to 36 percent and in 1982 to 27 percent. Union affiliation has since continued to decline at a slower but unalterable pace. The latest figures that we have, taken with the reservations always necessary with this kind of data, show union affiliation for Spain at no more than 15 percent.

Strikes in Spain reached their height in 1979, after the Constitution was adopted and freedom for unions and for the mobilization of workers in defense of their legitimate rights was fully guaranteed. The strength of the unions was great at that time, because so many of the demands of the transition were channeled through the unions. In those years strikes were the principal tools for obtaining better salaries and working conditions and also instruments of political pressure to promote change in the institutions of the state, maintaining the momentum of political struggle that had engaged the unions in the years prior to the transition.

At that time, strikes affected nearly half of the working population and nearly 19 million work days were lost each year. Since then, these figures have been dropping steadily. In 1995, the latest year for which we have data, there were the fewest strikes, workers affected and workdays lost recorded since 1977. The unions have not only lost members but, to a large extent, the support of the workers and the capacity to mobilize. Collective bargaining is now the principal channels used by the social partners to resolve the maladjustments that arise in a labor market ever more restricted by the constraints of a market economy where profit and free competition have priority. Under these conditions, the new structure of the labor market forces the unions to adapt themselves to the intolerable pressure of 20 percent unemployment, increasing demand for jobs and the insignificant rate of creation of new jobs.

Terrorism

The terrorist phenomenon results from two historical circumstances: on the one hand, from Basque nationalism and, on the other, from the urge for revolutionary change. Both types of terrorist violence arose in the sixties, although in Spain individual terrorism of an anarchical character goes back as far as the last decades of the nineteenth century and the first years of the twentieth. Anarchosyndicalism was well established in Spain during that period and in the first third of the twentieth century, but was literally erased from the map of ideologies during Franco's reign.

The groups that advocated revolutionary change and that used armed conflict to advance their cause (such as FRAP and GRAPO[22]) attracted antifranquist workers and students, while ETA (Euskadi ta Askatasuna) was created in July 1959 by a group that broke away from the Basque Nationalist Party (PNV), and has attracted followers from the same sectors and from those committed to peripheral nationalism and even from the so-called Basque anti-establishment clergy.[23] Since then it has been a constant disturbance on the Spanish political scene with responsibility for nearly a thousand murders.

The process of change in which Spanish society has been involved for the past twenty years has not substantially changed the main problems that Spaniards consider important: unemployment, drugs, crime and terrorism. Unemployment, terrorism and drugs are the three problems on which, on a national scale, we concentrate our greatest concerns. Some events of 1998 (ETA's murders and the people's mobilization against terrorism) have served to increase awareness of the problem, which had evoked a certain apathy because of the frequency of terrorist actions and the inefficacy of response.

While terrorism continues to be seen as an important problem, the efforts made towards ending it are now considered satisfactory. An indefinite unilateral ceasefire was proclaimed by ETA in 1998.

Crime

At the heart of our society, other conflicts are expressed in criminal behavior. In 1980, 222 murders were committed; in 15 years, the number has been halved. In 1995, there were 116 murders. However, the number of crimes against property has increased markedly. From 9,918 robberies registered in police statistics in 1980 the figure rose to more than 35,000 in 1995. The theft of cars has evolved differently. The highest number of vehicle thefts occured in 1990, with 135,559 cars stolen, while in 1995 the number had fallen to 98,847.

These trends have not, as one would expect, created a greater sense of security. Crime continues to be a major concern of Spanish citizens and its elimination a maximum priority. Paradoxically, the insecurity felt by most Spaniards contrasts with the relative personal securiy shown in social investigations. The sense of personal security is relatively high in the areas in which everyday life unfolds and where the only appreciable risk is petty theft and acts of hooliganism and vandalism.

In 1996, there were 16,378 complaints of abuse of women by their husbands, although the variation from year to year is not very pronounced. Another useful factor for getting to know a society is how way it protects its children and what aid it offers for their development and integration into society. Spain has a level of education, sanitation and social services that adequately covers the needs of its population, but has not reached a level of protection where child abuse has disappeared. The Services for Child Protection in Spain opened 32,483 files in 1991 and 1992 and found 8,565 cases of child abuse, mostly by negligence, while emotional and physical abuse were not uncommon.

Xenophobia

A form of violence that seeks to weaken the democratic State, its institutions and its values has emerged on the scene in recent years; its common elements are the attack against a person, the negation of his dignity and the weakening of his rights; violence organized by extremist groups in defense of their identity against diversity and difference.[24] The paradigmatic case is violence against foreign immigrants, particularly Africans, and against minorities, particularly gypsies.

The information gathered by Professor Calvo Buezas, already referred to, reveals the frequency of xenophobic attitudes among students. However, as indicated in one of the most recent studies on this subject prepared by the Ministry of Employment and Social Affairs and similar studies by other institutions, the rate of xenophobia in Spain has fallen in recent years, although a third of Spaniards over 18 still show some degree of racism. The latter group includes older people and those with a more conservative attitudes, as well as persons of low socioeconomic status who see the immigrants as competitors for jobs and are most likely to have them as neighbors.[25]

Juvenile Delinquency

The proportion of young people (between 16 and 25 years old) convicted by the Provincial Criminal Courts and the Examining Courts remained close to 50 percent of all convictions up until 1988. From that year on, the percentage of young people convicted has steadily diminished. The rate of juvenile delinquency legally defined, i.e. the number of young people convicted in relation to the total population of youths, increased gradually to a maximum in 1986, later decreasing and stabilizing at about 500 young people convicted for every 100,000 youths 15 to 25 years old. The incidence of crime among young people is greater than in the general population but the increase in recent years simply follows that of crime in general, especially that of crime against property.[26]

Victimization

Another way of analyzing criminality is to focus on the victims. Through surveys of victimization, the social incidence and characteristics of crime can be analyzed better than with police and judicial statistics that merely show administrative and police efficiency. The surveys of victimization prepared by the CIS in 1978 and 1980 asked respondents if they had been victims of crime during their lifetimes. 11% of the people interviewed answered yes to this question.

In 1996, another survey of the Center for Sociological Investigations repeated the question and showed that the increase in crime or attempted crime had been dramatic. Of the people surveyed, 46 percent answered that they had, indeed, been the object of a crime at some time and 2 out of 5 of these in the preceding year. The progress of victimization is clear.

The rate of victimization in communities of more than a million inhabitants nearly doubled in 1980 that of smaller communities. In 1996 the difference between large and small communities lessened, at least with regard to lifetime victimization. However, the data collected by the CIS in 1996 were from a sample taken in communities of more than 50,000 inhabitants, which reduces the possibilities for comparison with earlier studies made by the same Institute which included a wider range of community sizes.

Degree of Satisfaction

The capacity of a society to generate those conditions without which life's expectations are incomplete sustains the self-confidence with which people face life and the everyday problems. The satisfaction and happiness of a society's members reflect the hope with which they face the future and this is related to stability and a lack of anxiety with respect to the future. To satisfaction with health, housing, income, etc, must be added the aspirations, expectations, and values that shape the overall level of satisfaction with life.

The relationship between level of income and satisfaction with life is complex. Once a level of resources has been reached that is sufficient to cover basic needs decently, other factors related to the quality of life such as environment, interrelations, culture, safety, etc, become important, which does not impede income and level of earnings from continuing to play a role in satisfaction. According to a CIS report,[27] "the groups with a higher position with respect to level of earnings or income tend to be more satisfied than those less favored because of their lower status and lower level of access to the system of social compensations. Thus, satisfaction increases with income, education and professional status. In general, satisfaction with life seems to be associated with the more favorable social and economic positions."

There is no doubt that the standard of living as well as the conditions of life of Spaniards have improved notably. Their satisfaction with life is very high and has increased continuously since 1980. That year 70 percent were very or fairly satisfied with the life they lead and in 1990 the percentage rose to 80 percent. One aspect that has contributed to the positive evolution of satisfaction of Spaniards with the life they lead is the political change of the past 20 years and the consolidation of a democratic system. Satisfaction with the functioning of the system has increased gradually. In 1983, at the start of the socialist government, the number of people satisfied with how democracy was working was less than 50 percent of the population, today it is much higher.[28]

According to the European Survey on Values, in 1990 nearly half of the Spaniards considered themselves satisfied with their achievements and because things were going as they wanted, and a little more than a third declared having felt particularly excited or interested by something in the last week, but these proportions were lower than those of ten years before, although the number of Spaniards content with how things are going for them on the whole is increasing and this satisfaction goes hand in hand with the higher level of expectations and oportunities that Spanish society has generated.[29] There are authors who surmise that the Spaniards feel better, but live less intensely than they did ten years ago: "It seems manifest that Spanish society has less psychological vivacity, is less motivated, a bit more tranquil and integrated, with less tension, happier but less passionate."[30]

Recent investigations whose aim was to compare the evolution of certain values related to tolerance, solidarity, respect, etc., have confirmed how, year after year, the level of community spirit of Spanish society has risen slowly but unmistakably. At the same time Spanish society appears more fragmented and distrustful of the institutions charged with safeguarding and strengthening the democratic system so laboriously achieved.

The tolerance and respect that Spaniards now show towards behaviors or conducts that until very recently were socially rejected and even criminalized is an example of the change in collective attitudes and behaviors. The greater satisfaction with our surroundings and the willingness with which we face the future lead us to reduce tensions and conflicts.

Divorce has become a part of Spanish family life without great shocks and has had a slow and steady rise – far from the destruction of the family that some predicted and without altering the Spanish concept of a couple. Homosexuality is an increasingly legitimate option and the epithets that until recently stigmatized it are avoided.

Finally, another indicator of changes in Spanish society is the willingness of different groups to share common spaces such as housing, where the closest face-to-face relations occur and where there are greater possibilities for rejection. But drug addicts still meet with rejection. Much of the population resists their presence in nearby living spaces, perhaps more because of their life-style and easily transmitted diseases than their condition as addicts. However, for other disease carriers and those ill with HIV, awareness campaigns have promoted a change in attitudes.

4   DEFENSE

Spanish sentiments with respect to national defense are closely linked with the role that the Spanish army has played in our history, remote as well as recent. At present, no serious threat is perceived to territorial integrity, so the role of the army has, consequently, lost relevance in comparison with earlier times, when the existence of the "interior enemy" also justified its power. In recent years, three factors have conditioned the trajectory of the army as the guarantor of the independence and unity of the nation: entrance into NATO, the recognition of conscientious objection and the professionalization of the armed forces. The debate on its present responsibilities, and on its modernization, is still open. Spaniards are not very favorable with regard to increases in the defense budget, possibly because they anticipate no exterior threat and because of the changes in the international scene since the disappearance of the Soviet bloc.

Arms Industry

Nearly ten years after the end of the Cold War, the arms industry has largely overcome the crisis when demand decreased, programs for new systems were frozen and the very existence of the industry was questioned. At that time, uncertainty abounded in a market that survives mainly by contracts signed with foreign governments. The Spanish arms industry barely survived the crisis in the world armaments trade. While private industry adapted, the large public enterprises of Spain were the most affected by the international economic crisis that imposed drastic budget limitations on their best clients.

The Spanish arms industry has never been very important when compared to that of neighboring countries. In the economy as a whole, the weight of the defense industry has some importance, or at least Spaniards think so; 30 percent believe it is important, while a relative majority believe that it is not important enough to significantly affect the economy as a whole. Its limited dimension corresponds to the country's not very large economic capacity and to the scant effort it makes towards defense.

This opinion has changed little over the years. At present, the Ministry of Defense seems willing to unblock three large programs for the renovation of armaments that will give an important respite to two enterprises that are in an extreme situation: Santa Barbara and Bazán. CASA, the third aeronautic enterprise, is in the best position to collaborate in the manufacture of the European combat plane (EF-2000).

Aside from ethical questions connected with the production and sale of arms, the military industry has used international markets to obtain resources with which to develop its own armament systems. For Spaniards, this fact carries a heavy ethical charge that is reinforced by the movement against the manufacture of anti-personnel landmines.

To evaluate this question, we have used a scale of 0–10, where 0 means that respondents condemn the sale of arms to third countries completely and 10 means that they fully approve this commerce.

Having thus posed the question, we see that the Spanish population considers the sale of arms very negatively and this position has intensified even more since 1991. At present, Spaniards grade the sale of arms with an average of 2.16 points, while six years ago the assessment was 2.8. As can be seen, the variation over the years has been slight, but it clearly reflects an ethical rejection of the sale of Spanish armaments abroad.

These opinions run parallel to those expressed by the majority of respondants on the budget allotted to national defence. They are not in favour of augmenting these expenses and consider that their present level should be reduced or at most mantained. The majority consider that the budget allocated to the country's defence should not change in the immediate future and they believe it preferable to reduce the military budget than to increase it.

NATO Membership

The adjustments required by Spain's incorporation into NATO and the new missions that our armies have taken on abroad are beginning to affect the need for modernizing the armed forces. Since the referendum on the incorporation into the Alliance, held in 1986, was approved by a slight margin, Spain has become more integrated in NATO's various structures, and the decision to integrate fully into NATO's military structure was formalized at the Brussels Summit. Until then, we had maintained a situation similar to the one France has had since 1967, taking part in the civil and military activities of the Alliance but not in its commands.

Spaniards continue to display a certain mistrust towards NATO, although the opposition has weakened since 1991. In that year, 42 percent of Spaniards opposed the Alliance: the same percentage as those favoring membership. The tie between the two opposing positions was repeated in 1992, but from that year on those who approve Spain's membership in the Alliance started to gain ground until in 1997 they were a majority. Today, Spain's presence in the alliance is taken for granted.

The advantages and disadvantages of Spain's membership in NATO are fundamentally related to the country's security. Full integration into the supranational organization is beginning to provide some additional benefits, or at least that is how the Spaniards see it. In recent years the conviction that NATO improves national security has increased as there is no longer the need to depend on our own forces to resolve armed conflicts, although it would be worthwhile asking just what it is we are confronting. As allies, integration in the military structure will allow us to locate one of the subregional commands in our territory and to have a greater power of decision with respect to the disposition of our own forces, although the question of who will take the strategic command of the southern zone to which we will belong is still open, as France insists that it be in European hands and not, as has been the case until now, under the command of a North American admiral.

The opinion in favor of NATO that these results reveal is strengthened when the necessity of its existence is taken into account. The disappearance of the Soviet Union and the incorporation into the Alliance of countries that until recently had been its satellites makes us wonder about the need for a defensive Alliance that has lost its principal enemy. Spaniards, however, see the Alliance as a good means of protection against possible but vague threats from abroad. The changes that NATO intends to make are aimed at clarifying a new strategic position for the West in order to give new meaning to the Alliance.

The fact that Spanish troops are collaborating abroad, integrated into multinational peacekeeping forces – or stabilizing and dissuading armies if we use NATO's terminology applied to the Bosnian war – is a significant development. The presence of Spanish troops in Bosnia, the symbolic presence of our army in the Gulf War and the collaboration of our navy in the economic blockade of Iraq, go beyond the simple military control of a strategic area. A delicate balance between the factions in conflict was needed by the Spanish troops in their work in Bosnia and there were numerous obstacles to overcome, which enabled them to gain important experience that will be useful in other zones in the future.

The Dayton and Mostar Agreements, that ended the confrontation between the various states of the former Yugoslavia, have generated a change in the attitude of Spaniards regarding the presence of our armed forces abroad. The risk has been reduced and their peacekeeping intervention in the Balkans are increasingly approved.

In 1997 the situation took a positive turn as the conflicting parties reached a delicate peace agreement with relations still tense between those who until recently were open enemies. The work carried out by the Spanish troops contributed, without a doubt, to the settlement of the struggle and the stabilization and reconstruction of a region devastated by war. On this occasion, however, the question asked was not, as in 1995, the degree of agreement with the presence of Spanish troops on UN peacekeeping missions in Bosnia, but for the degree of agreement "with the presence of Spanish troops abroad, collaborating in UN peacekeeping missions." Accordingly, it must be noted that in recent years opposition to the presence of troops abroad has lessened markedly and support for collaboration with UN peacekeeping missions has increased.

There is an important nuance to these results, since it is clear that "support for the presence of Spanish troops abroad will depend above all on the aim of the possible intervention as well as the circumstances that surround each case." Presumably, the indiscriminate dispatch of Spanish troops abroad would not receive wide support.

The armed forces are undergoing an in-depth renovation to adapt them to the military demands of our condition as a full member of NATO and to the needs of modern war. One of the subjects that has generated the most debate and controversy is the professionalization of the armed forces with the consequent elimination of obligatory military service.

The present government's electoral promise to achieve the gradual professionalization of the armed forces has not altered the widepread support that already existed among Spaniards in favor of the elimination of conscription. Spanish society clearly demands a model in tune with new concepts of defence based on the specialization of duties and the flexible adaptation of the armed forces to the country's real strategic needs.

The majority of the population believes our armed forces should be made up of voluntary and professional soldiers replacing the annual drafts of recruits. In 1997, 69 percent of Spaniards were in favor of this solution which continues to gain more and more support. This figure is slightly higher, discounting the differences in approach that make the questions difficult to compare, than that obtained by Amando de Miguel in an investigation on the army. According to his data, "60 percent of Spaniards support the elimination of the obligatory military service and the establishment of a completely professional army, versus a third that is in favor of continuing the present mixed model."[31]

The Government's decision to initiate the process of professionalization has reduced support for the present situation of the obligatory military service. It is mainly older respondants with ideological positions close to the right and those with a lower level of education who favor the present composition of the armed forces. Nevertheless, and in spite of the wide social consensus on this matter, interesting variations can be detected. The youngest are most attracted to professionalization, which is least accepted by those over 60 years of age. Young Spaniards are not known for enthusiasm about national defense, although neither do they show rejection nor outright oposition to military matters.[32]

Young people's rejection of obligatory military service is one of the arguments most used by the media to support professionalization of the armed forces. The rise of conscientious objection and the refusal to do military service must be examined carefully. The number of those who claim problems of conscience about taking up arms has been steadily increasing. According to data from the National Council of Conscientious Objection, from January to October 1997, 109,041 aplications were submitted compared to 93,000 in 1996 and 72,000 in 1995. This annual increase of conscientious objection is putting defense in a dilemma. If this increase continues, the next years will see a lack of sufficient recruits for the needs of the armed forces, especially the army.

The data on refusal to do military service vary in accordance with the wording of the question. According to A. de Miguel, refusal to do military service "although illegal, has a certain social legitimacy. 60 percent of Spaniards consider refusal to do military service a valid personal option as opposed to 10 percent who describe it as a crime. The remaining third consider it a lack of solidarity."[33]

5 WELFARE

Until the seventies the concept of welfare in Spain was closely linked with economic welfare, a direct relation being established between production, economic growth and consumer capacity and individual and social welfare. However, although economic factors tend to be crucial in times of want, the role played by other factors increases in importance as poverty is reduced It may be said that "only after the sufficient resources are available to cover basic needs decently is it posible to begin to speak about quality of life and social welfare.[34]

For this same reason the direct relation between earnings or level of income and welfare cannot be considered alone. In the eighties, other factors that are distributed unequally and are more closely related to quality of life, began to acquire more importance. However, this does not keep income from continuing to play a major role in the satisfaction with life or in the perception of welfare. Various studies of the Centre of Sociological Investigations have repeatedly revealed, as noted earlier, that "the groups with a higher position with respect to level of income tend to be more satisfied than those less favored because of their lower status and lower level of access to the system of social rewards. As a whole, satisfaction with life seems, therefore, to be associated with the better social and economic positions in the social structure."[35]

Income conditions the possibilities of spending, saving and access to material and nonmaterial goods. But it is not only the level of present income that matters but also the expectations for future income, because the latter is highly influenced by the confidence raised by the economic system and by the enthusiasm with which we lead our lives. In an excellent newspaper article on family spending, Carmen Alcaide stressed the importance of the spending patterns in order to appreciate how an economy behaves: "The family decisions on saving and consumption depend basically on the evolution of their disposable income and the degree of confidence, influenced by future expectations for income and employment."[36]

Extremadura is still the region with the lowest level of GDP per capita, with a deficit with respect to the Spanish average of 34 percent, while at the opposite extreme are the Balearic Islands, whose GDP per capita exceeds the average for Spain by 42 percent. However, both figures must be considered in their local context. As Julio Alcaide shows,[37] if from the distribution of GDP per capita one passes to the distribution of disposable family income per capita, as corrected by the relative price levels, the differences are reduced considerably. In this case, Extremadura is only 15 percent below the national average, while the Balearics exceed it by 25 percent. Indeed, disposable family income per capita, as corrected by relative prices, is the variable that best expresses the average level of welfare, and the lessening of the differences is due basically to the redistributive action of the public sector through taxes and transfers.

Moving from the regional or local context to the national distribution of these indicators, we see that since 1970 a real redistribution of income has occured whatever the indicators that we use. In 1970, the richest 10 percent of the households had 41 percent of the disposable family income. In 1994, the richest 10 percent of households had only 28 percent of aggregate income. It must be remembered that the figures for 1970 were the consequence of the key period of Spain's policy of development at all costs that visibly deteriorated the personal and functional distribution of income as "the fruit of growth went to the highest layer of society in a higher proportion."[38]

The Economic Report prepared annually by the *Servicio de Estudio* ("Think Tank") of the BBV indicates that "between 1986 and 1994 Gini's index fell continuously which reveals that inequality in income distribution is diminishing. However, the relative differences of income by deciles are still high; the average income of the highest decile is nearly ten times higher than that of the lowest decile.

Although poverty has decreased, the perception of it is very strong in a country where inequality generated great injustices in the past, and continues to do so. The idea of poverty should not be simply equated to the lack of economic resources. Other variables must be taken into consideration. At the end of the day, poverty is always a referent of social inequality.[39]

However, when dealing with international comparisons, a purely economic description of poverty must be used. With this indicator, we see a decrease since 1973 in the percentage of poor people and households in Spain (below 50 percent of the median income), as well as a decrease in extreme poverty (below 25 percent of the median income). Both facts tally with improvement in the distribution of disposable family income.

The economic crisis of the early nineties added new forms of poverty stemming from unemployment and social exclusion. Unemployment has become a structural component in our society, generating new life-styles at the fringes of the established economic system. The rate of unemployment in Spain is one of the highest in the European Union at about 20 percent of the active population, according to the official statistics (Survey of Active Population, prepared by the National Institute of Statistics, and the Statistics of Registered Unemployment, prepared by the National Employment Institute) and offers a bleak panorama. However, some writers[40] are of the opinion that unemployment is overestimated and that the working active population is underestimated, i.e. we have unemployment closer to 12 percent than the 22 percent given by EPA in 1996.

Even with such questionable data as this, we find enormous differences in activity, employment and unemployment within the Spanish population. The most flagrant discrimination with regard to unemployment affects women and young people[41]: "Unemployment is a largely feminine phenomenon: women represent close to 50 percent of the unemployed and only 1/3 of the employed." The probability of being unemployed has decreased among men and increased among women since 1992. On the other hand, the highest rate of unemployment obtains among the younger groups, although it was they who benefitted most by the temporary recovery of employment for both sexes between 1985 and 1992.

In view of the figures, it is no wonder that the underground economy is thriving. In the absence of stable employment, and with increasingly precarious employment, uncontrolled types of employment become attractive means for generating earnings at the fringe of the regulated channels. The underground economy has undergone a dramatic growth since 1986. According to Juan Velarde, the underground economy represented 14 percent of the GDP in 1997. The Basque Country and Navarra, whose fiscal system is different form the rest of Spain, registered the lowest index of irregularity, while the highest was found in the Balearics, Galicia and the Valencian Community. Aragón, Asturias and Cantabria are below the average.[42]

In one of the latest studies by the Center of Sociological Investigations of the underground economy, 34 percent of those surveyed in June 1997 knew of people working in enterprises without a contract or social security and more than half considered that these working conditions occurred frequently or fairly frequently. The main way Spaniards justify this situation is with the lack of work alternatives.

Although the distribution of income has, in recent years, reduced the extreme differences, this has not been the case with the perception of inequalities. The elements that contribute to the perception of that inequality are more visible today than in the past. 63 percent of Spaniards see social inequalities as very or fairly great, while only 6 percent see them as small.[43] Since 1985, when economic comentators announced the end of the crisis that had begun in 1973, there has been talk of the scandalous ostentation of new wealth obtained by speculation. A precarious dual model of the economy has developed. The economic growth generated since 1985 widened the gulf between social sectors and between regions. As Vidal-Beneyto indicates,[44] "the essential economic agent is no longer the worker but capital on the one hand and the consumer on the other. In the field of production proper, technological innovation comes first and increasingly supersedes the workforce, as productivity depends directly on the efficiency of the technology. This causes a reduction of jobs that brings unemployment as an unavoidable dimension of contemporary reality and separates society into two large groups: those who have a visible and permanent job and those who don't and who become second class citizens."

Although various economic indicators point to an improved distribution of income among Spanish households in the past twenty years, the difference between 20 percent of households controlling 7.5 percent of the income and 20 percent controlling 43 percent is still vast. It is not that the gulf has widened but that the elements that contribute to the perception of inequality are much more visible today than they were before.

These observations lead us to believe that the perceived inequalities are symptoms of a weakened social structure that creates class tensions beyond those of the traditional social classes. In an earlier work,[45] and quoting Corey, we stressed the growing presence of a new middle class, made up of salaried workers and very different from the classic proprietors and professionals that composed the old middle class.

The middle class today is composed of four sectors: a) administrators, including supervisors and mid-level civil servants who function as advisors or executives in the technical division of work; b) service professionals who are mostly state employees; c) semiautonomous employees, such as scientific and technical personnel and many professionals whose "semiautonomy" refers to their situation in the work process; and d) independent workers, the remains of the old lower middle class that has been greatly transformed during this century. Thanks to Professor Tezanos,[46] who in 1984 prepared an estimation of the growth of these four ocupational groups between 1950 and 1981, we can draw a trend line characterizing the future social structure Spain. The size of these groups rose from 14 percent to 33 percent of the labor force during those years. He also found that the liberal professionals, plus service personnel, plus administrative, comercial and technical personnel, plus businessmen, managers, directors, and independent workers increased between 1965 and 1984 from 35 percent to 52 percent of the active population while the sum of unskilled workers, agricultural workers, farm owners without employees and skilled workers decreased during those years from 65 percent to 46 percent. In 1984, according to his estimations, the sector of self-employed and independents, within the block he calls proprietary classes, and the sector of non-manual and services workers, within the block of salaried classes, included 60 percent of the labor force without counting the 82,400 professionals of the armed forces.[47]

In a study by the Centre of Sociological Investigations[48] already mentioned, a classification of category or socioeconomic status was used that reflects these new and old categories, although it doesn't coincide exactly, as an important sector of skilled workers was not included.

In recent years, the transformation of Spanish society has been closely linked to economic development. These changes have been very rapid and opinion has adapted to them more slowly. Opinion lags behind in its adjustment to expansive cycles of the economy and the economic indicators seldom coincide with the perceptions of the population, much more cautious and slower to recognize positive cycles. In spite of this, opinions about the trajectory of the economy are not illusions that can be dismissed. They have a direct effect on the economic orientations and behaviors of individuals.

Welfare and satisfaction with personal or family economic situations are relative concepts that allow us to identify and weigh the differences in perception from one group to another. The differences are important, since one usually estimates his personal economic situation better than that of the country as a whole.

6 FREEDOM

The Spanish state has, since 1977, provided itself with adequate instruments for guaranteeing the fundamental liberties of a democratic society. The forty years of Franco's regime forged conditions in which the liberties common to advanced democracies did not exist or were very much reduced. The transformation that occurred when the former head of state died was not abrupt. Changes in structure, culture and mentality had begun to occur during the period prior to his death. The transition was successful in part because of the changes that had begun to develop in the last years of Franco's regime, in a political and social model that had already been worn out. As early as 1966 the proportion of Spaniards who preferred political decisions to be made by those elected by the people was more than three to one, and this view was maintained until after the death of the dictator, when it began to increase.

After the adoption of the Constitution on 6 December 1978, mechanisms were initiated to guarantee the freedoms that had been denied Spaniards for so long. The right to asociation and political participation, religious freedom, the right to organize trade unions, etc., were included in the Magna Carta as fundamental rights putting Spaniards on the same level as the citizens of societies that had long been enjoying them. The democracy attained and guaranteed by law has played a key role in changing Spaniards' mentality. We must not forget that "democracy is not simply a set of institutions and mechanisms but also an ethic, a form of political conduct or, as some say, a culture. It can't be improvised nor can it be learned in a day or a few years."[49]

Once these formal liberties had been obtained and the institutions that guarantee them put in place, the concept of freedom lost for us its priority over other basic aspects of democratic coexistence. This relation is fundamental to the understanding of Spaniards' attitudes towards the State and its intervention in our lives. A welfare state must guarantee access for all its citizens to the necessary means of making individual freedom effective.

The concepts of freedom and equality have changed their meanings in our society. It is no longer a question of achieving what our forbears pursued as ends in themselves. The strength of our democracy is based, precisely, on the fact that it has transcended the concepts of freedom and equality in favor of a polity in which welfare and quality of life do not end with these basic freedoms. In the first and most difficult moments of the transition, the recuperation of those basic elements served to sustain the institutions that would regulate and arbitrate from then on, our future political, social and economic life. As a society moves from an interventionist and autocratic model, as ours was before 1975, to one which aspires to the same level as the advanced western democracies, concerns become more centered on freedom than on equality. This was the case in Spain until well into the 1980s. Thereafter, the concepts of freedom and merit have tended to prevail over the concept of equality in a market economy where work and personal effort take precedence.

The crisis of the 1990s has made manifest the deficiencies that a purely liberal system can create in a short period of time. (The corruption and rapid enrichment of certain economic and political elites have influenced this tendency).

Since 1992, equality has been favored over liberty. What happened to turn the earlier trend that valued freedom over equality? The two *idées-force*, freedom and equality, act in all settings, from private life to the work organization. As Orizo indicates in his comentaries on the *Encuesta Europea de Valores* ("European Survey of Values") "in economically and politically developed societies, freedom consists in not being subject to restrictions and in personal autonomy, while the egalitarian impulse has lost some of its economic contents along the way. Its manifestation as social justice for the disinherited is giving way little by little to the absence of discrimination."[50]

This seems to be the opinion of Spaniards today, who perceive great inequalities in our society.[51]

On the other hand, liberty and equality have traditionally been considered the two main pillars on which the democratic political spectrum rests. Norberto Bobbio,[52] in one of his latest works, discusses the different attitudes that right and left wing parties hold with respect to equality: those who describe themselves as left wing concede greater importance to what makes men equal. Those who describe themselves as right wing are convinced that the inequalities are unavoidable and that, in the end, their disappearance is not even desirable.

On this ideological spectrum, we Spaniards are situated, predominantly, in positions left of center and our present inclination is towards avoiding abrupt jumps in the social model by advocating slow and gradual change, such as has oriented the reforms that have gone so well for us in the past twenty years. We want the changes and transformations to be slow so as not to cause radical modifications of the existing order. This moderation in our attitudes and our ideological positioning strengthen the tendency to give priority to equality over freedom, especially in the economic sphere.

It should also be noted that solutions to present problems no longer correspond to rigid ideological approaches. The political and social transformation of Spain has generated a new culture that doesn't respond to the parameters that defined society in the 1970s. There is a generational and ideological gap between the new right and the traditional Spanish right that is widening. The same could be said for the traditional left with respect to the new generations of the left in which ideological references act more and more as an historical identifier and less as a model for political action. Pragmatism has substituted for utopia; the immediacy of everyday problems has made the idea of a worldwide transformation of society more and more remote.

The application of the concepts of freedom and equality to the relationship between public and private is very important. At present, we are witnessing an alteration in the relationship between the public, i.e. state intervention in some fields of the economy and services, and the private, i.e. the tendency to a lesser presence of the state in certain sectors. We can not ignore our excessive dependence on the state: in 1988, ten years after the adoption of the Constitution, only 23 percent felt "responsible for their own welfare," while 75 percent considered that this was the responsibility of the state.[53]

The relationship between public and private was one of the elements differentiating the political proposals of the Spanish parties in the elections of 1996, although without explicit support for a position that would exclude either of the two options completely. The idea of state intervention in the economy makes less sense now, especially when tied to certain traditional ideological tendencies. At present there are other, more moderate, views that propose that the state continue to take care of certain activities, while others should be prevailingly private, but without excluding the presence of both types of management in specific sectors.

The defenders of the privatization model hold a modernizing vision of the public sector, centered on improvements in administrative efficiency and restraint in public spending. Against this dominant idea, the detractors of privatizations consider the role of the state to be valid in sectors considered strategic, as well as in others with market deficiencies and advocate the improvement of public enterprise management rather than its disappearance.

In fact, the business sector, either publicly owned or with state participation, is formed by a group of enterprises with very different activities. Spaniards tend to prefer public or shared management rather than strictly private enterprise in many of the essential economic sectors. In some, the three options (state, private initiative, mixed management) are very balanced. Public management is conceived as appropriate in the traditional sectors of state intervention such as education, health care, the defense industry, rail transportation and is appreciated also in the postal service, the aerospace industry and, to a lesser degree, in energy.

As can be seen, the sectors clearly assigned to the public sphere are those that have a tradition in Spain of administrative intervention or those that are too important to be left in the hands of the private sector. Mixed management is preferred in the research sector, while private management is preferred in finance. Some other sectors show no clear tendency one way or the other.

The fundamental attitudes of Spaniards towards the operation of public services leads us, on the one hand, to desire greater autonomy, and, on the other, to mistrust the restrictions that the free market would place on the state. Spaniards lean more towards state intervention for regulating and controlling the activity of certain sectors rather than direct intervention. On the whole, in regressive economic cycles, economic recovery is linked to greater state activity, while in expansive economic cycles, there tends to be more distrust of state intervention in economic activity.

It is precisely these economic cycles that periodically reopen the debate on the advisability, or need, to augment the public sector by nationalizing enterprises or reducing the public sector by privatization. Telecommunications, electricity and finance companies have, in recent years, passed into private hands as the state gave up its participation in them.

A study done in Madrid in 1996 on these questions showed distrust of dismantling the public enterprise sector. Of those interviewed, 30 percent opted for the expansion of state presence through the nationalization of enterprises, 27 percent would leave things as they were and 31 percent chose privatization for most public enterprises. The indecisiveness and ambiguity of the answers should not make us forget that there is a long-standing tradition of state interventionism in Spain. There are still sectors in which the role of the state is not questioned and it should not surprise us that in 1995, in a nationwide survey, three-fourths of respondents supported greater state intervention outright.[54]

In any case, the debate is still open and the results of this and other studies do not clear the horizon. Perhaps the ambiguity with which Spaniards face the public-private issue is an indication of their ambiguous attitudes towards freedom and equality. As Beck wrote: "Only those people who have a home and a secure job and, therefore, a material future, can be the citizens who make democracy theirs and revitalize it. The plain truth is that, without material security, political liberty does not exist. There is no democracy – only the threat to all by the new and old regimes and totalitarian ideologies."[55]

In egalitarian social policies, education and health care, together with housing, are perceived as worthy of special protection by the public authorities. In this sense, Article 27 of the Constitution, in addition to recognizing education as a fundamental right of the individual, establishes, in paragraph 2, that the aim of education is the full development of the human personality, while respecting the democratic principles of coexistence and fundamental rights and liberties. Thus, education becomes essential for the transmission of the values and principles consecrated in the Magna Carta.

The Spanish educational system has undergone numerous changes in the past 30 years. Since 1970, there have been two large scale reforms: the General Education Law of that same year, and the Law for the Regulation of the Education System (LOGSE) in 1990, that regulates non-university education. Between those dates, two other regulations completed the transformation of the education system: in 1985, the Basic Law Regulating the Right to Education established the regime of agreements through which public funds are used to finance educational institutions that comply with certain conditions. The other was the Law of University Reform of 1983.

The level of instruction that is reached by the population beyond obligatory schooling measures their capacity to participate fully in the benefits of a democratic system. The progress observed during the last quarter of a century has been remarkable. The highest percentage of illiterates, or of those without studies of any kind, are concentrated in the older age groups, while the rates decrease towards zero among the youngest age groups who have enjoyed a system that allows them to accede to levels of training suited to their efforts and to their intellectual capacities.

Similarly, nearly 100 percent of the population is covered for health care (Social Security covers 95 percent and the remaining 5 percent ise covered by charitable organizations, mutual benefit societies, and private insurance).[56] This nearly universal coverage has greatly taxed the public authorities in their effort to meet the demand. Since 1981, the differential of health care spending compared to the EU average has been lessening, from 1.5 to 1.

But education and health care are only two aspects of the importance that is given to state provision of essential services in order to overcome basic inequalities. In its third chapter, the Spanish Constitution develops the basic principles of social and economic policy mandating the public authorities to promote favorable conditions for social and economic progress (Article 40) and to guarantee sufficient aid and social security benefits in situations of need (Article 41). The cost of Spain's Social Security system increased progressively from

1980 until 1994 in absolute as well as in relative terms. Since then, the percentage of the GDP represented by this spending has leveled off.

But not all social protection relies on Social Security. In 1996, Spain dedicated 22 percent of its GDP to social protection as measured by SEEPROS (European Statistics System for Social Protection). Following this system, social protection benefits are classified into eleven functional groups. Spain dedicated 40 percent of this spending to old age and widow's pensions, 26 percent went for ill health benefits and 12 percent to unemployment protection. All in all, in 1996 Spain spent 234,472 pesetas per inhabitant to cover those needs.

One of the integral elements of the European image is the extensive state services that supposedly go with high taxation. In spite of the high level of taxes collected in Spain, there is agreement that state services remain below the European average. There is general support for increasing spending in those areas of state action in which Spaniards observe an evident deficit: education, health care and social security. Those most critical of the tax level conform approximately to the following profile: secondary level of studies, right wing ideology and religious beliefs. At the other extreme, though not necessarily giving full support to the present tax level, are people with a higher education, left wing ideologies and no religious beliefs.

The importance given in the state's budget to various sectors reflects public support of public spending and how that spending is distributed. Budgetary allocations for certain services are considered scant, especially those for health care, housing and unemployment. Allocations for education, pensions and welfare are also considered scant, though to a lesser degree.

Spaniards regard some public services as sufficiently funded; infrastructure, public order and justice are among these. Others, such as defense, are considered to receive excessive funding.

Spaniards are inclined to the opinion that the present level of services should be maintained and improved but in no way, however, at the cost of higher taxes. Modifications in taxation should be linked to improved fiscal management of the funds collected. A reduction of taxes with the same level of services would obtain wide support. Limiting public services in order to improve their quality obtains much less support.

Another indicator of the ambiguity of public opinion with respect to the role of the state is the proposal that private initiative replace the state for some social services. The case of pensions is symptomatic since they are one of the pillars of the welfare state. Several studies by public and private institutions show that the present system of social security cannot be sustained in the middle and long term. The scenario for which it was designed has changed radically: a deficit, a low birth rate and an aging population have created a new situation without a promising future. If present trends continue, the ratio of pensioners to workers will increase by a factor of 2.4 in the next 50 years. In the 1970s there were three workers for every retiree. Today, the ratio is 1.7 per retiree. In the year 2030 the projected ratio will be 1 to 1.

Most Spaniards would choose a mixed system for pensions, in other words, an obligatory public system (that guarantees a minimum pension for the least favored groups), supplemented by a private system (in which criteria of individual preference are applied). Only 35 percent would choose a public system and a scant 6 percent an exclusively private one. This data reflect what many citizens are already doing to supplement their future social security pensions.

Our democracy, still young, has important issues it must resolve. Democracy must be upheld by tradition and by institutions that permit its defense and that is only possible with time and good fortune. Spaniards are aware that the Constitution does not resolve every problem that time has brought to light. Thus, an important number of citizens[57] believe that constitutional reform is necessary in order to correct the flaws that have become patent as the country has matured. The problem of regional autonomy is unresolved and European integration has created new relationships that need to be considered.

Despite wide public support for, and satisfaction with, our democratic system, there are many matters left unresolved. A CIS report states that the motives for dissatisfaction with the democratic system "do not constitute criticism from without, since they are not brought forward nor can be interpreted as attacks on the democratic system by sectors of our society in disagreement with its essence. They are specific complaints about deficiencies or imperfections made from within, criticism of the faulty functioning of something that should be perfected and corrected."

Amando de Miguel, in his research program for the Complutense Foundation, claims that the best way to measure support for the democratic system in our country is by a direct question about the consolidation of democracy. In his survey of Spanish society, he obtains the following results: "13 percent state that Spanish democracy is *well established*, 37 percent say that *there is still work to be done* and a residual 12 percent maintain that *there is no real democracy*."[58]

Young people might be more critical of the system, having neither had the experience of a different form of government nor participation in public life. However, from the beginning of the transition, democracy, with all its imperfections, has received solid support from the young.

Many of the imperfections are being corrected as they arise. Satisfaction with democracy has been increasing with time. By 1985, there was wide satisfaction with the functioning of the democratic system, despite many uncertainties.

Free expression is one of the basic values of any democracy. Spaniards report a noticeable improvement in freedom of speech.[59] In 1992, 56 percent of survey respondents considered that it had improved compared with ten years before, while 29 percent were of the opinion that the situation was at least the same. Spaniards also value the freedom that the media have now as compared to before. The credibility of the media is closely linked to its independence. Credibility seems highest for radio, while public TV ranks far behind in second place (in 1992 when this data was obtained)[60] and the press in third place. Private TV was in fourth place and magazines last.

Towards the end of the eighties, a great commotion was caused by the appearance of private TV. Since then, the private channels have become a normal part of everyday life and the controversy has calmed down. Since private initiatives have never been questioned in other media (radio, press, etc.), why was this so controversial? The answer is that television is the medium to which the population is most exposed. But, on the whole, private television has brought competition to the field and some improvement in quality.

7 CONCLUSION

The Constitution of 1978 required the conversion of our legal order to democracy, either by adapting elements from European and Atlantic countries or by restoring traditional institutions and norms. At the same time, innovations involving great risks were introduced, such as the territorial organization of the autonomous regions and localities that in some ways goes beyond federalism. The state has not only shared powers with its autonomous communities but is also involved, at present, in the cession of powers to the governing bodies of the European Union as required by the international treaties that have been signed.

There is no doubt that the public liberties exist not only in the constitutional text but in everyday life. Equal protection of the laws, the right to life, ideological and religious freedom, the right to personal liberty, the right to intimacy, inviolability of the home, freedom of residence and movement, educational entitlement, freedom of speech, freedom of assembly, the right of association, due process, academic freedom, the right to organize trade unions and the right to strike and to petition are expressly listed in the Constitution and are protected by it.

Likewise, the welfare of Spanish citizens has unquestionably improved since 1978, even though a high rate of unemployment persists as compared to the European average and women, and above all young people, suffer most intensely from it. Little by little, we are advancing towards the European average of per capita income, and will probably reach it in the first years of the twenty-first century, although equalizing the living conditions of the country's regions will take longer.

In defense, there has been a great transformation of the armed forces, reducing their size and adjusting them to the needs of a society without enemies. They have introduced modern technologies and participate in peace-keeping operations, mainly in NATO missions. They are also becoming totally professional so that conflicts arising from conscientious objection and the refusal to do military service will soon be obsolete.

There is, in all fields, a general and visible effort towards eliminating inflexibilities and adapting the instrument of the state to the needs of its citizens. This is not easy considering the authoritarian history from which we have emerged. Leviathan is becoming flexible and sharing its legislative and executive powers, although it still conserves a monopoly of judicial power.

The administration of justice seems, precisely, to be the least satisfactory aspect of the Spanish state today. It is too slow and insufficiently equitable, which is surprising because for the first time in the history of the country, the courts are not governed by the executive power. But its flexibility borders on ineffectiveness. The reform of the Penal Code excluded or lightened the punishment for some crimes against the person as well as economic crimes whose seriousness and frequency in Spain has increased the population's sense of insecurity.

Despite these critical observations, the final balance of everything considered in this paper is unquestionably positive. Despite the flaws pointed out here and others not mentioned, the leading characteristics of Spain's democratic experience since the publication of the Constitution is flexibility and the willingness to take into account the needs and demands of a modern society. Spain is at present such a society, emerging from the long period of dictatorial rule prior to 1975.

NOTES

1 Suarez, A., "Apuntes sobre la transición política" ("Notes on the Political Transition"), in *Cambio* 16, No 1000, 16 January 1991, 14–17.

2 Garcia Ferrando, M. et al, *La conciencia nacional y regional en la España de las autonomías* (National and Regional Consciousness in the Spanish State of the Autonomies), Madrid: CIS 1994.

3 Lamo de Espinoza, E.: *El lugar de España en Cataluña y Euskadi* (Spain's Place in Catalonia and the Basque Country/Euskadi). *El País*, 20 July 1998.

4 Centre of Sociological Investigations, study 2211, March 1996.

5 Garcia Ferrando, M. et al, *La conciencia nacional*, 92ff.

6 Del Campo, S., *Estado Actual y Perspectivas de la Sociedad Española ("Present State and Perspectives of Spanish Society")*, Madrid: Fundación Independiente 1994), 81.

7 Touraine, A.) *Podemos vivir juntos? Iguales y diferentes* ("Can We Live Together? The Same and Different"). Madrid: PPC, 1997.

8 Peces-Barba, G.: " *)Qué Constitución, qué nacionalismo, qué lealtad?"* ("What Constitution, What Nationalism, What Loyalty?"), *El País*, 15 September 1998.

9 Marias, Javier: "*Don y daño de lenguas*" ("Gift and Damage of Languages"), *The Weekly Supplement*, 26 July 1998.

10 Arnaiz Villena, A. and Alonso García, J. *El origen de los vascos y otros pueblos mediterráneos* ("The origin of the Basques and Other Mediterranean Peoples"). Estudios Complutenses, 1998.

11 Olabarría Agra, J. "*Juego limpio*" ("Fair Game"). *El País*, 18 Sept. 1998.

12 Jon Juaristi. *El bucle melancólico* ("The Melancholy Curl"). Madrid: Espasa Calpe, 1997.

13 Martín Rodriguez, A. M., and A. Rodriguez Pérez, "El estereotipo del delincuente y la teoría del etiquetado social ("Criminal Stereotypes and the Theory of Social Labeling"), *Revista de Estudios Penitenciarios* 243 (1990): 45–55.

14 Del Campo, S. *La opinión publica española y la política exterior* ("Spanish Public Opinion and Foreign Policy"). (Tecnos, Madrid: Informe INCIPE 1998, 20ff.

15 Calvo Buezas, T. "Inmigración, cultura y salud" ("Immigration, Culture and Health"), *Ofrim, supplements*, December; Health and Wellfare Council of the Community of Madrid, 95–110.

16 El País, 2 March 1998.

17 Colectivo IOE. "La inmigración extranjera en Madrid" ("Foreign Immigration in Madrid"), *Ofrim, Supplements*, December, Council of Health and Welfare of the Community of Madrid, 1997, 17–72.

18 This matter is taken up in greater detail in the article "El proyecto europeo de España en el siglo XX" ("Spain's European Project in the 21st Century"), Documents and Memorias of the Royal Academy of Moral and Political Sciences 1 (1998): 86–99. The aforementioned Incipe Report 1998 can be consulted in the same way.

19 López Pintor, R., *Sociología industrial* ("Industrial Sociology"). (Madrid: Alianza Editorial, 1986, 324ff.

20 Alcobendas Tirado, M.P., *Datos sobre el trabajo de la mujer en España* ("Data on the Work of Women in Spain"). (Madrid: CIS, 1983).

21 Pérez Díaz, V. *Clase obrera, partidos y sindicatos* (Working Class, Parties and Unions) (Madrid: Sociological Research Programme of the INI, 1979); Pérez Díaz, V. *"Elecciones sindicales, afiliación y vida sindical de los obreros españoles hoy"* ("Union Elections, Affiliation and Union Life of Spanish Workers Today"), *Revista de investigaciones sociológicas* ("Sociological Research Review") (1979).

22 FRAP, Antifascist Patriotic Revolutionary Front; GRAPO, First of October Antifascist Resistance Groups

23 Reinares, F. *"Sociogénesis y evolución del terrorismo en España"* ("Sociogenesis and Evolution of Terrorism in Spain") in Salvador Giner (ed), *España: sociedad y Política* (Spain: Society and Politics). Madrid: Espasa Calpe, (1990): 357.

24 Temas para el Debate (Subjects for Debate), Editorial, no. 16, January 1996.

25 El País, 15 September 1998

26 Camacho, J.M.: "Delincuencia" (Crime), in Del Campo, Salustiano (ed.) *Tendencias Sociales en España, 1960–1990* ("Social Trends in Spain, 1960–1990"), vol. 3 (Bilbao: Fundación BBV, 1993), 405–16.

27 Center of Sociological Investigations, *Relaciones interpersonales, actitudes y valores en la España de los 80* (Interpersonal Relations, Attitudes and Values in Spain in the 80's) (Madrid: CSI, 1988).

28 Del Campo, S.; Camacho, J.M.: "Grado de satisfacción" (Level of Satisfaction) in Del Campo, Salustiano (ed.) *Tendencias Sociales en España, 1960–1990* (Social Trends in Spain, 1960–1990), vol. 3, 453–67.

29 Villalain, J.L. et al. *La sociedad española de los 90 y sus nuevos valores* (Spanish Society in the 90's and its New Values), Fundación Santa María, 1992.

30 Orizo, F.A. *Los nuevos valores de los españoles* (The Spaniards' New Values), Madrid: Fundación Santa Maria, 1991.

31 Amando de Miguel and Marta Escuin, in Del Campo (ed.), *Tendencias Sociales en España, 1960–1990*, 269.

32 Centre of Sociological Investigation, Study no. 2234, February 1997.

33 De Miguel, A. and M. ESCUIN, *ABC de la opinión española* (Madrid: Espasa Calpe, 1997), 272.

34 Blanco Albarca, A. "La calidad de vida: supuestos psicosociales" (Quality of Life: Psychosocial Hypothesis) in VVAA, *Psicología social aplicada* (Applied Social Psychology) (Bilbao: Desclée de Brouwer, 1985), 181.

35 CIS, *Relaciones interpersonales, actitudes y valores en la España de los 80* ("Interpersonal Relations, Attitudes and Values in Spain in the 80's"). (Madrid, CIS, 1988), 181.

36 Alcaide, C. "El gasto familiar" (Family Spending), *El País*, 12 July 1998.

37 Alcaide, Julio (1994): "El ciclo expansivo-recesivo de la economía española desde la óptica regional" (The Expansive-recessive Cycle in the Spanish Economy from a Regional Viewpoint) Papeles de Economía Española (Papers on Spanish Economy) 59 (1994): 2–36.

38 Cazorla, Perez J. *Sobre los andaluces* (Málaga: Agora, 1990).

39 Navarro, José, "Pobreza y desigualdad en España" (Poverty and Inequality in Spain) in Vidal-Beneyto, J. (de) *España a debate. Tomo II: La sociedad* (Spain under Debate, vol. 2: Society) (Madrid: Tecnos, 1991).

40 Gaviria, M. *La septima potencia: España en el mundo* ("The Seventh Power: Spain in the World") (Barcelona, Ediciones B., 1996), 201ff.

41 Castillo. S. and L. Toharia, "Las desigualdades en el trabajo" ("Inequality at Work") in *Mercado de trabajo y desigualdad* (Labour Market and Inequality), vol. 4 of Symposium Equality and Distribution of Income and Wealth, Fundación Argentaria, 1993.

42 José Mª Serrano: *Desigualdades territoriales en la economía sumergida* (Territorial Inequalities in the Underground Economy) *El País*, 9 July 1998.

43 Campo, S. del, *Estado actual y perspectivas de la sociedad española* (Present State and Perspectives of Spanish Society) (Madrid: Independent Foundation, 1993).

44 Vidal-Beneyto, J. *España a debate* (Spain under Debate) (Madrid: Tecnos, 1991).

45 Campo, S. del *La Sociedad de Clases Medias* ("Middle Class Society") (Madrid: Espasa-Calpe, 1989).

46 Tezanos, J. F. "Cambio y modernización en la España actual" (Change and Modernization in Spain Today), in *Revista Española de Investigaciones sociológicas* (Spanish Review of Sociological Investigation) 28 (Oct.–Dec.) 1984: 44–5.

47 del Campo, *La Sociedad de Clases Medias*.

48 "Actitudes ante la economía sumergida" (Attitudes towards the Underground Economy) CIS, study No 2,249.

49 Anguita, M. F., "*Mirando hacia atrás sin ira*" (Looking Back without Anger), *El País*, 29 July 1998.

50 Orizo, J. F. *Los nuevos valores de los españoles* (The Spaniards' New Values) (Madrid: Santa María Foundation-SM, 1991), 205.

51 del Campo, "Estada actual," 59; CIRES, June 1992.

52 Bobbio, N. *Derecha e Izquierda: razones y significados de una distinción política* ("Right and Left: Reasons and Significance of a Political Distinction") (Madrid: Taurus, 1995).

53 Campo, S. del and J.M. Camacho, "Valores sociales" (Social Values), in Campo, S. del, ed, *Tendencias Sociales en España, 1960–1990* (Social Trends in Spain, 1960–1990), vol. 3. (Madrid: Fundación BBV, 1993).

54 Survey on public and private enterprise, Eudox.

55   Beck, Ulrich, "Kapitalismus ohne Arbeit," *Der Spiegel* 20/1996, in Hans-Peter Martin and Harold Schumann: *La trampa de la globalización* (Deception of Globalization) (Madrid: Taurus, 1998).

56   Health, Medicine and Health Care Yearbook (Madrid: El País, 1997).

57   CIS, study 2201, December 1995.

58   De Miguel, A. *La Sociedad Española, 1996–97* (Spanish Society, 1996–97), (Madrid: Alianza Editorial, 1998), 338.

59   Campo, S. del: *Estado actual y perspectivas de la sociedad española* (Present State and Perspectives of Spanish Society) (Madrid: Independent Foundation, 1993), 64.

60   Campo, S. del, ibid., 64ff.

The U.S. Government at the Turn of the Century

THEODORE CAPLOW

1 INTRODUCTION

The founding document of the United States (1787) begins, "We the People of the United States, in Order to form a more perfect Union, establish Justice, insure domestic Tranquility, provide for the common Defense, promote the general Welfare, and secure the Blessings of Liberty to ourselves and our Posterity, do ordain and establish this Constitution for the United States of America."

In this chapter, I presumptuously propose to evaluate the current performance of the U.S. government with respect to union, justice, tranquility, defense, welfare, liberty.

2 UNION

The framers, with the failure of the Articles of Confederation fresh in their minds, were aware of the danger of conflict among the states about to be joined together in the new union, but they could go only so far in limiting state sovereignty and stopped short of declaring the union indissoluble. Subsequent events showed how critical that omission was. But since the end of the Civil War, the national government has become steadily more powerful in relation to the states. The movement continues to this day as Congress and the judiciary expand the federal role in education, health care, crime control, the environment, product safety, tort liability, retail sales, contracts, and every other jurisdictional area formerly reserved to the several states.

Despite much talk of devolution, a few contrarian Supreme Court decisions, and some shifting of administrative responsibilities, the states are now so firmly under federal control that serious conflicts between states or between a state and the federal government have become unthinkable.

The only vestige of state sovereignty that matters is the equal representation of states in the U.S. Senate, which gives the citizens of sparsely populated states like Nevada and Wyoming much more influence per capita in that body than the citizens of New York or California. Only a few political scientists seem to mind.[1]

With respect to *union*, the U.S. government deserves an A.

3 JUSTICE

The two words "establish justice" of the Preamble cover a multitude of activities – civil, criminal, and military courts at every level from justices of the peace to the Supreme Court, thousands of local, state and federal law enforcement agencies and hundreds of thousands of police officers, an intricate network of tax agencies and tax collectors, nearly a million lawyers, millions of pages of statutes and of regulations with the force of law, and perhaps most important, the confidence of the people at large in the fairness of the authorities.

Although each of the fifty states has its own laws, courts, and enforcement agencies, these are so closely supervised by the federal courts, so frequently overborne by congressional mandates and decisions of federal judges, and so often involved with federal enforcement agents that the justice system can be viewed as a national entity.

This is the category in which the performance of the federal government shows the steepest downward trend and the least hope for the immediate future. The symptoms of trouble include:

- An ongoing change in the character of statutes and regulations, whereby they become ever more numerous, longer, more detailed and less flexible, with less and less scope for the application of practical judgment and common sense.

   For example: the OSHA regional office in Chicago, after visiting a construction site, sent a citation to the brickmaker for failing to supply a Material Safety Data Sheet with each pallet of bricks. If a brick is sawed, OSHA reasons, it can release small amount of the mineral silica. The sawing of bricks, however, does not release large amounts, and bricklayers don't spend much time sawing bricks. Bricks, after all, are not used like lumber. Brickmakers thought the government had gone crazy ... Brickmakers dutifully began sending out the MSDS form, which describes for the benefit of workers how to identify a brick (" a hard ceramic body ... with no odor") and gives its boiling point (above 3500° F.) The problem, at least as seen by the brick manufacturers, is the implication that the material is, in fact, hazardous ... these forms were an invitation to lawsuits.[2]

- As the law became increasingly rigid, its agents became increasingly indifferent to outcomes:

  For example: Take the case of Grace Capitello, a 36-year-old single mother with a true talent for parsimony. To save on clothing, Ms. Capitello dresses herself plainly in thrift store finds. To cut her grocery bill, she stocks up on 67 cent boxes of saltines and 39 cent cans of chicken soup ... Ms Capitello's stingy strategies helped her build a saving account of the more than $3000 in the last four years. Her goal was to put away enough money to buy a new washing machine and maybe one day send her daughter, Michelle, to college ... But there was one catch. Ms Capitello is on welfare – $60 a month, plus $60 in food stamps – and saving that much money on public aid is against the law ... The Milwaukee Department of Social Services took her to court, charged her with fraud, and demanded that she return the savings.[3]

- The indifference to outcomes that has become characteristic of the American legal system is compounded by a degree of judicial discretion that verges on frivolity:

  For example: In Maryland, Timothy Sherman, 17, was convicted of the shotgun murder of his mother and stepfather. The murder occurred in the middle of the night when Timothy was in his mother's home. His fingerprints were on the shotgun's trigger. The shotgun was found in a tree where he had hidden objects before, a tree between his mother's house and the house to which he ran to report the murders. A box of shotgun shells with two missing was under his mattress. Sherman appealed his conviction because a juror had made an unauthorized visit to the crime scene ... two members of a three-judge panel, evidently believing that defendants have a right to perfect trials, not just fair ones, overturned Sherman's conviction.[4]

- In the tort liability system, the premise that liability is created by negligence or malfeasance, has been replaced by the premise that when an injury occurs, some affluent person or entity should be made to pay compensation. Common sense takes a real beating here.

For example: Chevron Chemical was sued in federal court by an employee who contracted pulmonary fibrosis, allegedly as the result of long-term exposure to a chemical called paraquat. The Federal Environmental Protection Agency requires a label on this product warning among things, against "prolonged exposure" and "repeated contact." Chevron had put this label on the product. The company was held liable for a defective warning, although the court acknowledged that Chevron had no legal right to change or to supplement the warning prescribed by EPA.[5]

- From 1980 to 2001, the number of inmates in the state and federal prison systems of the United States increased from 317,000 to 1,500,000. Counting jail inmates, there are currently more than 2 million people behind bars in the U.S. Elsewhere in the developed world, incarceration rates range from about 35 per 100,000 residents in Japan to about 100 in Canada. The U.S. rate is above 500 – an unprecedented level for a civilized country. The increase has been largely driven by the war on drugs, which features draconian sentences for relatively innocuous acts.

  For example: In June 1991, the U.S. Supreme Court sustained the sentence of Ronald Harmelin, a first offender sentenced to life imprisonment without the possibility of parole in Michigan for the possession of half a pound of cocaine.[6]

- As the number of federal prosecutors more than doubled in recent years, many of them developed a ruthless style in keeping with the disparity of power implied when cases are labeled *The United States v. John Doe*. Some prosecutors are extraordinarily insensitive to the sufferings they inflict.

  For example: At the time of his sentencing Anthony F. Zak was seventy-one and his ailing wife, Peggy, was seventy-six. Zak was a World War II veteran with no prior criminal history. Some months before, however, federal agents had discovered that he was growing 112 marijuana plants in his garden. Now it was time for District Court Judge Alan A. McDonald – sitting in Yakima, Washington – to pronounce the sentence. McDonald was upset because the mandatory minimum sentences approved by Congress required him to send Zak to federal prison for five years. Referring to the "very sad issue at hand" – the imposition of a five-year prison term on a seventy-one-year-old man – McDonald turned to Pamela Byerly, the assistant U.S. attorney who was handling the case.

  "Now I'm informed by Mr. Zak's attorney that the government has gone farther and they've forfeited all his property, is that correct?"

the judge asked the prosecutor, "Who in the world called that shot?" "Your honor," Byerly replied, "we have a separate forfeiture attorney and I don't know how that – I was not involved in the case at that time. I do not know how that decision was made."[7]

- It is often remarked that the United States has an excessive supply of lawyers and that their number is growing by leaps and bounds. But the oversupply of lawyers in this country has not lowered the price of legal services. Quite the contrary. Resort to the law has become a penalty rather than a privilege for the average citizen and the differential ability to pay legal fees is the weapon of choice for large corporations and public agencies seeking to punish individuals.

  For example: When 11 Fort Worth residents learned that a couple in their neighborhood planned to sell their house to a county agency that was going to turn it into a group home for the mentally retarded, they complained that this move would violate local restrictions. When they filed suit, a state judge gave them a temporary injunction against the sale ... These apprehensive residents dropped their lawsuit eight days after it was filed when their attorneys discovered a Texas statute that excluded group homes from deed restrictions on sales of single family homes. Four years later, the U.S. Justice Department – on referral from HUD – sued the residents who opposed the group home but then withdrew from combat ... The majestic US government charged that the lawsuit filed four years earlier was "frivolous, baseless and discriminatory" ... Should the defendants – now down to eight – lose, they are likely to be hit for some $12,000 in actual damages, together with possible punitive damages. Their legal fees will be more than $200,000.[8]

- In areas of popular hysteria, like child abuse, the courts and law enforcement agencies have not hesitated to set aside the most basic safeguards of due process.

  For example: [There is] the story of a young mother outside Syracuse whose two-year old daughter was taken away from her after she naively confided to an uninformed stranger that she had become aroused while breast feeding. She had called a community volunteer center to find out how to contact the local chapter of the La Leche League support group. Anyone at La Leche could have assured her that such feelings were utterly normal. Instead, the community volunteer center referred her to a rape crisis center, which in turn reported her to a child-abuse hotline. She was arrested and subjected to a five-hour police interrogation, and was separated from her daughter for an entire year.[9]

• The confiscation of property has become the most gratifying and profitable branch of law-enforcement activity. Neither the Fifth Amendment nor ordinary notions of fairness are allowed to stand in the way:

For example: The Supreme Court ruled in March 1996 that the government can seize cars, houses, and other property used for criminal activity even if the actual owner of the property did not know about the wrongdoing. It ruled against a Michigan woman whose family car was confiscated when her husband used it for sex with a prostitute. The five to four decision, which surprised lawyers on both sides, enhanced the power of states to take property connected to crimes and, according to dissenting justices, could lead to the seizure of vast amount of property from innocent owners.[10]

• Should the property-owner be black or otherwise disreputable, law-enforcement can be even more high-handed.

For example: Jones, a second-generation African-American nurseryman in his family's Nashville florist business, was about to board an American Airlines flight. As he had done many times before, Jones was on his way to Houston to buy flowers and shrubs. Because the wholesalers prefer cash, he was carrying $9600. This time, however, apparently because Jones fit a "profile" of what drug dealers are supposed to look like, two police officers stopped him, searched him and seized his $9600. The businessman was given a receipt and told he was free to go ... After a long legal battle and a lot of publicity, Jones got his money back.[11]

• The most flagrant witch hunt of recent years – the trial and imprisonment of hundreds of daycare workers and parents for imaginary ritual abuses of children – was directly sponsored by federal agencies.

For example: In cases where recordings [of children] testifying for the prosecution were made, preserved, and given to the defense, juries often handed down not-guilty verdicts. Where there were no tapes, defendants were typically convicted ... Child-protection authorities institutionalized their phobia about interview records when the National Center for the Prosecution of Child Abuse (NCPCA) published a voluminous manual instructing district attorneys how to handle child-abuse cases ... INVESTIGATION AND

PROSECUTION OF CHILD ABUSE contains reams of advice on how to gather pro-prosecution expert witnesses; how to discredit those who testify for the defense; how to pick juries sure to vote guilty; and – perhaps most important – on not videotaping interviews with children, since doing so may help the defense. The text was published by the National District Attorneys Association, and was federally funded by the Justice Department and the National Center on Child Abuse and Neglect.[12]

Thousands of such incidents contribute to the widespread impression that the power of government is often exercised abusively and without much regard for ordinary standards of fairness. The most celebrated episodes – the assault on the Branch Dravidians, the Ruby Ridge shootings – are less important than the daily occurrence of small events that shock the neighbors – the freezing of a merchant's bank account by the IRS without prior warning, the dawn raid by the FBI on the wrong apartment, the eviction from her home of the old woman whose husband went to prison for growing marijuana.

With respect to the public perception of the system's fairness, the evidence is fairly conclusive. A series of national surveys taken between 1964 and 1995 included the question, "How much of the time do you trust the government in Washington to do the right thing?" The proportion of respondents agreeing to "just about always" or "most of the time" declined from 76 percent in 1964 to 25 percent in 1995[13].

On *justice*, the nation's performance is clearly substandard.

D+ might be an appropriate grade.

The downward trend is likely to continue for some time to come, since the futile war on drugs continues unabated while the persistence of the incarceration mania is guaranteed by such reforms as mandatory sentencing guidelines, three-strikes-and-out measures, the abolition of parole and by the growing political influence of the prison construction and private prison industries.

4 TRANQUILITY

The goal of domestic tranquility implies:

- that riots and insurrections are prevented;
- that persons and property are safe;
- that private and public transactions are conducted with civility;
- that citizens are mutually respectful.

Riots and Insurrections

This nation has a long tradition of violent local conflicts. From the Whisky Rebellion of 1794 to the Seattle riot of December 1999, every decade has witnessed episodes of violent confrontation between hostile groups of citizens and between citizens and the law.

The dispute over slavery was the principal stimulator of violence in the years leading up to the Civil War, and Southern resistance to enfranchisement in the years afterward. Labor-management conflicts provoked serious violence from the Haymarket riot of 1886 to the soft-coal strikes of the 1930s, and although labor relations are generally peaceful nowadays, violent confrontations still occasionally occur. The Vietnam decade provoked three distinct series of violent episodes – student protests against the war that extended to other issues, the civil rights demonstrations that began in Birmingham and spread throughout the South, and the less articulate, but more destructive riots in black inner-city districts during the long hot summers of the 1960s. Between 1964 and 1968, by one estimate, there were 329 serious riots in 257 American cities.[14]

Since the end of the Vietnam War, many of the large-scale demonstrations for black civil rights, women's rights, gay rights, against the Gulf War, for and against immigration, and for political causes and candidates have been peaceful.

By historical standards, the United States has been relatively peaceful in recent years, but there were shocking exceptions: the Los Angeles riot and its echoes in other cities, the bombing of the New York Trade Center by foreign terrorists, the bombing of the Federal Building in Oklahoma City by native terrorists, and the Seattle riot against the World Trade Organization.

In contrast to previous eras, there are no organized parties of any consequence on either the left or the right of the political spectrum that presently seek to change the American form of government. Although the level of complaint is high, the rules of the game are supported by a massive consensus.

Public Safety

A great surge of crime occurred between 1967 and 1975 when the murder rate, the number of murders divided by the population, increased by 52 percent in only eight years, while robberies increased by 112 percent and burglaries by 85 percent.[15] Thereafter, there was no clear cut trend until the early 1990s when crime rates began to decline from year to year.

The total rate of the seven index crimes included in the Uniform Crime Reports of the FBI (murder, rape, robbery, aggravated assault, burglary, larceny and motor vehicle theft) was lower in 1999 than in 1975, although higher than in 1967.

The popular impression of continuously rising crime in the U.S. during the 1980s seems to have had no factual basis except for a significant increase in the rape rate. But that offense is subject to serious reporting errors. The great majority of rapes go unreported so that fluctuations in the official rate are more likely to be due to shifts in the propensity to report than in the incidence of the offense. The National Victimization Surveys, conducted annually by the Department of Justice since 1973 and thought to provide more accurate measures of trends in crime, show *declines* in both rape and aggravated assault between 1975 and 1993.[17]

The rising crime rate that fueled so many political careers between 1975 and 1995 was apparently an illusion. There is not even any evidence for the belief that citizens were increasingly apprehensive about their personal safety. Almost annually, since 1972, the General Social Survey has put this question to its national sample of respondents: "Is there any area right around here – that is, within a mile – where you would be afraid to walk alone at night?" The distribution of responses has been essentially flat for all that time.[18]

But although rates of violent crime did not rise appreciably after 1975 and have recently fallen, the U.S. homicide rate is much higher than those of other modernized countries and represents a serious deprivation of tranquility for law-abiding citizens.

The incarceration mania already mentioned, whereby the number of prison inmates in the U.S. quadrupled in just seventeen years, is driven by the futile, expensive effort to prohibit the use of certain psychotropic drugs, by increases in prosecutorial efficiency and by the lengthening of sentences for common offenses that were already longer in the U.S. than in any other modernized country.

The incarceration mania has had dramatic effects on the African-American population. More than half of the inmates in state and federal prisons are black. Black men are eight times as likely to be imprisoned as white men. How much of this over-representation is attributable to discriminatory treatment by the justice system is a long-debated and still unsettled question, but there is no doubt that the over-representation is a demographic catastrophe; 32 percent of black men aged 25 to 29 were in jail, in prison, on probation, or on parole in 1995.[19]

These are the men who are not available as husbands for black women, whose fatherless children will grow up in mean conditions and furnish new recruits for street gangs, and who will themselves commit new crimes when they are eventually released and find no other opportunities open to them.

Civility

It is difficult to measure trends in civility with any precision. Political rhetoric was extremely uncivil in the early days of the Republic but the level of civility seems to have improved throughout the nineteenth century. The factions debating slavery before the Civil War used somewhat more courteous language than the factions debating abortion today. For much of the twentieth century, national politics were conducted on a fairly high level between parties that did not seriously challenge each other's legitimacy. Colorful epithets and implausible accusations were mostly associated with the left and right fringes of the political spectrum.

In recent years, the passions aroused by the ongoing controversies over abortion, homosexuality, sexual harassment, political correctness, affirmative action, gun control, pornography, animal rights and school prayer have filtered into electoral contests and lowered the level of civility so that nasty language is commonplace and the spreading of false accusations on the eve of an election is regarded as a normal campaign tactic.[20]

Such practices have been reinforced by the development of the paid television advertisement as the principal form of political communication and the reliance of that form on misrepresentation of one kind or another.

Mutual Respect

During the administration of Lyndon Johnson, there were two important shifts in federal policy that profoundly transformed the daily experience of Americans.

One was a rapid unplanned change in the goal of the civil rights movement. Martin Luther King's dream envisaged a color-blind society in which individuals participated freely without regard to race or ethnicity. What developed with amazing speed instead, out of ambiguous language in the Civil Rights Act of 1964 and the Voting Rights Act of 1965 and the regulatory initiatives undertaken by the Equal Opportunity Employment Commission and other federal agencies with the enthusiastic approval of the federal courts, was a system of racial classification that divided the whole population into five officially recognized – and scientifically meaningless – races: American

Indian or Alaskan Native, Asian or Pacific Islander, Black, Hispanic, and White, and that mandated preferences in employment, education, and government contracts for the first four of these groups as against the fifth.[21]

Women were eventually added to the four "racial groups" entitled to preference. Despite widespread opposition to affirmative action, the federal government currently operates nearly five hundred programs of affirmative action based on this strange taxonomy and it is effectively illegal to apply for a job or admission to college, to enlist in the armed forces, ask for a passport, or compete for promotion in a public agency without identifying oneself by "race." In an ironic reversal of earlier Jim Crow practices, white policemen have recently been known to claim reclassification as black on the strength of a newly discovered great-grandmother.

The other great shift in ethnic policy came about with less deliberation as unintended consequences of the Immigration Act of 1965 and subsequent modifications of it. "The bill will not flood our cities with immigrants. It will not upset the ethnic mix of our society," said Senator Edward Kennedy at the time.[22] His brother, Robert Kennedy, then attorney general, told a congressional committee that Asian immigration would be approximately 5000 during the first year, after which immigration from Asia would virtually disappear.[23] As it turned out, more than 5,000,000 Asians were admitted in the next two decades.

Legal immigration figures do not include the huge bulge from 1988 to 1991, as some three million illegal aliens took advantage of an amnesty offered by Congress to obtain resident status. Nor do they reflect the continued presence of some four million other illegal aliens and the annual arrival of perhaps a half million more. Nor the annual comings and goings of some hundreds of thousands of contract laborers from below the border.

Of the 18.4 million legal immigrants who entered the country between 1968 and 1996, nearly half came from Latin America and the Caribbean, a third from Asia, and 2 percent from Africa. They were entitled to the benefits of affirmative action as soon as they set foot on U.S. soil.

There are several interesting aspects to these numbers. First, the nation has lost control of its borders. Any enterprising Mexican who wishes to do so can enter the United States, buy a fraudulent birth certificate and social security card in downtown San Diego for a few dollars, use these to obtain a driver's license, and settle in for good. In the states where illegal immigrants are concentrated, they account for a high proportion of crime and welfare and educational and health expenses. The children they have after arrival are citizens by birth.

A more respectable method than sneaking across the border is to arrive at a port of entry by air or ship and claim political asylum. Persons who do so are released into the population with instructions to return for a hearing at some later date. About one in twenty actually do so; the others are not heard from again.

Most of the legal immigrants are admitted for purposes of family reunification; that is, they are relatives, or claim to be relatives, of previous immigrants. Once admitted, they can admit others by a sort of chain-letter process. Most of the current immigrants have few discernible skills to contribute to the national economy.

According to one calculation, post-1970 immigrants (and their descendants) account for about two-thirds of this country's present population growth and are projected to account for nearly all of it hereafter.[25]

Included in the ramshackle structure of immigration law are all sorts of special arrangements – for Cubans, for Russian Jews, for young people from Ireland, for wealthy persons with money to invest, for government witnesses in drug trials.

Ramshackle or not, the structure commands tacit bipartisan support. The most recent toothless bill to reform enforcement of existing immigration laws failed of passage in the spring of 1999. Democrats expect to get most of the votes of new citizens and fear the power of the strong Hispanic lobbies that have appeared since the Hispanic race was invented by government fiat and of the Asian lobbies that have copied them; they even fear the diplomatic pressure exerted by the Mexican government on behalf of its ex-nationals. Republicans are keenly, if privately, aware that unchecked immigration helps to keep wages low. Some liberals see diversity as an end in itself. Some conservatives welcome the growth of new minorities capable of checking African-American demands.

But nothing in the nation's history suggests that an increase in ethnic diversity will promote tranquility. Three hundred years of black-white relations provide abundant evidence on that point. And the problem is compounded by the inequities built into the racial preference system, the increasing defensiveness of the white majority and the increasing alienation of the designated minorities.[26]

The criterion of tranquility can not be considered satisfied at more than the minimal level. C would be a fair grade.

5 DEFENSE

The United States emerged from the Cold War as the sole superpower. We have the capability to project military force to any part of the world as no other state can do. We spend more on defense than all European states combined. Our army and air force are better equipped than any other and use more advanced technologies. Moreover, they are volunteer forces with high morale. The U.S. Navy sails unchallenged through every sea.

Three significant problems remain:

The first is the unresolved nuclear threat. Since it would be technically feasible – indeed easy – to destroy New York or Chicago with a few nuclear explosives mounted on intercontinental ballistic missiles, or on submarine-launched ballistic missiles, or on low-flying cruise missiles, or dropped from high-flying planes, or smuggled in by ship or truck, the nation's security is not well assured.

There are still many thousands of nuclear weapons in the arsenals of the United States and of the states of the former Soviet Union, and hundreds more deployed by Britain, France, China, Israel, India and Pakistan. The U.S. and Russia are committed by treaty to reducing their stocks to 3500 strategic weapons apiece by 2002, but it is clear that the deadline will not be met by either party; the other nuclear states are not committed to reduction.

No one has been able to imagine an effective defense against nuclear attack. Yet the American response to the window of opportunity opened by the end of the Cold War and cooperative relations with the Russian military establishment, has been almost lackadaisical. The mutual reduction of nuclear weapons was dutifully undertaken, but with a notable lack of enthusiasm or haste.[27]

The second problem is the want of a suitable enemy.

In the long run, it is probably not possible for the U.S. to maintain a huge and costly military establishment without a singular enemy which presents an unequivocal threat. The three most likely candidates are a resurgent Russia, China, and a Pan-Muslim military federation. Russia inherited most of the armed forces and nuclear arsenal of the Soviet Union and its conversion to a peaceful democracy is still imperfect. Russian chauvinists are active and influential and close to the centers of power. On the other hand, the threat of a Russian invasion of western Europe is unlikely to be renewed for the foreseeable future. The Russian armed forces are in disarray and the resources for rebuilding them are not available. Other than by a suicidal nuclear attack, it is difficult to see how Russia could seriously threaten the security of the United States.

China, with five times the population of the United States, a rapidly expanding economy and a bellicose regime, is a much better candidate. A Chinese invasion of Taiwan would be difficult for the U.S. to accept but difficult to counter by military means. A Chinese invasion of Japan, or a North Korean invasion of South Korea with Chinese support, would require an American military response under existing treaty obligations, and that too might not be easy. We are a long way from 1950. China is presently restrained by a combination of economic and nuclear deterrence and by the limited popularity of its rulers. But U.S. policy towards China is ambiguous, and the role of military force in that policy is deliberately undefined.

A union of Muslim states, with seven hundred million people in a continuous belt from Morocco to Indonesia, would introduce a formidable new element into world affairs, particularly if that entity were ruled by Islamic fundamentalists hostile to the American way of life. This would indeed be a serious threat but the deep divisions within the Muslim world, between Shia and Sunni, Arab and Persian, modernized and backward, oil-rich and dirt-poor, make it unlikely.

The unpleasant possibility, of course, is that the need for an enemy to justify our high state of preparedness will lead in a non-deliberate and reflexive way to policies that provoke the emergence of one or another of these hostile forces. A book titled *The Next War*[28] and co-authored by a former secretary of Defense (Weinberger) almost gleefully projected five imminent wars: with North Korea and China in 1998, Iran in 1999, Mexico in 2003, Russia in 2006 and Japan in 2007.

The third problem is the expanding U.S. share – about 60 percent in 1996 – of the international arms market, pursued as a national policy for the purpose, among others, of "maintaining the defense industrial base." According to a Pentagon estimate quoted in the press, 90 percent of the 50 armed conflicts under way in the world during 1993–94 involved one or more parties that had recently received U .S. weapons or military technology.[29] And in most of their recent encounters with armed adversaries, our own forces have faced weapons and technology exported from the United States.

This is a difficult sector of performance to grade, setting the high quality of U.S. forces and U.S. military technology against the neglect of nuclear dangers, the vagueness of strategic policy, and the continuous stoking of the arms trade. B+ is the highest possible grade.

7   WELFARE

The word was long used to refer to one of the most mischievous and counterproductive of federal programs, Aid to Families with Dependent Children (largely reformed in 1996), but its proper sense is much broader and includes both economic management and the provision of human services.

Economic management is a sphere of activity in which modern nations directly compete and in which quantitative scoring is highly developed. Some indicators of successful economic management are (1) a continuous rise in Gross Domestic Product per capita; (2) a continuous rise in average earnings; (3) low inflation; (4) low unemployment; (5) favorable trade balances; (6) high savings rates; (7) the gradual reduction of inequality.

These indicators conceal a political paradox. The modern welfare state accepts the responsibility of achieving these difficult goals without necessarily having the capability to do so, since it shares responsibility for the national economy with millions of private decision-making entities. But the Soviet Union and other states that tried to dispense with private decision-making had even less success in economic management.

Gross Domestic Product.   The U.S. trends are a mixed bag. Per capita GDP has risen steadily since 1960, but at a slower average rate than most of the other advanced countries. U.S. productivity grew at a slower rate from 1990 to 1995 than in any previous peacetime period since the Civil War, except for the Depression of the 1930s.[30] Thereafter there was marked improvement.

Earnings.   The nearly continuous upward trends in average hourly wages and in family income that had been maintained throughout the nineteenth and most of the twentieth century came to a jarring halt in the early 1970s. In constant 1996 dollars, the median income of U.S. households rose by an average of only one-quarter of one percent per year between 1970 and 1996,[32] and that slight increase was entirely attributable to the increased employment of married women. The median income of married-couple families with non-working wives actually declined over the same period.[33] Since then, there has been some slight improvement.

It has been argued that the stagnation of earnings was illusory, because the fringe benefits received by employees (principally health insurance, vacation and sick leave, and retirement contributions) increased more than enough to offset the small decline in dollar income. On the other hand, tax rates were increasing at the same time so that the median after-tax income of American families declined by 8 percent between 1977 and 1987 alone.[34]

From about 1800 to about 1970, American industrial wages were the highest in the world. By the 1990s they were nearly the lowest among the advanced, industrial nations.[35] If the hourly compensation costs for production workers in U.S. industry are taken as 100, French and Japanese wages stood recently around 120 and German wages at 180, while in eleven smaller countries, production workers are better paid than in the U.S.

There is considerable debate about the causes of the relative immobility of earnings after 1973. But two factors stand out – the decline in the rate of economic growth and the diminishing membership and influence of labor unions.

Inflation has traced a markedly uneven course since 1960, driven in part by industrial and market factors and in part by the gyrations of government policy. The worst recent year for inflation was 1980, at 13.5 percent. The best was 1986 at 1.9 percent. In the past few years, the Federal Reserve's efforts to minimize inflation have been conspicuously successful.

Unemployment Since 1960, the U.S. unemployment rate has oscillated in the range between 3.4 (in 1969) and 9.5 (in 1982 and 1983).[38] As of this writing in 2000, it stands at 4.0, confuting the received wisdom of economists that a rate lower than 6.0 would be inflationary. The unemployment rate of African-Americans runs about twice that of the national average. Hispanics and young workers also experience higher than average unemployment.

Superficially, unemployment in the United States compares very favorably with most of the other advanced industrial nations. They have more unemployment and, in particular, more long-term unemployment. But exact comparisons are impossible because the U.S. figures, unlike those of other countries, exclude discouraged workers who have given up looking for jobs, exclude the huge prisoner population, and count part-time workers as fully employed. Moreover, there is some evidence that even the short-term unemployed are undercounted.[39]

Trade Balance In most of the years from 1790 to 1840, imports exceeded exports, with a maximum trade deficit of $65 million in 1816. From 1840 to 1875, exports and imports stayed in rough balance. Then the growing industrial strength of the country made itself felt. From 1889 to 1970, the only years in which exports failed to exceed imports were the Depression years of 1934 to 1940, although the differences in both good years and bad were relatively small. The favorable trade balances of the 1960s, for example, ranged from $1.7 billion to $8.2 billion. In the early 1970s, some modestly negative trade balances were recorded. Then the picture changed completely. Beginning in 1977, the U.S. has imported a great more than it exported in every single year, with the deficit exceeding $150 billion in 1986 and 1987 and again in every year from 1994 to 2000.[40]

These deficits were partly offset by a favorable balance in travel and financial services but what remained was sufficient to convert the United States from the world's largest creditor to its largest debtor, indeed the largest debtor the world has ever known.

Savings   The rate of saving has fluctuated irregularly since 1950. The gross domestic savings rate in the U. S. in 2000 was both the lowest in its history and the lowest in the developed world.[41]

Moreover, the U.S. has a higher rate of consumer indebtedness than any other country. These mortgage and installment loans, credit card balances and unpaid bills are equivalent to negative savings. The trend is alarming. Private household debt increased from year to year from 1980 to 1999. In 1992, the financial assets of the 91 percent of the U.S. families who had such assets had a median value of $13,100. But the median debt of the 73 percent of all U.S. families who were indebted was $17,600.[42] Millions of families owed more on their houses and cars than their houses and cars were worth. Tens of millions had negative net worth, and the situation has since deteriorated.

Inequality   There is no accepted formula for optimum inequality in the distribution of wealth and income. The classic socialist formula of "from each according to his ability, to each according to his need" has not proved workable under socialist regimes. An equal distribution is totally implausible in a modern economy. A moderately unequal distribution is held to promote the general welfare better than an extremely unequal distribution but there is no consensus about how much inequality is moderate. However, it has been taken for granted that income inequality tends to decline over time in democratic polities. A 1988 study showed a significant inverse relationship in a sample of 55 countries between income inequality and the total duration of democratic regimes, even with the level of economic development controlled.[43]

The attitudes towards income inequality that command the most agreement in advanced, industrial societies seem to be these: (1) the poorest residents ought to enjoy a decent living standard; (2) the income of workers afflicted by unemployment, injury or sickness should be protected; (3) living standards should not be a function of age; (4) inequality should decline with economic progress.

Poverty   The trend of poverty in the U.S. tells a simple story. During the decade of the 1960s, strong economic growth, together with the federal government's War on Poverty, reduced poverty by nearly half. But the effort faltered in the 1970s and poverty worsened in the 1980s and the early 1990s.

The overall figures mask enormous differences between social categories. In 1992, poverty afflicted 12 percent of whites, 29 percent of blacks and 27 percent of Hispanics;[44] and in 1993, 25 percent of persons without a high school diploma, 12 percent of high school graduates and only 2 percent of college graduates.[45] In 1970, 25 percent of elderly people and 15 percent of children were poor. Subsequently, their positions have been reversed so that by 1997 only 10 percent of the elderly but 20 percent of children were classified as poor. The most extreme figure was attained for black and Hispanic children – 37 percent were poor in 1997.[46] But the poverty rate for all American children far exceeds that of any other advanced country; it runs about three times as high as the corresponding rates in Germany, France and Italy.[47]

Poverty is not easy to measure. The figures above are based on per capita money income, without taking account of taxes, food stamps, school lunches, rent subsidies, Medicare, Medicaid, and so forth.

When the Social Security tax is reckoned in (the poor are not much affected by income taxes), the poverty population increases by more than 50 percent; if health services are factored in at full cost, the poverty population decreases.[48]

The official U.S. poverty threshold is set by an arcane formula based on the changing cost of a basket of food. Other countries set the threshold at half the median income. Fortunately, the two methods produce similar results. In 1995, a group of private scholars sponsored by the Russell Sage Foundation published a comparative analysis of poverty and poverty polices in the United States, Canada and western Europe.[49] The findings were generally unfavorable for this country. The American poor were found to be both more numerous and poorer than those of other advanced countries.[50] This was largely because the benefits they receive are less generous than those of other countries. The percentage of poor households lifted out of poverty by tax and transfer programs ranged from 62 percent in the Netherlands down to 0.5 percent in the U.S.![51] The proportion of families with children below the poverty level in the 1980s was greater in the U.S. than in Canada, France, Germany, Ireland, Luxembourg, the Netherlands, or Sweden – 20.7 percent in the U.S. compared to 2.7 percent in the Netherlands and in Sweden. In the U.S. black population, it stood at 49 percent, worse than any other segment of an advanced, industrial nation.[52]

As of 1996, more than five million American families spent more than half of their incomes on housing or lived in "severely substandard" housing and that proportion was rising.[53] One reason for this was the extraordinarily inept design of the federal programs intended to alleviate poverty. The centerpiece program, Aid to Families with Dependent Children, was ostensibly devolved to the states and reformed in 1996, but it still includes perverse incentives for unmarried mothers to remain unmarried, avoid stable relationships and avoid employment. The effective tax rate imposed on them for marrying or taking a job is always high and sometimes exceeds 100 percent. The programs that provide subsidized health care and housing for a fraction of the poor are much more advantageous for the providers than for the clients.[54] In social surveys, the basic premise of the welfare state – that the government should provide a basic income for all – is accepted by only about one in five American respondents, compared to sizeable majorities in other countries.[55]

The U.S. has another unenviable distinction. It is the only member of the set of advanced industrial nations in which full-time work at the minimum wage produces less than half (43 percent) of the median family income, compared, for example, to 79 percent in the United Kingdom and as much as 94 percent in France.[56]

The situation is somewhat more favorable with respect to the duration of public assistance, which is relatively brief in the U.S., and with respect to such facilities as household appliances and telephones, where the American poor are not conspicuously worse off than their foreign counterparts. But when it comes to collective amenities, there is nothing in contemporary western Europe that matches the squalor and insecurity of inner-city neighborhoods in the largest American cities.

Income Protection   Unemployment insurance, first installed by the New Deal, is managed jointly by the federal and state governments. Unlike the parallel systems in other countries, it has never undertaken to cover all of the unemployed or to replace their lost wages. It provides a meager cash income for a period of weeks while the recipient looks for work. It has never covered those who fail to find new jobs, and those who eventually give up looking or who settle for part-time work are not even counted as unemployed.

By 1975, the system had been liberalized several times and covered almost three-quarters of the officially unemployed. Since then, coverage has been gradually reduced and only about a third of the unemployed receive any benefits today.

Another major source of income insecurity is the reduction of income associated with involuntary job loss. The long slow shift from manufacturing to service employment has compelled millions of laid-off factory workers to move to lower-paid service jobs. The downsizing of corporate and private bureaucracies in the 1990s has had similar consequences for middle-level managers, whose new positions often pay less and offer fewer fringe benefits than they had before.

Workers' compensation is another insurance plan whereby employees injured in the course of their work are reimbursed for lost wages and medical expenses. The premiums are paid by employers and are experience-rated. Except for railroad workers and federal employees, this is a state rather than a federal responsibility.

American health insurance has some unique features that threaten the income security of most of the labor force. Coverage can be lost by the discovery of a pre-existing condition or by the failure of an insurer or simply by exceeding the dollar limits of a policy, and in any of these cases, medical and surgical expenses can reduce a middle-income family to destitution. It happens to thousands of families every month. By early 2000, more than 40 million Americans had no health insurance at all.

Incomes and Wealth   The most surprising trend in the American economy is the spectacular increase in inequality observed in the recent past, which deviates both from previous American experience and from the current experience of other modernized nations.

From 1900 to 1972, the steady increase in the Gross National Product per capita was accompanied by a gradual equalization of income. At the beginning of the century, the richest five percent of American families enjoyed about three times the aggregate income of the poorest forty percent. By 1972,the two groups were approximately at parity. Since then, the gap has widened again so that the share of the small top group is nearly double the share of the large bottom group. To take another comparison, the median real income in the lower fifth of the income distribution is a bit lower today than in 1972 while the median income in the upper fifth of the income distribution has effectively doubled during the same interval. Between 1977 and 1999, according to a study by the Center on Budget and Policy Priorities, the after-tax income of the richest one percent shot up by 115 percent while the poorest fifth suffered an income loss of 9 percent.[57]

Only in America are corporate executives likely to be paid 500 times as much as as their rank-and-file employees. Meanwhile, the unequal distribution of wealth becomes more unequal from year to year – we have hundreds of thousands of multi-millionaire families and tens of millions of families with negative net worth, while there is more poverty in the U.S. (less than half the median income) than in any peer nation and also much more extreme poverty (less than one-fourth of the median income.)

There was a parallel trend in the distribution of wealth, as the share of the top 1 percent rose from 31 to 37 percent between 1983 and 1992, by which time their net worth exceeded the combined net worth of the lower 90 percent of the population.[58] The disparity is even greater today.

What caused the gradual progress of equality to go so sharply into reverse here while it continued in many other countries? Some factors are unmistakable: the reduction of effective tax rates on high incomes and the increase of effective tax rates on low incomes; the declining membership and bargaining power of labor unions; the effects of immigration and globalization in restraining wage increases. Other factors are buried deep in the national psyche. The most curious feature of this massive trend is that it occurred in an era of exceptional domestic tranquility without provoking any resistance except for scattered and so far ineffective objections to global free trade.

Disequalization still goes merrily on today, when the most frequently proposed changes in the federal government's income policies are the further reduction or elimination of the capital gains tax, the privatization of Social Security, a national sales tax, and a flat income tax. By no coincidence at all, each of these measures would have the effect of further widening the existing inequality of income and wealth.

Human Services   The two most important human services provided by modern welfare states are education and health. With respect to both of these, the American welfare state is unique in denying universal access and imposing heavy and unpredictable costs on individuals and families.

While primary and secondary education are offered at public expense, the poor quality and disorderly condition of the public schools drive millions of pupils into private schools that charge substantial fees, while the colleges and universities that formerly offered free or low-cost instruction have been forced by financial stringency to shift more and more of their costs to students. In contrast to other advanced countries, where higher education is essentially free and admission to elite institutions is based on merit alone, the American system is expensive and inequitable and becomes more so with every passing year.

If the educational situation in the U.S. is troublesome, the health care situation is disastrous. The federal programs intended to provide health care to the elderly and the poor respectively – Medicare and Medicaid – have had the unintended effect of inflating the price of medical services and supplies for the entire population and encouraging predatory practices by health insurers and providers. As a result, the U.S. health care system now consumes a far larger proportion of GDP than that of any other country, shows relatively unfavorable results in life expectancy and morbidity and excludes a large fraction of the population from coverage.

Given the contrast between the enormous assets – natural and human – of the U.S. economy and the several unfavorable trends noted above, the government's performance on welfare must be characterized as mediocre, C at best.

7 LIBERTY

The liberties enumerated in the First Amendment to the U.S. Constitution include the free exercise of religion, and freedom of speech, of the press, of assembly and the right of petition. The right to bear arms is established by the Second Amendment. The Third Amendment, concerning the quartering of soldiers in private houses, is obsolete. The Fourth, Fifth and Sixth cover various aspects of due process – immunity from unreasonable searches and seizures, the requirement of an indictment for infamous crimes, the double jeopardy clause, the powerful right against self-incrimination, the blanket right of due process, and the requirement of just compensation for private property taken for public use. The Sixth Amendment enumerates the rights of criminal defendants, beginning with the right to a speedy and public trial and ending with the right of counsel. The Seventh Amendment requires jury trials in civil suits.

The Eighth prohibits excessive bail or fines, and cruel and unusual punishment. The Thirteenth prohibits slavery, the Fourteenth mandates the equal protection of the laws for all residents and the equal right of all citizens to unenumerated privileges and immunities, and repeats the due process clause of the Fifth with special reference to actions of the several states. These two clauses enabled the Supreme Court, in a long series of twentieth century decisions, to make most of the restraints imposed on the federal government by the Bill of Rights applicable to state and local governments also.[59]

The Fifteenth Amendment forbids the denial of voting rights because of race, color, or previous servitude. The Nineteenth gives equal voting rights to women. The Twenty-fourth prohibits the denial of voting rights for failure to pay taxes. The Twenty-sixth extends voting rights to citizens eighteen or older.

Freedom of speech and press are very often denied by private or local authorities, for example by college administrators enforcing speech codes, by editors censoring articles, by school boards removing books from libraries, but infrequently by federal agencies, except with regard to their own employees.

The free exercise of religion by individuals is universally respected in the U.S. today, including religions that involve snake handling, animal sacrifice and sorcery. The federal courts have been consistently vigilant with respect to this right. But the establishment clause of the First Amendment, "Congress shall make no law respecting an establishment of religion," has proved as baffling for the courts as for legal scholars. At various times the Supreme Court has ruled that transporting parochial students to and from schools at public expense is constitutional but transporting them on field trips is unconstitutional, that the loan of a public school textbook to a parochial school is constitutional but the loan of audio-visual equipment is not, that a state may provide guidance counseling to parochial schools in a mobile unit but not on their school grounds. And an extraordinary number of lawsuits about Christmas decorations in and around public buildings are still wending their way through the courts.

Over the years, a remarkable division has developed between the theistic practices and symbols of the American republic and the insistence of the federal courts that state and local governments be totally secular. Thus, while both houses of Congress have salaried chaplains and open their sessions with prayer, public schools are not permitted to sponsor prayer in any form. While the Ten Commandments are displayed on the walls of the Supreme Court building itself, their display in state or local public buildings is unconstitutional. While U.S. currency bears the motto "In God we trust," no state or local government is allowed to make any overtly religious statement. These judicial gyrations have much more symbolic than practical importance.

The same can not be said for the hundreds of state and federal programs that come under the general heading of affirmative action and that violate the apparent intent of the Fifteenth Amendment by distributing rights and privileges according to race and color.

The bundle of rights that constitute due process are more elaborately defined and generate more litigation in the United States than in any other democratic society. Refinements of due process account for the strange American custom of freeing offenders whose guilt has been established beyond any reasonable doubt when a procedural error is discovered in the investigation or trial of their cases and the even stranger customs associated with capital punishment, whereby the actual risk of death from being sentenced to death in the U.S. is less than the risk of death in some outdoor sports.

Nevertheless, the elementary requirements of due process are commonly disregarded – with the full blessing of the federal and state courts – in areas where the passions of the public have been sufficiently aroused. Persons accused of child abuse are not allowed to confront their accusers. The property of persons accused of drug trafficking is confiscated without trial. The rule against self-incrimination has been held not to cover compulsory urine-testing. The prohibition of double jeopardy is overcome by charging an acquitted defendant with conspiracy or racketeering in connection with the same incidents.

Over and above the legal niceties, there is a widespread impression that law enforcement agents – especially in the IRS, DEA, OSHA, FBI, CIA, and the offices of federal prosecutors – are not especially scrupulous about individual rights that might obstruct agency purposes. The body of laws and regulations they enforce is so vast and so inchoate that it is possible to find authority for almost any action they wish to take. And individuals, unlike large corporations and organized social movements, are not well-positioned to litigate with the government.

The nation's current performance with respect to liberty is neither very good nor very bad – a typical B.

8 CONCLUSIONS

We begin to understand why the American government is not vulnerable to revolution or even to drastic reform. If we average the grades proposed above for each of the six criteria of governmental performance, giving them equal weight, the average is B minus, a mediocre but passing grade. Yet this great Leviathan performed much better in earlier years and in the fullness of time it may do so again.

NOTES

1 See, for example, Lazare, Daniel, *The Frozen Republic: How the Constitution Is Paralyzing Democracy* (San Diego: Harcourt Brace, 1996).

2 Howard, Philip K. *The Death of Common Sense: How Law Is Suffocating America.* (New York: Random House, 1994), 37.

3 Rose, Robert L. *Wall Street Journal,* 2 June 1990, A1, A10.

4 Wills, George. *Washington Post,* 3 March 1996, A27.

5 Ferebee v. Chevron Chemical Company, DC Federal District Court, 1984.

6 *Washington Post,* 11 May 1991, A1, A8.

7 Burnham, David, *Above the Law: Secret Deals, Political Fixes and Other Misadventures of the U.S. Department of Justice.* (New York: Scribner, 1996), 188.

8 Hentoff, Nat. *Washington Post*, 2 April 1996, C7.

9 Oxenhandler, Noelle. "The Eros of Parenthood." *The New Yorker*, 19 February 1996, 48.

10 *Washington Post*, 3 August 1996, A1, A7.

11 Burnham, *Above the Law*, 189.

12 Nathan, Debbie, and Michael Snedeker. *Satan's Silence: Ritual Abuse and the Making of a Modern American Witch Hunt* (New York: Basic Books, 1995), 225, 226.

13 *Washington Post*/Kaiser Family Foundation/Harvard University Survey Project (Menlo Park CA: The Henry J. Kaiser Family Foundation, 1996).

14 Lind, Michael, *The Next American Nation: The New Nationalism and the Fourth American Revolution* (New York: The Free Press, 1995), 111.

15 SAUS79 (Statistical Abstract of the United States 1979).

16 SAUS79, Table 291; SAUS98, Table 335. *Washington Post*, 12 May 1999, A3.

17 U.S. Department of Justice, *Criminal Victimization in the United States* (Washington, DC: Bureau of Justice Statistics, 1993), 99.

18 National Opinion Research Center. General Social Survey, Cumulative Codebook, 1972–1994. (Chicago: NORC, 1995).

19 The Social Change Report (Muncie, IN: Center for Middletown Studies, 1996), 6:1:2.

20 For example, campaign workers representing themselves as pollsters telephoned Maine voters late in the 1994 campaign to ask if their opinion of congressional candidate Rick Bennett would change if they knew he had defaulted on his student loans. Mr. Bennett had not defaulted on any student loans. Larry Sabato and Glenn Simpson, *Washington Post*, 3 March 1996.

21 The document that enacted this weird classification was the Office of Management and Budget's directive #15, prepared in 1973. For a detailed account of the shift from individual to group rights in the civil rights movement see Lind, *The Next American Nation*, 109 et. seq.

22 Cose, Ellis, *A Nation of Strangers: Prejudice, Politics, and the Populating of America* (New York: William Morrow, 1992), 109.

23 Brimelow, Peter, *Alien Nation: Common Sense about America's Immigration Disaster* (New York: Random House, 1995), 78.

24 SAUS59, Table 109; SAUS79, Table 123; SAUS87, Table 7; SAUS98, Table 5.

25 Brimelow, *Alien Nation*.

26 For an abundance of anecdotal evidence on these points, see Johnson, Haynes, *Divided We Fall: Gambling with History in the Nineties* (New York: W.W. Norton, 1994).

27 Presidential Decision Directive 34 (PPD-34), 1995.

28 Weinberger, Casper, and Peter Schweizer. *The Next War* (Washington, D.C.: Regnery, 1996).

29 Isenberg, David. *Washington Post,* 18 February 1996, c5.

30 For a full discussion of the causes and consequences of this slowdown, see Madrick, Jeffrey, *The End of Affluence: The Causes and Consequences of America's Economic Dilemma* (New York: Random House, 1995).

31 SAUS98, Table 721.

32 SAUS98, Table 739.

33 SAUS95, Table 738, SAUS98, Table 740.

34 Phillips, Kevin, *Boiling Point: Republicans, Democrats, and the Decline of Middle-Class Prosperity* (New York: Random House, 1993), 48.

35 Madrick, Jeffrey, *The End of Affluence: The Causes and Consequences of America's Economic Dilemma* (New York: Random House, 1995), 82–3.

36 SAUS95, Table 761.

37 SAUS95, Table 628; SAUS87, Table 637.

38 Phillips, *Boiling Point,* 98–9.

39 SAUS95, Tables 1334 and 1335; Historical Statistics of the United States: Colonial Times to 1970, Series U187-200.

40 SAUS79, Table 728; SAUS99, Table 1322, and subsequent press reports.

41 SAUS99, Tables 730, 731 and subsequent press reports.

42 SAUS95, Table 744.

43 Muller, Edward N., "Democracy, Economic Developmentand Income Inequality," American Sociological Review 53 (1988): 50–68.

44 SAUS99, Table 763.

45 SAUS99, Table 767.

46 See also, Sawhill, Isabel V.,"Young Children and Families," in Shultee, Henry J. and Charles L., *Setting Domestic Priorities: What Can Government Do?* (Washington, DC: Brookings Institute, 1995) 147–84.

47 Weick, Stefan, "Zunehmende Kinderarmut in Deutschland?" ISI 15 (1996): 1–3, Table 1.

48 McFate, Katherine, Roger Lawson, and William Julius Wilson, *Poverty, Inequality, and the Future of Social Policy: Western States in the New World Order* (New York: Russell Sage Foundation, 1995).

49 Greg J. Duncan et al., "Poverty and Social-Assistance Dynamics in the United States, Canada, and Europe," in McFate, Lawson, and Wilson, *Poverty, Inequality, and the Future of Social Policy,* Table 2.1.

50 McFate, Lawson, Wilson, *Poverty, Inequality, and the Future of Social Policy,* 29–66.

51 Department of Housing and Urban Development, press release, 15 March 1996.

52 For a full discussion of the perverse incentives built into these programs, see Caplow, Theodore, *Perverse Incentives: The Neglect of Social Technology in the Public Sector* (Westport, CT: Praeger, 1994).

53 Duncan et al, "Poverty and Social Assistance Dynamics," Table 2.9.

54 Ibid., Table 2.8.

55 Phillips, *Boiling Point*, Table 1.
56 Strobel, Frederick R., *Upward Dreams, Downward Mobility: The Economic Decline of the American Middle Class* (Lanham, MD: Rowman and Littlefield, 1993), 47–8.
57 *Washington Post* 9 May 1999, A8. This was a sharp change from the previous trend, which had remained approximately level since 1949. See Levy, Frank, *Dollars and Dreams* (New York: Russell Sage Foundation, 1987), 14.
58 Ibid. See also Frank, Robert, *Luxury Fever* (New York: The Free Press, 1999).
59 The free expression clause of the First Amendment was "incorporated" (Justice Brennan preferred "absorbed") so as to apply to state and local authorities in the same way as on its face it applies to Congress in Gitlow v. New York 1925 when the Court declared in passing that the 14th Amendment requirement of due process made the states subject to the same requirement. Subsequent Supreme Court decisions in 1940, 1947 and 1958 incorporated the remainder of the Bill of Rights except for the 7th Amendment. I am indebted to Professor Robert O'Neil for this account.

The Contemporary Canadian State: Redefining a Social and Political Union

SIMON LANGLOIS

1 INTRODUCTION

The Canada that has just entered the third millennium does not much resemble Canada of the year 1867. The composition of its population has changed radically. Its economy and culture have been profoundly transformed as well. One may say that this is in no way exceptional, because other countries analyzed in this book have undergone similar changes in many aspects. What is surely different in the case of Canada is that even the values upon which the country was founded have changed. Peace, order, and good government as presented in The British North America Act were the values of the Dominion of Canada, founded in 1867 as a union of four British colonies, and as a pact between two founding peoples. One hundred and thirty-four years later the new fundamental values of the Canadian society are: equality of persons, equality of the provinces, multiculturalism, two official languages, respect for individual rights, welfare and social security.

Canada's performance in respect to these values makes it a model for other states. Canada has been recently classified by UNESCO as one of the world leaders in social development. However, the state was close to collapse in November 1995 when 49.6 percent of Quebecois voted for the mandate to negotiate the sovereignty of Quebec. That was a sign of an evident crisis. From 1992 to 1997, the official opposition in the Canadian Parliament was a party advocating the sovereignty of Quebec. The parliamentary elections of 1996 and 2000 were strongly influenced by regional differences. As a result of those elections the Reform Party (another regional party) became the official opposition in the Canadian Parliament in 1996, and is now known as The Canadian Alliance. This was a signal that the West was going to play an increasingly important role in Canadian affairs. It announced as well the emergence of a new, quite radical neo-conservative political discourse close to the rhetoric of the U.S. Republican Party. The Canadian Alliance broke away from the previous Canadian conservative right. The party proposed a radical reduction of the role of the state in the economy, a radical re-orientation of Canadian welfare policy, a re-examination of official bilingualism, and a "tough course" in relations with Quebec. The emergence of the Canadian Alliance and the continued strength of the sovereignty movement in Quebec show a profound social cleavage and make it evident that Canada is undergoing a transformation. Finally, the division of power between the federal and the provincial governments in such areas as health care, education and social services is being renegotiated. The federal state is no longer disposed to limit its activities to the distribution of money to the provinces so that they can define and run their own social programs. It wants to play an active role in defining national standards and to be seen as important where social programs are concerned, since welfare state institutions have become the key elements in the identification of Canadians with their state. For reasons of national unity, the federal government would like to become more visible.

The Canadian state is undergoing a profound change. Historical relations between its two founding linguistic communities – French and English Canadians – are being redefined as well as their relations with the aboriginal population. Long-repressed aboriginal issues are coming to the surface. Meanwhile, Canada is searching for a new balance of power between the provinces and the federal state. The need for a new division of power results from the growing demographic and political importance of the western provinces as well as from the need to redefine the welfare state in the context of globalisation. Canada is becoming more integrated within North America with the signing of the free trade agreements with the United States and Mexico and as a result of globalisation. The Canadian economy is more narrowly integrated with that of the continent as a whole. The same thing may happen to Canadian culture, and that would put Canadian identity into question.

The text which follows is divided into three parts. In the first part we shall consider the macrosociological context in which the new values emerge. We shall pay particular attention to Canada's new self-representation, which is marked by a breach with its past. We will then analyze Canadian performance with respect to the great national goals common to all democratic polities identified in the conceptual framework adopted for this book: union, justice, tranquility, defense, welfare, and liberty. We shall finish by examining a number of challenges that seem to be particularly acute in Canada.

2   NEW MACROSOCIOLOGICAL CONTEXT

Canada forms a new collectivity, in the sense given to that term by Gérard Bouchard (2000), that is a collectivity "born of migratory international or intercontinental transfers from the old populated zones (mainly European), to the new territories (more precisely territories considered and treated as new), so that the immigrants could have the feeling of a certain zero point of social life" (Bouchard, 1998: 220–1). International immigration and internal migrations have played a central role in the transformation of contemporary Canada. Six tendencies seem to characterise the evolution of the structure of Canada: increase in immigration, linguistic polarisation, recognition of the aboriginal peoples, changes in the regional balance, increased continentalism and the emergence of a post-industrial economy. We shall discuss each of these briefly.

Increase in Immigration

The population of Canada is now over thirty million, half as large as the populations of France or Great Britain. If its growth continues at the present rate, the Canadian population will, in the course of the 21st century, equal the number of inhabitants of these two countries, which have in a way given birth to it. Who would have predicted that one day the population of Canada might attain the same size as that of France or Britain?

Canada is a country of immigration, so considerable during the past fifty years that it has profoundly transformed the country. The average number of immigrants has fluctuated since 1951, depending on economic conditions. In 1990 the Federal Government took steps to increase the annual number of immigrants. Since 1990, an average of 230,000 have been admitted annually. Between 1951 and 2000, about eight million people settled in Canada, which is roughly equivalent to the population of Switzerland or Austria. Taking into account its size, Canada is, of all the industrialised countries, the one most open to immigration and in the 1990s it showed the highest rate of population growth, higher than that of the United States or Australia, two other countries that currently encourage mass immigration (Statistics Canada 1993).

The percentage of Canadians born abroad was about 15 percent according to the census of 1996. In most of the big Canadian cities, especially in Ontario and in the West, the foreign-born proportion is even larger (more than 20 percent in Calgary, Vancouver, and Victoria, and about 18 percent in Edmonton and Winnipeg, not to mention Montreal and Toronto, which have become multicultural cities).

In the 19th century and for most of the 20th, most immigrants were of European origin. Before the 1960s, they came predominantly from the United Kingdom, western and southern Europe (France, Germany, Italy, Greece), and from Eastern Europe. Canada modified its immigration policy in 1962, making the country more accessible to people of non-European origin. In the 1980s, about half of the immigrants came from Europe, and the other half from Third World countries (Africa, South America, the Caribbean) or from Asia. This diversification was heightened in the 1990s when the number of immigrants from Asia exceeded that from Europe. Thus, contemporary immigration is culturally and ethnically heterogeneous. The Canadian population census now allows respondents to identify themselves as belonging to a visible minority. The data reveal that 11 percent of the population place themselves in that category and that they are heavily concentrated in Toronto, Montreal and Vancouver.

The Relative Regression of the Francophone Population and Linguistic Polarization

Originally occupied by the aboriginal people, Canada was colonised and developed by French-speaking and English-speaking peoples. Their populations were nearly equal in number after the Rebellion of 1837. Afterwards, immigration sustained the demographic growth of English Canada, while the lesser growth of French Canada depended almost exclusively on the high fertility rate of French Canadian families. The number of francophones in relation to the whole of the Canadian population has been in regression since the second half of the nineteenth century. People who declare French as their mother tongue now represent a little less than one fourth of the Canadian population, compared to 29 percent in 1951. The proportion declaring English as their mother tongue was 60 percent in 1996. Because of immigration, the proportion of people who declare a language other than French or English as their mother tongue has increased as well (passing from 12 percent in 1951 to 16 percent in 1996). Finally, many of the aboriginal peoples who constituted 3.4 percent of the

Canadian population in 1996 chose one of fifty-two Amerindian languages as their mother tongue, although most of them speak English as a first or second language, or French in several communities in Quebec.

Quebec is predominantly francophone while the rest of Canada is predominantly anglophone. In Canada minus Quebec, English is the mother tongue of 77 percent of the population. New Brunswick is an exceptional case: the francophone Acadian community is concentrated there and although slightly declining, still comprises a third of the population of the province. In other Canadian provinces the position of francophones is weak and in decline. Francophones in Ontario, the largest Canadian province, are only 5 percent of the population, even though their number has been growing. The provinces situated on both sides of the Rocky Mountains – Alberta and British Columbia – have the smallest francophone minorities – less than 4 percent of their respective populations.

While the number of francophones has diminished outside Quebec, the number of anglophones has been diminishing in Quebec, falling from 14 percent in 1951 to 9 percent in 1996, as many anglophones moved to Ontario or the western provinces in the 1970s and 1980s. At the same time, as previously noted, the number of people whose mother tongue is neither French nor English has been increasing. A similar trend is observed in Ontario, where the population declaring English as a mother tongue has diminished, while those whose mother tongue is other than English or French have increased. The relative importance of anglophones in Quebec and francophones in Ontario is affected by the large number of immigrants whose mother tongue is other than English or French. Despite important migrations to other provinces, the number of anglophones in Quebec rose from 558,000 in 1951 to 659,210 in 1996 – and even to 817,540, if one considers the language spoken at home as indicative. Similarly, in Ontario the number of francophones increased from 342,000 in 1951 to 500,000 in 1996.

The French-speaking population of Canada has more than doubled since 1951, but its relative size has diminished because the English-speaking population has grown much faster. The francophones are heavily concentrated in Quebec. Only 8 percent live in Ontario, 4 percent in New Brunswick – the homeland of the Acadians – and 4 percent in the rest of the country. These data illustrate in another way the linguistic polarisation of Canada: the tendency of francophones to concentrate in Quebec is more and more marked, while their importance elsewhere in Canada is in decline. This condition threatens the survival of several French-speaking communities.

The language used at home is the most significant indicator of linguistic affiliation, and an important indicator of identity. The majority of Quebeckers (84 percent) speak French at home. In New Brunswick, 30 percent of the population do so, but a very slight proportion in the rest of Canada, where many other languages are spoken, reflecting the multicultural character of the country. It is important to note that the number of citizens who use English at home in Québec is higher than the number of those who declare it as a mother tongue. This proves the dynamism of the English language in Quebec, despite concerns to the contrary.

The language transfers to English have permitted the anglophone minority in Quebec to increase in number, in contrast to what happened to francophones elsewhere in Canada. We have analysed the extent of language transfers by comparing the mother tongue still understood and the language normally spoken at home, which enabled us to construct an indicator of linguistic continuity. The anglophone community in Quebec has grown thanks to the integration of immigrants who adopted English as the language of communication at home, according to data from the 1996 census. But forty percent of all such changes were made to French and there is a generation effect: young immigrants choose French more frequently because of language laws. Outside Quebec in 1996 there were a million people whose mother tongue was French, but only 650, 000 of them reported using French at home, which suggests that their assimilation is under way.

The immigrants and their descendants outside Quebec nearly all choose English as their language of daily use. Very few opt for French in an environment largely dominated by English. This contributes even more to the increase of linguistic polarisation observed with respect to the mother tongue. In addition, a considerable number of francophones assimilate with the majority while living outside Quebec, to such an extent that half of the francophones outside Quebec and Acadia are assimilated within two generations.

There are two contradictory interpretations of the situation of the two official languages. The first one, expressed by Heritage Canada and the federal Commission of Official Languages, points to the growth of the absolute number of francophones outside Quebec as well as to the progress of French as the second language in Canada and of English as the second language in Quebec. These two trends are presented as indicators of progress in bilingualism. Studies by the Ministry of Canadian Heritage minimise the considerable rate of assimilation of francophones outside Quebec. The author of one such work writes, "Finally, it is good to remember that most of these so called assimilated francophones can still speak French" (O'Keefe 1998: 37). It may be so, but if French is replaced by English at home, that seems to be a prelude to assimilation or anglicisation in the course of the next generation.

The second perspective emphasizes the regression of the proportion of francophones in Canada. Three factors may explain it: assimilation, the declining birth rate of francophones, but above all the massive immigration from abroad, which has lowered the proportion of francophones in relation to anglophones since the majority of immigrants integrate with the English-speaking majority.

The rate of bilingualism has considerably risen in Canada since the 1960s. Today, 17 percent of the Canadian population is bilingual. This rate for the whole of Canada is biased by the high frequency of bilingualism in Quebec (38 percent), which is the only really bilingual province. Outside Quebec the rate of bilingualism is only 10 percent. Bilingualism is increasing among young people, which suggests that it may expand in the future. French immersion courses at primary and secondary levels of education are more and more popular outside Quebec. The number of students enrolled rose from 20,000 in 1976 to 250,000 in 1990.

The Federal state has played a key role in the expansion of bilingualism. It has instituted bilingualism in the government agencies of the capital (Ottawa) although the project has not been entirely successful. All high officials working in Ottawa are required to become bilingual by the year 2002. The everyday work of the government in the Canadian capital is certainly done mainly in English, but all the documents are translated into French. The Federal state gives financial support to French-speaking communities outside Quebec, and its policy promotes bilingualism in the public institutions under its jurisdiction, such as ministries and crown corporations in Ottawa. The Federal state would like to play a more important role on the symbolic level as well, stressing the bilingual character of the country, even though bilingualism is in fact very limited in Canada except for Ottawa, Quebec and some regions near Quebec.

The government of Quebec is also active in the sphere of language but it follows a different model. It wants to assure a dominant position for French in Quebec, as is the case for English elsewhere in Canada. The francophone Quebeckers try to encourage immigrants to integrate with the francophone majority. Anglophone Canadians follow a parallel model of integrating immigrants with the anglophone majority. Immigrants of diverse origins now represent about 10 percent of the Quebec population. Historically, the majority of newcomers who settled in Quebec chose English. However, things began to change in the 1970s after the adoption of language laws and policies aimed at the integration of immigrants to the francophone majority. Since the effects of language laws will be visible only over a long period of time, it is too early to assess their real impact, but early indicators, such as language used in higher education and knowledge of French, suggest that the integration of immigrants in Quebec is done more and more in French, even though English is still attractive.

Will the integration of immigrants to the francophone majority of Quebec (which is presently underway) transform Quebec society, just as their integration with the anglophone majority outside Quebec has transformed Canadian society? There is no doubt about that, even if this transformation is just beginning. Possibly, a new francophone identity, different from the Quebec national identity of the 1970s and 1980s, is about to emerge, as illustrated by the vigorous debate on how to define identity in Québec.

Recognition of the Aboriginal Peoples

In Canada there are 608 groups of Amerindians who speak 52 different languages. The aboriginal population was 642,414 in 1998, which represents 2 percent of the whole Canadian population. The percentages are higher in the Prairies, the Northwest Territories and the Yukon. In two western provinces – Manitoba and Saskatchewan – Amerindians represent about 10 percent of the population. The majority live on reserves (58 percent). The aboriginal population is relatively young (half of them are under 25 years old), but their living conditions are much worse than those of the rest of the Canadian population. In spite of diverse living conditions and heterogeneous interests, Amerindians share a common identity as the first settlers on Canadian soil.

Changes in the Regional Balance

Since the fall of the Soviet Union, Canada is the country with the largest land area in the world, but its population is very unequally distributed. Three out of four Canadians live less than 150 kilometers from the U.S. border, most of them in urban areas; 62 percent live in Ontario and Quebec, the two provinces which have always been the most important for demographic, political and economic reasons. However, this situation is now changing. The population of the two provinces on either side of the Rocky Mountains (Alberta and British Columbia) are increasing rapidly and their importance in Canada almost equals the importance of Quebec. The relative demographic importance of Quebec and of the Atlantic Provinces has been in decline since the 1950s, while Ontario's has grown. While the demographic growth of the western provinces partially re-establishes the balance between the regions, the high rate of demographic growth in Ontario threatens a new desequilibrium. Thirty-eight percent of the Canadian population now live in this province, compared with 33 percent in 1951. The importance of Ontario in the Canadian Federation is enormous; it produced 41 percent of GDP and elected 60 percent of all liberal members of parliament – 101 out of 103 ridings in Ontario – in the 2000 election. The position of Quebec and of the Atlantic region in the Canadian economy is declining, while that of British Columbia is rapidly increasing.

The problem of regional inequalities has always been very important in Canada. The country has developed from east to west although natural conditions favored exchanges with the south. The Federal state has played a key role in the development of the country. Construction of railways, and of a seaway on the St Lawrence River, tariff and energy policies, regional development programs, as well as the distribution of tax burdens between rich and poor provinces are examples of central government intervention. In spite of such interventions, the Atlantic provinces seem somewhat peripheral, while the west of the country is developing rapidly. Frustrated under the Trudeau government, those provinces are now trying to play a more significant role in Canadian affairs, in contrast to Quebec which is seeking greater autonomy. The representation of political parties in the federal parliament reflects this regional diversity.

Increased Continentalism

The Canadian state in the twentieth century has been more interventionist than its U.S. counterpart. It intervened in the economic sphere, in order to develop a national economy by tariff barriers that long disfavored the west of the country. It also intervened to redistribute resources among the provinces, a policy non-existent in the United States. The energy policy adopted by the Federal Government after the oil crisis of 1973 was another example of interventionism , as was the creation of the welfare state. Over a short period of time, social welfare programs have come to be regarded by Canadians as a characteristic differentiating them from Americans (Clement 1996). The Canadian state was also interventionist in the cultural sphere, founding such national institutions as public radio and television, the National Film Board and the Council of Arts of Canada, institutions that have influenced the way English Canadians perceive themselves.

Since the Quiet Revolution those institutions have also contributed to the self-representation of Quebecois culture.

The Canadian economy is increasingly integrated with that of the rest of the North American continent. The free trade agreement, first with the United States, then with Mexico (NAFTA), and the new context of globalisation have further opened up the economy. In the 1960s and 1970s continentalism was regarded as the very negation of Canadian identity. It is no longer so, even though the Canadian left still believes that Canadians lost a part of their identity when they opened the borders. State capitalism is in decline and large public pan-Canadian enterprises, which had played a major role in the for-mation of the country, have been privatised (Air Canada, Canadair, Canadian National, Petro-Canada, etc.). Do all these changes indicate that Canada and the United States are drawing closer together and that as a result specific characteristics at the heart of the Canadian identity are being abandoned? Only the future will tell, but the ten-dency is certainly there. It must be noted however, that in spite of being well integrated within the continental economy, Canada is also showing considerable cultural dynamism – in literature, popular music, film and painting – which allows it to affirm its own identity, dif-ferent from that of the United States (Conlogue, 1996; Smith 1997). If this analysis is correct, economic and cultural trends are developing along divergent lines. The Canadian State would like to promote a policy of cultural exceptionalism in negotiations concerning interna-tional economic exchange, in line with the *politique d'exception culturelle* promoted by France. It is in open conflict with the U.S.A. at this point, since it aims at protecting the Canadian cultural industry from Amer-ican competition.

End of Lumberjacks and
Emergence of a New Post-Industrial Economy

For a long time the development of Canada was based on the exploita-tion of its rich natural resources and thus the primary and secondary sectors used to constitute the basis of the Canadian economy. World War II accelerated industrial development and modernisation. A long period of prosperity followed, known as the Thirty Glorious Years (1945–75). In a few decades, Canada passed from an economy based on the exploitation of natural resources to a post-industrial type, dom-inated by services and new technologies, though natural resources remain important. Agriculture is no longer primarily a way of life and farms have become real commercial enterprises, in most cases highly mechanized and capitalized, while the extraction and processing of natural resources such as wood and metals have adopted new technologies and are now extensively computerised. High-technology industries have multiplied, especially in the sectors of energy (hydro-electricity), transport (planes, trains, cars, leisure vehicles), communication (telephones, cable television, radio, television), electronics, and biotechnology, to cite just a few examples. More than two thirds of all jobs are now in the service sector.

The economy based on the exploitation of natural resources nourished the social and cultural imagination of Canadians and largely influenced the way they were perceived by outsiders. Whether he spoke English or French, the Canadian was most often represented in literature or painting as a frontiersman or a lumberjack (Atwood 1971). This representation, like that of the Canadian economy, must now be corrected.

Having discussed the context of the activity of the Canadian state, we shall briefly examine its performance with respect to six main goals of the contemporary state, common in fact to all developed countries. These are national unity, justice, tranquility, defense, welfare and liberty.

3   UNION

We shall pay particular attention to the evaluation of Canadian unity, which is presently undergoing a profound transformation (Létourneau 1996). Three aspects will be considered. First, we shall stress the emergence of a new Canadian identity from the multiplicity of structural changes described above. The second aspect concerns the transformations of francophone identity, as well as conflicts between Quebec and the rest of Canada, and changes within that call for a revision of the terms of co-existence for two different national societies within one state. Finally, the Canadian Federation is confronted with the difficult question of redefining the status of its Amerindian peoples.

The new Canadian Identity

Canada is probably questioning its identity more than any other developed country. The structural changes mentioned above have stimulated the emergence of a new Canadian identity, based on values which are in clear contradiction with the traditional ones. In a book entitled The Continental Divide (1990), the American sociologist Seymour Martin Lipset suggests that the North American continent began to divide itself more than two hundred years ago into two opposed entities: one of them made a revolution and the other a counter-revolution. At their origins, the first was liberal, egalitarian and rebellious, the second conservative, authoritarian and loyalist (see also Banting, Hoberg and Simeon 1997). While the frontier has been the most significant symbol in the American imagination, survival and heritage dominated the Canadian mental universe for about two centuries. Desmond Morton insists upon the "loser mentality" which has marked Canadian identity, "An important element of Canadian identity is the place given to losers, whether they be the defeated Loyalists from the American colonies or the inhabitants of New France conquered by England, the Irish immigrants fleeing the famine or recently arrived political refugees" (Morton 1994, B-1).

Evidently, it is no longer possible to sustain a collective self-image characterised by a "loser mentality." Canada is constructing a new identity. Today, John Diefenbaker's dream of *one* Canada has practically come true outside Quebec. We suggest that a new meaningful entity has been under construction in Canada, following the adoption of the Constitutional Law in 1982. This Law recognised on the juridical level the sociological transformations that had been underway since 1945 (Langlois 1999).

Multiculturalism has become one of the principal elements of Canadian identity (LaSelva 1996; Kymlicka 1995; Angus 1997). By adopting multiculturalism, Canada has chosen a policy adapted to its new structure but in Quebec that policy has been perceived as diminishing the importance of the Quebecois identity and as treating francophone Quebeckers as just another ethnic group. Elsewhere in Canada multiculturalism is considered to be an effective way to integrate newcomers and to distinguish Canada from the United States. This approach is different from those adopted by other countries of immigration. France has opted for a Jacobin model of integration, which eradicates differences and emphasises equality. The United States has privileged a liberal model of integrating individuals into the great American dream of a free society, regardless of origins, language or culture, a society where everyone is responsible for himself.

Multiculturalism is an essential element of the new official definition Canadians give themselves. Certain analysts have criticised the official policy of diversity as tending to isolate cultural communities by promoting only their differences (Bissoondath 1995). But such criticisms remain marginal, probably because that view is not shared by the immigrants themselves who eagerly integrate with the anglophone society and culture (outside Quebec), as shown by John Conway (1992), who goes on to assert that Canadian multiculturalism is a myth.

Then there was the multiculturalism myth – that Canada was a mosaic of many cultures and national identities of which the Québécois were but one and English Canadians another. The effect of this was to deny the essential binational, bicultural reality of Canada while effectively masking the continuing hegemony of English Canada. Official multiculturalism ignored the sociological reality that immigrants have largely joined – and uniquely and often dramatically influenced – one or the other of the English-Canadian or Québécois nations through a sort of functional integration (while resisting assimilation). (Conway, 1992, 140)

An analysis by Bibby (1990) goes in the same direction. Even if public discourse on immigration is different in Canada than in the United States, the two countries resemble one another in practice; the so-called melting pot is at work in both and the challenges posed by a harmonious integration of immigrants of diverse origins are in fact the same. The great diversity of origins of Canadians living outside Quebec and their integration with the anglophone majority are probably the two most powerful factors which stimulated the formulation of a new self-definition now underway in Canada, and the abandonment of the binational model of the state, which was a francophone dream from the beginning of the century until the end of the 1960s (see Kymlicka 1995).

In 1982 Canada gave itself the Charter of Rights and Freedoms, which has taken on an enormous symbolic significance (Cairns 1992; Taylor 1992). Probably more then any other factor, its reference to the rights of the person has changed the political culture of the country and contributed to the construction of a new identity, at the heart of which lies the emphasis on individuals rather than collectivities. This is a major change. There are a number of clauses in the Charter of Rights and Freedoms that are directed towards the promotion of collective rights, but in practice individual rights are central.

The third principal point is the equality of provinces, despite the evident disparities between Ontario (10 million inhabitants) and Prince Edward Island (135,000 inhabitants). The concept of provincial equality has supplanted that of equality between two founding peoples, professed since the beginning of the century by French-Canadian ideologists and politicians. From the birth of the Confederation in 1867 until the election of Trudeau in 1968, Canada was not defined in the same way by francophones and anglophones. The former considered Canada to be a binational country, and French Canada as a cultural and normative entity based in Quebec. In the 1950s and especially at the beginning of the 1960s Canadian federalism evolved to recognise to some extent the binational and dual character of the nation. The government of Quebec obtained new powers and began to exercise new jurisdictions. The federal government transferred to Quebec the right to collect certain taxes. In just a few years the amount of tax paid by Quebeckers to their provincial government rose significantly and now exceeds the amount paid to the federal government. When it came to the introduction of a universal state-based pension system, the Quebec government created its own system – le Régime de rentes du Québec – while the rest of Canada adhered to the Canada Pension Plan. The government of Ontario led by Robarts played for a time in the 1970s with the idea of officially adopting the thesis of two nations, which would have given Quebec a special place within a redesigned confederation. During the electoral campaign of 1968 the Conservative Party of Canada led by Robert Stanfield, then the official opposition in Ottawa, adopted the thesis of two founding nations and promised to give it official recognition. The Liberal Party, which had just chosen Pierre Elliott Trudeau as its leader, was re-elected, and as a result the policy of Ottawa towards Quebec moved in another direction.

The strategy of national unity launched by Pierre Trudeau after his election in 1968 marked a halt in the recognition of national duality. Trudeau's strategy emphasised new principles, such as the equality of provinces, equality of all citizens and equality of francophones and anglophones as individuals. Trudeau's strategy sought to promote bilingualism in Canada and to impose bilingualism in federal public administration, rather than to consolidate the development of French language and culture in Quebec.

In a well-documented work, Kenneth McRoberts, maintains that the concept of Canada developed by Trudeau's government was misconceived. He rejects the argument that the recognition of Quebec in a multicultural Canada would have led to an intensified demand for the autonomy of Quebec within the federation. He maintains instead that such recognition would have checked the growing support for the sovereignty option. He argues that Quebecois nationalism was defeated in 1980 by Canadian nationalism: "this new Canadian nationalism was different from Quebec nationalism. Rather than an 'ethnic nationalism' it was a 'civic nationalism,' which rose above ethnicity, and other social divisions. None the less it was nationalism and, moreover, it was one in which the nation consists of individuals who first and foremost are Canadian. As such this Canadian nationalism directly contradicts the vision of a federal, dualist Canada with distinct societies and multiple identities which has been so important to generations of Quebec francophones" (McRoberts 1997, 172).

Several attempts to reform the Canadian Constitution had failed between 1968 and 1980. In 1980 the First Referendum on sovereignty-association took place in Quebec. The proposal was rejected (the sovereignists obtained 40 percent of the votes) and after that Ottawa unilaterally repatriated the Constitution from England without the consent of Quebec. What followed is well known – two other attempts to recognise the status of Quebec within the Canadian Federation failed as well (the Meech Lake Accord and the Charlottetown Accord) while the second Referendum almost gained a simple majority (49.4 percent of votes in favour of sovereignty). The constitutional impasse still persists (see Robertson, 1991).

In short, a new Canadian identity – an imagined community (Anderson 1983) – is presently being consolidated (Resnick 1995). While this new Canadian identity can be considered a successor to the English-Canadian, it represents a break with the country's history, especially with the French-Canadian dream formulated at the beginning of the century, the dream of a binational country based upon the recognition of two founding peoples. Latouche (1995), Laforest (1992, 1995) and other political analysts insist that the contract agreed to in 1867 – the Federal Union established by the British North America Act – was unilaterally broken when the Constitution was repatriated from London in 1982. As Latouche has put it: "It was decided that the country could no longer allow itself to exist without being a nation" (Latouche 1995, 81).

Not being of British stock, new immigrants who have settled in Canada could not define themselves as English-Canadians (Tully 1995). Instead, they have defined themselves simply as Canadians, and they have learned English to participate in the civic life of their new country. In 1998 the prime ministers of the three prairie provinces were all of non-British stock, from families relatively recently settled in Canada. Like an increasing number of their fellow citizens, they define themselves as Canadians. The same is true for Amerindians, who proudly declare their distinct cultural identity and seek to obtain more power to develop their communities, but without calling into question their identity as Canadians. In short, Canadians have developed a strong national sentiment that is expressed in their attachment to their *great northern country* (Angus 1997) and the symbols which represent it – the maple leaf, the beaver, the flag and the national anthem.

Transformations of Francophone Identities

In this new context traditional French-Canadian identity has been shattered (Harvey 1995, Dumont 1997; Stebbins 2000). Francophones outside Quebec have managed to reconcile their own identity with the Canadian one by defining themselves as bilingual Canadians and not only as French-Canadians. The latter term is now disappearing and is being replaced by an explicit regional reference, such as Franco-Ontarians or Franco-Manitobans. The fact of defining themselves as bilingual emphasises that English and French are equally important as points of reference in their new identity (Langlois 1995). There seem to be three components of the new francophone identity outside Quebec – the fact of belonging to a specific region, the status of a minority and the fact of belonging to one of the two main linguistic groups. If this analysis is correct, it is possible to characterise francophone minorities outside Quebec as national minorities distinct from ethnic minorities formed by immigrants of diverse origins.

The unilateral repatriation of the Constitution in 1982 is perceived in Quebec as a breach of the federalist pact agreed on in 1867 and as breaking away with the historical Canada, a country defined by francophones as having a dual character. French-speaking citizens of Quebec – sovereignists but also some federalists – have developed a strong national sentiment of their own, a new Quebecois identity which is a national identity, open to integration of immigrants (Ignatieff 1993, 1995). This national sentiment, however, is not accepted in the new emerging Canada which is reluctant to acknowledge Quebec's special status in the Confederation, whether in the form of asymmetrical federalism, or by accepting Quebec's demands expressed in a variety of formulas: special status, distinct society, sovereignty-association (Conway 1992). The history of constitutional failures from the first constitutional conference in 1867 to the rejection of the Charlottetown Accord in the 1992 referendum suggests that this reluctance has become an obstacle impossible to overcome (R. Cook 1994; C. Cook 1994). It follows that the new Canadian identity and the Quebecois identity coexist and develop along parallel lines, but within different universes of reference, to use the concept proposed by Fernand Dumont (Bourque and Duchastel 1996; Fortin and Langlois 1998).

The Amerindian Question

The Amerindians of Canada are officially the wards of the federal state in accordance with the Indian Law. The Ministry of Indian and Northern Affairs has a considerable annual budget, a part of which goes directly to Indian Councils which are responsible for the management of everyday affairs on the reserves. The Indians are listed in state registers according to the rule of blood – one must have at least one-fourth Indian ancestry to be classified as Indian.

The Constitutional Law of 1982 recognizes the old treaties signed with Amerindian nations, which gave them the right to territories as well as the right to hunt and fish all year round or the official right to trade freely without regard to customs regulations.

The status of Indians as defined in Canadian law is no longer adapted to the law-governed society based on common citizenship. As wards of the state, the Amerindians living on the reserves are in practice unable to borrow money from banks to start their own businesses nor are they entitled to mortgage their property. On the other hand, they do not pay any income or sales tax if they live on a reserve. The reserves have become too small for their current populations and thus the possibilities for their economic development are limited. However, if their borders are extended, it would raise the question of joint management of these territories with non-Indian residents, since the traditional rules of Indian self-government will no longer be applicable. This may threaten Amerindian identity itself, protected until now by the system of reserves.

The Amerindian nations demand autonomy to manage their everyday affairs. They also claim the right to ensure their economic, social, and cultural development and extend their demands to establishing a new order of government which remains to be defined in each case, since the situations of particular Amerindian nations groups vary greatly. Authority must be delimited and the forms of government determined. Will non-Indians have the right to vote? How much autonomy? What new entities? The list of questions could easily be prolonged.

New problems are emerging. Amerindian villages in the far North are underdeveloped, especially in the north-west; some do not even have a basic municipal infrastructure. The increase in the number of educated Amerindians, the emergence of a political and business elite, but above all the high level of fertility will force the aboriginal, provincial and federal governments to negotiate new agreements in the coming years. The aboriginal communities presently face a demographic boom. For example, ten years from now the community of Crees in Quebec will have grown from 15,000 to 25,000 people. How will it be possible for young people to live and earn their living in villages of the Great North far away from the cities? The problems are even more challenging in certain provinces of the Canadian West where the aboriginal population is more numerous.

The search for solutions of the Amerindian question raises many practical problems and some basic questions as well. How is it possible to maintain and develop Amerindian identity based upon blood relations and at the same time affirm the existence of a law-governed state in which all citizens are equal without distinction of race, sex, language, or origin? Negotiations between Amerindian leaders and superior levels of government are under way, but they proceed very slowly. There are considerable obstacles to overcome but the completion of a few new treaties and agreements – with the Crees of James Bay in Quebec in the 1970s and with the Niguas in British Columbia in 1998 – seems promising.

4 JUSTICE

The exercise of civil and criminal justice does not cause serious problems in Canada. Nevertheless, in this sphere as in any other, there are changes under way. Two major changes are the emergence of a new juridical culture emphasising personal rights and the new role of the Supreme Court. According to Judge Brian Dickson the passage of Canada from a parliamentary to a constitutional democracy, necessarily gave more power to judges.

New Role of Courts of Justice and
Especially of the Supreme Court

The role of courts of justice and above all the role of the Supreme Court has changed profoundly since the beginning of the 1980s. With the adoption of the Charter of Rights and Freedoms which has been an integral part of the Constitution since 1982, the courts of justice acquired a new function; they may declare whether the laws passed by the federal or provincial parliaments are in accordance with the Charter. By deciding whether laws are constitutional, the judges assume an important political role since they now solve problems which formerly belonged in the strictly political sphere.

Courts of justice are more and more expected to resolve conflicts between groups of citizens and the state. In the past such conflicts used to be resolved by negotiation or as a result of public protests. The examples are numerous. A divorced woman from Trois-Rivieres has managed, by a decision of the Supreme Court, to avoid the income tax imposed by the ministry on the child support paid by her ex-husband for their children, basing her claims on the Charter of Rights and Freedoms. Labor unions have successfully opposed several laws concerning work. Women in Ontario demanded and obtained the right to walk topless in municipal parks, thus invalidating municipal regulations. Amerindians have had their territorial claims confirmed by the courts. The Supreme Court decriminalized abortion. It has also established a body of rights for homosexuals (pensions, discrimination at work, etc.) and in 1998 overturned some clauses of an Alberta law on the grounds that it allowed for discrimination against homosexuals.

There is no constitutional court as such in Canada. This is a significant deficiency of the federal system which is susceptible to conflicts of jurisdiction between different levels of government since the Constitution inspired by the British tradition is not specific about the division of all powers. Which level of government will pass laws pertaining to telecommunications? This was difficult to foresee in 1867. But, as noted above, the Supreme Court does act as a constitutional court. In 1982 it declared as legitimate the unilateral repatriation by Ottawa of the Canadian Constitution from England despite the opposition of Quebec, since this decision was supported by the majority of the provinces. The Supreme Court has also judged unconstitutional certain clauses of the Law 101 concerning the official language of Quebec. Since the Canadian Constitution does not include any provision for the secession of a province, the Canadian government asked the Court for a ruling on the legality of a unilateral declaration of independence by Quebec. The 1998 ruling holds that Quebec cannot unilaterally declare its independence, but it allows for the secession of Quebec from Canada after gaining approval in a referendum (the referendum question must be clearly formulated) and obliges the federal government to negotiate with Quebec. This judgment is interpreted differently by the two levels of government, since the problem of Quebec's right to secede can not be confined within a strictly juridical framework.

The fact that the procedure for nominating judges to the Supreme Court has not been changed raises the question of their legitimacy. The Prime Minister has the exclusive personal privilege of naming Supreme Court judges, the only constraint being that they must be citizens of a given region. Quebec for instance has the right to be represented by three out of the nine judges because the legal system (the Napoleonic civil code) existing in Quebec is different from that of the rest of Canada (common law). Since there is no public examination of candidates, the nomination procedure has come under intense public criticism as anachronistic and undemocratic, considering the expanded role of the Court. After the last nomination of four judges to the Supreme Court, there was an outburst of protest and demands for a more transparent procedure.

The New Juridical Culture Centers on the
Promotion of Individual Rights

There exists in Canada a real culture of equality among citizens, which was reinforced by the inclusion of the Charter of Rights and Freedoms in the Constitution. This Charter has radically modified the Canadian political culture. Several authors have demonstrated that a constant reference to rights leads to the emergence of a culture of special rights that tends to replace the common public culture (Gagné 1992; Loney 1998; Mackey 1999).

We shall cite one example of the new problems raised by divergent assertions of rights. After the massacre of seventeen young women students of the Polytechnic School in Montreal in the 1990s, citizens' groups launched a campaign to restrict access to personal firearms and to oblige their owners to register them with the police. Such measures are widely accepted in the Atlantic provinces, Quebec (especially) and Ontario, but not in the Western provinces, where people regard gun control measures as infringements on their liberty, thus sharing an attitude popular in the U.S. The Canadian Alliance vigorously opposes this law and favors freedom of possession of firearms. This example, though limited in itself, illustrates the kind of disagreement that occurs within Canadian political culture between groups of people who claim incompatible rights as well as a characteristic division of opinion between the East and the West.

Traditionally, judges have always enjoyed high prestige, as demonstrated by surveys of occupational prestige. However, public opinion has become more critical of their work, as the social representation of crime has changed. Thus, women's groups demand more severe punishment for assault, rape and other crimes of which they are victims and the work of certain judges has been much criticized in recent years on the grounds that they were not sensitive enough to the gravity of the offenses.

Incarceration in Decline

The total rate of incarceration in Canada fluctuates around 100 prisoners per 100 000 residents and has risen only slightly since 1980. Penal sentences for less serious offences have tended to be less severe in recent years, in contrast to sentences for more serious crimes. Generally, offences are more severely punished in Canada than in European countries, but much less severely than in the United States, which has a very high rate of incarceration. The federal state favors more severe criminal laws. Quebec, which prefers resocialization, is opposed to that project.

5 TRANQUILITY

Canada is a relatively peaceful country. Crime exists there as everywhere else, but it does not seem to result in any serious deprivation of tranquility for law-abiding citizens. The same is true of violent confrontations (dangerous street demonstrations, violent strikes, and acts of terrorism), which are few and far between. There were racial riots in Toronto in the 1980s and acts of senseless violence at the end of 1980s when the Montreal hockey team won the Stanley Cup, but these were isolated events.

Labor-Management Conflicts

A certain number of labor – management conflicts resulted in violence in the 1970s, especially in Quebec (strike of the Front Commun in public administration, strike of firemen in Montreal, plunder of a building-site in James Bay, etc.). Such conflicts have since become less frequent and they are no longer characterized by violence.

Few Ethnic Conflicts

There are no major conflicts between ethnic communities in Canada, in contrast to the United States. There is some residential segregation in large Canadian cities, but the groups involved are not in open conflict with one another.

An exception must surely be made for Amerindian communities. Relations with Amerindian communities remain troublesome and sometimes very tense. Some of them want to defend territories they have traditionally occupied against what they consider to be attacks from outside. They do so most often by opposing projects of economic development like forest-cutting (in British Columbia) or hydroelectric dams (Churchill and Ste-Marguerite Rivers, James Bay, etc). They often choose spectacular means of protest to attract public attention, like the blocking of bridges or roads, the occupation of buildings or demonstrations during international meetings.

There are tensions between some of the 608 Indian groups and neighboring communities about access to animal and fish resources, about lumber exploitation, and about smuggling. The situation on several reserves continues to be very strained. There have been violent confrontations between the forces of order and armed Indians. The crisis in Oka (a village near Montreal) was widely publicized in the summer of 1990, but there have been similar incidents, not without victims, in Ontario and British Columbia. Such violent confrontations seem less probable now, since different levels of government have begun to negotiate with Indian authorities and the Amerindian question is under discussion at a high political level. Nevertheless, a potential for trouble remains.

Evolution of Crime Rates

The number of violent crimes rose significantly between 1960 and 1980. In recent years the rise has been smaller (Cusson 1990). The homicide rate is the most analyzed indicatory in criminology because homicide is the most serious of common offenses and also the best reported. The rate was level in Canada from 1920 to 1960, then it rose substantially until the end of the 1970s, with a remarkable surge of murders (Ouimet 1994:23). The rate has since declined, passing from 2.5 homicides per 100,000 residents in 1980 to 2.0 in 1995. A large number of these homicides were due to war between criminal groups, such as Hell's Angels.

Other acts of violence have been increasing, especially simple assault where the increase has been dramatic during the past fifteen years. The main factors appear to be the deteriorating living conditions of a part of the population, increased unemployment, and increased drug-trafficking as well as the criminalization of violence against women. Aggravated theft for financial gain varies with economic cycles but has tended to increase. Less serious crimes against property have been in decline for fifteen years, except for motor vehicle theft. Criminologists observe a correlation between age structure and crime rates. "The sharp rise in crime in the 1970s coincided with the increased proportion of teenagers and young adults in the population" (Ouimet 1994:36). Other factors like dwellings that are empty during the day (due to both partners working), and increases in the number of stealable goods (electronic equipment, leisure vehicles) contribute to an increase in larceny.

The number of police per 100,000 residents rose in the 1970s in response to the general increase in crime. It was 201 in 1970, 235 in 1975, and 229 in 1980 and has been slowly decreasing since that time. It does not appear that the security of the population in general is more endangered than before. Canadian towns and cities are relatively safe and crime tends to be concentrated in specific social milieus.

War between Motor Gangs and Battles between Clans

Juvenile delinquency is above all a group activity, as has been repeatedly shown. About two thirds of all convicted young offenders are gang members, according to a study of juvenile delinquency in Montreal (idem p. 284). The number of youth gangs has risen in large Canadian cities, with frequent conflicts between rival gangs, especially gangs of the same ethnicity. This type of conflict between gangs whose members have the same ethnic origin (Asian, Antillais, Latin-

American) is a recent phenomenon in Canada and is obviously attributable to the increase and diversification of immigration.

However, what attracted the most attention in the 1990s was the phenomenon of criminal motorcycle bands. There were real wars between rival gangs of adult motorcyclists, first in Quebec and then in other Canadian provinces. In particular members of Hell's Angels, Banditos and Rock Machine fought violently over control of the drug market, with several bombings and numerous murders.

Conjugal and Family Violence

Acts of violence against women and children are more visible and less tolerated than formerly. Women who are victims of conjugal violence are encouraged to report the abuses they suffer, leading the police to intervene more frequently. The witnesses of conjugal and family violence are also more inclined now to denounce the offenders to the police or to public organizations, such as the Youth Protection Organization or to centers for battered women. What is more, conjugal violence has been redefined as criminal, so that the police are now obliged to arrest those who commit it and to begin legal proceedings. At the end of the 1980s an increase in the incidents of conjugal violence was recorded (Lemieux 1994: 343). Conjugal rape is now considered a form of aggravated assault, and public sensibility towards this type of violence has changed.

It is difficult to calculate with precision the incidence of conjugal violence or to measure its evolution in time. Victimization surveys suggest that it is frequent, but estimates vary. A study by Statistics Canada early in the 1990s reported that one fourth of women over 16 had been or would be victims of a violent aggression in the course of their lives. However, men do not monopolize conjugal violence. One fourth of all murdered spouses are men. Those men who are victims of conjugal violence consider themselves badly protected by the law and victimized by the commonly accepted idea that in every case of conjugal violence the man is the aggressor and the woman is the victim.

Other categories of persons especially exposed to violence are the sick and the handicapped, the elderly and the very young. These are now the object of particular attention by the judicial authorities (Brodeur and Ouimet 1994).

6 DEFENSE

Canada has a professional army whose role was redefined in the early 1950s in order to orient it towards missions aimed at maintaining world peace. Canada first proposed to the United Nations the creation of a multinational peacekeeping force – the Blue Helmets – during the Suez Canal crisis of 1956. In recognition of this initiative, Lester B. Pearson received the Nobel Peace Prize. Since that date, the Canadian army has been very much involved in missions in all parts of the world under the aegis of the United Nations, for instance on Cyprus, in Egypt, in Somalia, in Indonesia, and in Bosnia. During the Gulf War Canadian participation was rather modest, limited to a supportive role far from the front lines. The role of the Canadian army is to maintain peace in distant zones of conflict, rather than to defend its own unthreatened frontiers.

But the army has been called upon to intervene on several occasions in interior affairs to maintain order, as in the crisis of October 1970 or the Oka crisis of 1990. After the proclamation of martial law by the Trudeau government in October 1970, troops deployed in front of main government buildings, in reaction to terrorist attacks by the *Front du Libération du Québec* (FLQ) which kidnapped a British diplomat (James Cross, liberated in December 1970), and assassinated Pierre Laporte, a minister in the Quebec government. In retrospect, this intervention may have been out of proportion to the threat and partly motivated by the federal government's desire to check the growing sovereignty movement in Quebec. In 1990, the army intervened to put an end to the Oka crisis, after Amerindian warriors had blocked access to a bridge connecting Montreal with the south bank of St. Lawrence River and had partially occupied a village north of Montreal.

Until recently, the army enjoyed a favorable public image. This image was somewhat blackened by the misbehavior of one of its contingents in Somalia and subsequent attempts at a coverup by high army officers. The incident exposed the shortcomings of the army command and reduced public confidence in that institution. The integration of women into the army became the topic of the day in 1998, when several cases of rape and sexual harassment in the ranks came to light. The male military culture has not adapted easily to the presence of women soldiers and to the reconstruction of the soldier's role. Complaints by women soldiers of abuse have been widely featured in the press and high army officials have been reticent about them. Public discussion of what the army considers its internal affairs is not inscribed in the military culture, a fact that does not match the new juridical culture described above, with its emphasis on individual rights. The army is now going undergoing a struggle between its traditional culture and the new legal standards that demand more transparency.

Nevertheless, the favorable public image of the army has been to a large extent recovered thanks to its participation in humanitarian missions during natural disasters (floods in the Saguenay region in 1995 and in Manitoba in 1996, the black ice crisis in Montreal in 1998). Its interventions provide effective insurance in case of major disasters and reduce the tensions associated with the abandonment of the military's traditional responsibilities.

7 WELFARE

From the 1940s to the 1980s Canada developed a welfare state of the conservative type, according to the Esping-Andersen typology (1990). Important changes have been underway since the end of the 1980s. Some analysts speak of the deconstruction of the welfare state. This pessimism seems exaggerated , as several indicators show. The total expenditure of the state for health care, education, social services, leisure and culture amounted to 27 percent of the GDP in 1995, compared to 25 percent in 1980. Even though the federal and provincial governments still invest a large share of their financial resources in social programs, there have been significant attempts to rationalize expenses since the beginning of 1990s and cuts in public expenditure have affected the budgets of social programs and of the health care and educational sectors, as well as the number of employees in public administration.

A detailed analysis of the welfare state would have to be much more extensive. We shall restrict ourselves to certain recent tendencies on the microsociological level, in order to determine to what extent the well-being of citizens has been achieved. The welfare state is presently undergoing a profound transformation in Canada, partly because needs have changed (the aging of the population for example), but mostly as the result of a crisis in public finances and the new supply of costly advance care. The state, being a federation, has undertaken to reorganize the relations between its levels of government.

Tax and Transfer Payments as Means
of Reducing Inequalities

The state redistributes the income of households by means of two mechanisms which considerably reduce socio-economic inequalities. These are transfer payments directly to households and the income tax.

The average amount of these transfers is highest in low income households and diminishes with rising household income. Transfer payments represent about half of the financial resources of families in the lowest quintile of income. Transfer payments have increased significantly during the past fifteen years. This increase has been important for households at the bottom of the income range but also for middle-income households. In 1980, households in the lowest income quintile received 45 percent of their incomes from the state; fifteen years later this proportion reached 55 percent In the second quintile, the state's contribution rose even more during that period, from 13 percent to 25 percent.

The state also redistributes income by means of taxation. Two tendencies characterize this intervention. First, a family's tax rate increases sharply with any increase of revenue in a given year. Second, the rates in the upper quintiles have been rising faster than gross income for the past fifteen years. The average tax paid by families in the upper quintile rose by 42 percent between 1980 and 1995, while their incomes increased by only 4 percent.

It is therefore useful to take the average net income of families, after transfers and taxes, as the indicator of their economic position. According to this indicator, households in the lowest income quintile have experienced a slight financial improvement during the past fifteen years, but there has been no improvement for the other quintiles. Households in the middle ranges suffered the most income loss. Even though the middle-class has not grown smaller, according to data pertaining to households (Beach and Slotsve 1986), its disposable financial resources have diminished more than those of households with low or high incomes. A recent study by de Gardes, Gaubert and Langlois (2000) confirms this pattern for the period 1969–1992.

Is it possible to speak of rising economic inequality in the light of the trends described above? The answer is positive if we consider market income, and negative if we consider net disposable income of households.

We consider first the development of inequality in individual earnings, which has been increasing since the beginning of the 1980s. Morissette (1995) identifies three contributory factors. First , the real wages of young workers declined sharply in the 1980s for all levels of education and in all main sectors of industry. Betcheman and Morissette (1994) have shown that accounting for marital status, profession, level of education, union membership or province does not modify the observed decrease. Second, disparities in hours worked increased in the 1980s. This factor is related to income inequality between men and women, since the latter work fewer hours per week on average. Third, Morissette's study demonstrated the appearance of a new phenomenon in the 1980s: employees with the highest hourly wages tended to work more hours a week, while those with low hourly wages tended to work less. This correlation between the hourly wages and the number of hours worked has played a major role in the increasing inequality of earnings.

A greater disparity in work hours and an increased correlation between the number of work hours and hourly wages have been observed in all sectors of employment, for union members and non-members alike. It is clear, therefore, that neither de-industrialization, nor a slight decrease in union membership can explain the increase in income inequality (Riddell 1993).

Did the level of education of individuals play a role in this increase of inequality? It is known that technological progress resulted in an increased demand for specialized workers in the 1980s and that they benefited from higher wages (Freeman and Needell 1991). This was a very clear trend in the United States, where the ratio of the average salary of university graduates to that of non-graduates increased between 1978 and 1989 (Murphy and Welch 1992). A widening disparity between the incomes of graduates and non-graduates was not so marked in Canada, although clearly observable. Freeman and Needels (1991) explain this difference by four factors: the greater availability of university graduates in Canada, the rapid increase of GDP, flourishing international trade and the strong position of labor unions.

Labor unions managed to raise the wages of poorly remunerated workers in the 1980s. Between 1981 and 1988 the real hourly wages of male union members in the lower quintile rose by 17 percent compared to only 3 percent in the upper quintile. The same was true of female union members. "This suggests that in the context of slight increases in real wages which prevailed throughout the 1980s, negotiations led by labor unions succeeded in improving the situation of their poorly remunerated members" (Morissette 1995:13). It should be remembered that the proportion of labor union membership varied very little in Canada, passing from 32 percent in 1980 to 34 percent in 1993, while in the United States it fell from 30 percent in 1970 to 16 percent in 1990 (Riddell 1993).

The problem of inequalities presents itself differently if we examine the income of households rather than that of individuals. Inequalities in family market income (before taxation and transfers) have been undoubtedly rising in recent years; the Gini coefficient increased from 0.447 to 0.495 between 1970 and 1998. Individual earnings, market income, and investment profits are more and more unequally distributed. State intervention reduces this tendency. The equalization effect resulting from taxes and direct transfers is shown by a wide gap between the Gini coefficients for household income calculated before

and after taxes and transfers. The difference between the two coefficients measures the redistributive effect of state policies. A comparison
with other countries is instructive. In the United States for example,
the gap between the two coefficients is not very significant, which
means that the redistribution of income is less marked (Glatzer and
Hauser 1998). Murphy and Wolfson noted "a most dramatic contrast
between Canada and the United States: There was an unequivocal
increase in income inequality in the United States over both decades
[from 1975 to 1995], while there was an almost unequivocal *decrease* in
inequality in Canada" (Wolfson and Murphy 1998:14, underlined by
authors).

Two other indicators confirm the importance of redistribution in
Canada. We calculated the ratio of the average disposable income of
families in the upper quintile to the average disposable income of families in the lower quintile, for both definitions of income (that is
before and after transfers and taxes). The ratio for gross income
increased between 1980 and 1998 while the ratio for net income
decreased. We then calculated the shares of total income and the
shares of disposable income according to quintiles, which is a classic
indicator of distribution. We can see once again that families in the
lower quintile increased their share of the aggregate aftertax income
and that this tendency intensified from 1980 to 1998.

Even if the two devices for redistribution – the progressive income
tax and direct transfers to individuals and households – have func-
tioned well, the net result of state intervention has changed somewhat. In the 1960s and 1970s, it diminished the existing inequalities
among households; since 1980 it has worked to neutralize increases
in inequalities which might otherwise have occurred. From 1970 to
1980 the Gini coefficient for household income decreased (from
0.373 to 0.356). Since then it has remained quite stable. But the situation may change in the next few years. The distribution of income
from private sources is increasingly unequal. The best-qualified
workers and these who are employed in rapidly developing sectors
(new technologies, financial institutions, high-productivity industries) increase their incomes faster. The disparity between the
incomes of graduates and non-graduates is widening (although at a
slower rate than in the United States), as shown by Morissette (1995).
Free trade and globalization intensify the growth of inequalities. Less
qualified workers have to compete with lower-paid workers in developing countries, and labor unions find it more difficult to maintain
their bargaining power. Finally, certain political parties promote a
radical reduction of taxes, a policy that has now been adopted by
some provincial governments, notably in Ontario and Alberta. Such

tax reductions together with cuts in social programs in recent years, will probably contribute to inequality.

Reduction in the Number of Low Income Families

Poverty is not officially measured in Canada, but Statistics Canada calculates annually the so-called Low Income Cut-Off (LICO) which is (mistakenly) interpreted by some analysts as the threshold of poverty. The proportion of families below the LICO has been declining since 1980, followed by a slight increase. The low-income measure (LIM) characterizes poverty better and permits international comparisons. Households are considered poor if they receive less than half of the median disposable income, the disposable income being divided by the number of household members (the equivalence scale). These statistics show some reduction of poverty since 1980, consistent with the data on disposable income distribution.

However, social dependency has been high in Canada since 1980, with a slight decline at the end of 1990s. The proportion of social aid recipients more than doubled in fifteen years, from 6 percent of the population under 65 in 1980 to 10 percent in 1998, with a peak of 12 percent in 1994. It has since decreased somewhat but remains very high.

The Decrease of Gender Inequality

Women have steadily increased their participation in the labor market, while men are less and less active as a result of early retirement. The ratio of women's to men's earnings in full-time jobs has increased considerably in recent years, from 64 percent in 1980 to 72 percent in 1998. However, that ratio does not take account of the differences in education and in qualifications between the sexes, the differential preference for free time, the fact that women are more engaged in housework, or the total number of work hours. On average, employed men work more hours outside the home than employed women who use more hours for housework, a fact that affects the difference in income.

8 LIBERTY

The constitutions of all developed countries propose to protect the liberties of their citizens and specify their fundamental rights. Respect for rights is not a problem in Canada. The free exercise of religion, freedom of speech, freedom of movement, political freedoms and due process are universally respected. There are no political prisoners and parties of the extreme left are not suppressed in any way. The high degree of political freedom is dramatically illustrated by the existence of an officially recognized socio-political movement claiming sovereignty for Quebec. The political parties representing this movement – the Parti Québécois on the provincial level and the Bloc Québécois on the federal level – are a part of the Canadian political landscape. A few opponents in English Canada have wanted Quebec's secession to be declared illegal, but their marginal opinions have little, if any, support. The debate on Quebec's future is proceeding within a democratic framework. Referenda were held in 1980 and 1995. A recent judgment of the Supreme Court, alluded to above, recognizes the legitimacy of the democratic promotion of Quebec's sovereignty under certain rules.

In connection with the 1995 referendum, a movement demanding a partition of Quebec's territory emerged in the anglophone community of the province. It was supported by certain elements in English Canada, including some ministers of the federal government. Those who support the partition of Quebec argue that "If Canada can be divided, so can be Quebec." This movement remains marginal.

The state frequently intervenes to counterbalance inequalities and to block discrimination against disadvantaged groups: linguistic minorities, other visible minorities, aboriginal peoples, women, handicapped persons and homosexuals. So many actions of this kind have been taken since the 1960s that there is now a concern about the fragmentation of citizenship. Some of these interventions, in the context of the new juridical culture that emphasizes the protection of individual rights, deserve special notice.

In the 1960s and especially in the 1970s, the state intervened in favor of the francophone minority. The accessibility of public services in French was improved in the institutions of the federal government thanks to the adoption of the Law on Official Languages. Bilingualism was mandated in public administration and economic inequalities between francophones and anglophones were reduced. In Quebec, the anglophone community has a wide range of social and public services at its disposal (hospitals, social service centers, schools and universities, media,) as the law guarantees. The law on public advertising, which limits various forms of advertising in English-only and imposes priority to French, is however resented by some members of the anglophone community who regard it as a restriction of their liberty of expression. Nevertheless, measures to protect the French character of the province of Quebec are widely supported by the population of Quebec, including a majority of Anglo-quebecers. The law obliges immigrants to send their children to a French-language school at the primary and secondary level, and immigrants are informed of this obligation before entering Canada and Quebec. These laws are intended to insure the integration of immigrants with the civil society and the francophone majority and insure the possibility of full social participation, just as immigrants outside Quebec integrate with the anglophone majority.

Outside Quebec, the accessibility of services in French is more problematic, even though efforts are made to develop them. The only francophone hospital in Ontario is struggling (in 2000) to continue and its future is uncertain while francophones of the Ottawa region are suing the provincial government on this issue. Demands for services in French reappear from time to time here and there, but they no longer have the same importance as in the past; presumably because the new constitution offers a formal guaranty of services, especially in education at the primary and secondary levels.

Discrimination against women in the workplace has been the subject of extensive discussion and interventions in recent years. The best known of these are the measures that corrected systematic inequalities of earnings in public administration. The Commission on Personal Rights has obliged the governments of Quebec and Canada to award heavy compensation to members of employment units, mainly female, that formerly paid lower salaries than equivalent units, made up mostly of men. Another law requires private enterprises to correct their salary scales in order to eliminate discrimination against women; they are allowed a transition period of about ten years to achieve complete equality between the sexes.

The state intervenes as well to check discrimination against visible minorities and immigrants. Statistics Canada collects data on racial and even physical characteristics (handicaps) of the population – a procedure that surprises foreign, especially European, observers. The state, as well as various interest groups, is thus enabled to evaluate the effectiveness of its anti-discrimination measures.

Finally, the state intervenes, more timidly in this case, in favor of the recognition of rights for homosexuals. Different measures have been taken to oppose the discrimination of which they are victims, particularly the recognition of rights of homosexual partners (pensions, insurance, etc.), but such interventions are not of equal importance in different provinces, since several spheres of life fall under provincial jurisdiction.

State interventions in favor of particular groups inevitably provoke public debates, some of them quite vigorous, as the interventions in linguistic matters show, but the usual outcome is the recognition of a new group right.

9 CONCLUSION

Canada is going through transformations that are underway in other countries as well. Nevertheless, it must face its own peculiar challenges. Three such challenges can be clearly distinguished: the question of relations between Quebec and the rest of Canada, the question of the position of Amerindian nations in Canada, and the question of the future of the welfare state. All three issues imply a search for a new balance of powers between the provinces and the federal state. More generally, the very identity of Canada is at stake. Everything seems to suggest that Canada is now constructing a new national identity that moves it further and further away from the federal system established in 1867, which recognized regional differences, while one of the fundamental principles of the 1982 Constitutional Law is the strict equality of provinces. This principle has become a dogma in the public discourse of English Canada.

The redefinition of collective identity is occurring not only in connection with the status of Quebec but also in the context of globalization and North American free trade, not to mention the multiculturalism associated with recent immigration. Clearly the federal state is disposed to take a leading role in the search for responses to the challenges enumerated above.

Consider the first challenge is the question of Quebec's status within the Canadian federation. The present situation is inconclusive, as we have shown earlier (see Webber 1994; Lenihan, Robertson and Tassé 1995, among others). The present Constitution does not grant official recognition to the Quebecois nation on one side, and if the Parti Quebecois prevails in the coming elections, it could propose another referendum on sovereignty before long.

The second challenge is the future of aboriginal peoples in Canada. The present Constitution, recognizes both the ancestral rights of aboriginal peoples and their rights acquired by treaties, which forces the provincial and federal governments to negotiate new relationships. The problems are numerous and complex. Aboriginal communities differ in size and are unequally prepared for autonomy. The arrangements already negotiated – like that with the Niguas of British Columbia in 1998 – open new possibilities but global solutions will not be found quickly or easily.

The third challenge involves redefinition of the welfare state and promotion of a new social union. The federal government and most provincial governments have in recent years eliminated constant deficits and stabilized their finances, although the public debt remains high. A thorough revision of social programs has been undertaken.

The budgets for health care and education are being re-examined. It is certainly an exaggeration to speak of the dismantling of the welfare state, but the changes are profound. Neo-liberals press for more radical reforms, but a large part of the public and the labor unions (still an important political force in Canada) oppose such tendencies. Neo-liberalism has not won the game entirely and the debate will continue. It may divide the country along regional lines.

Canada is a very decentralized federation, in which provincial governments have important responsibilities, including the collection of direct taxes. The western provinces demand more powers and more freedom to act, but they acknowledge the central role of the federal government, which is accepted much more reluctantly by Quebec. The Atlantic provinces remain dependent on federal government subsidies and on the government's policy of equalization between richer and poorer regions. The leftist parties are stronger there and they counterbalance the conservative parties of the western provinces, which are opposed to policies of regional redistribution (see Hiller 1991).

While the federal state searches for a balance of power in a new social and political union, with national standards in health care, social assistance and education, Quebec views such projects as intrusions into the provincial sphere of competence.

The federal state has always played a central role in the economic and social development of the country. Even though its direct intervention into the economic sphere has diminished in recent years as a consequence of privatization, both federal and provincial governments continue to claim major roles in key sectors, like social development, welfare and culture. In the latter sphere, it will not be possible to avoid conflicts with the U.S, where the production of cultural products is relegated to private industry. In Canada, as in many European countries, cultural products and activities are closely linked to national identity and are a legitimate subject of state policy.

The construction and promotion of the national identity have become an important function of the federal state in recent years, for several reasons. First, the state attempts to counterbalance the sovereignty movement in Quebec by opposing it to Canadian identity. This is a new approach, devised after the second referendum on Quebec sovereignty. Second, in the new context of globalization, that identity is under continuous threat by the omnipresent southern neighbor, particularly with respect to the media and cultural products. Last, but not least, as a country open to immigration, Canada must modify its prior identity in important ways.

The federal state promotes a new Canadian nationalism based on national symbols and values. Canada no longer defines itself as a

British Dominion, although it still officially retains the symbols of the English Crown. Unlike Australia, there is no movement proposing to abolish these symbols. The question will surely be brought up one day, given the multicultural character of a country whose citizens no longer feel attached to the old-fashioned symbols of royalty, but it is not currently under discussion. Canada no longer defines itself as a dual nation, as proposed by the francophone elite in the 1960s. Both of these changes mark a break with history, as a new national identity slowly takes shape.

REFERENCES

Anderson, Benedict. 1983. *Imagined Communities: Reflections on the Origin and Spread of Nationalism.* London: Verso.

Angus, Ian. 1997. *A Border Within. National Identity, Cultural Plurality, and Wilderness.* Montreal: McGill-Queen's University Press.

Atwood, Margaret. 1971. *Survival. A Thematic Guide to Canadian Literature.* Toronto: Anansi.

Banting, Keith, George Hoberg and Richard Simeon (eds). 1997. *Degrees of Freedom. Canada and the United States in Changing World.* Montreal: McGill University Press.

Beach, R., and B. Slotsve. 1996. *Are We Becoming Two Societies?* Ottawa: C.D. Howe Institute.

Betcheman, G., and René Morissette. 1994. *Expériences récentes des jeunes sur le marché du travail au Canada.* Ottawa : Statistique Canada, Études analytiques numéro 63.

Bibby, Reginald W. 1990. *Mosaic Madness. The Poverty and Potential of Life in Canada.* Toronto: Stoddart.

Bissoondath, Neil. 1995. *Le marché aux illusions.* Montréal: Boréal.

Bouchard, Gérard. 1998. "Le Québec et le Canada comme collectivité neuves. Esquisse d'étude comparée" *Recherches sociographiques* 2–3: 219–248.

– 2000. *Genèse des nations et cultures du nouveau monde. Essai d'histoire comparée.* Montréal : Boréal.

Bourque, Gilles, et Jules Duchastel. 1996. *L'identité fragmentée. Nation et citoyenneté dans les débats constitutionnels canadiens 1941–1992.* Montréal: Fides.

Brodeur, Jean Paul, et Marc Ouimet. 1994. "Violence et société." In Dumont, Langlois, and Martin (eds), *Traité des problèmes sociaux,* 301–18.

Clement, Wallace. 1996. *Understanding Canada. Building on the New Canadian Political Economy.* Montreal: McGill-Queen's University Press.

Conlogue, Ray. 1996. *Impossible Nation. The Longing for Homeland in Canada and Quebec.* Toronto: The Mercury Press.

Conway, John F. 1992. *Debt to Pay. English Canada and Quebec from the Conquest to the Referendum.* Toronto: James Lorimer.

Cook, Ramsay. 1995. *Canada, Quebec and the Uses of Nationalism.* Toronto: McClelland & Stewart.

Cook, Curtis, ed., 1994. *Constitutional Predicament. Canada after the Referendum of 1992.* Montreal: McGill-Queen's University Press.

Cusson, Maurice. 1990. *Croissance et décroissance du crime.* Paris : Presses Universitaires de France.

Dumont, Fernand. 1997. "Essor et déclin du Canada français." *Recherches sociographiques* 3:3–49.

Dumont, Fernand, Simon Langlois, and Yves Martin. 1994. *Traité des problèmes sociaux, Québec.* Institut québécois de recherche sur la culture.

Esping-Anderson, Gosta. 1990. *The Three Worlds of Welfare Capitalism.* Princeton, NJ: Princeton University Press.

Fortin, Andrée, and Simon Langlois. "Présentation. Québec et Canada : deux références conflictuelles." *Recherches sociographiques* 39, 2–3 : 207–17.

Foster, James E., and Michael C. Wolfson. 1992. *Polarization and the Decline of the Middle Class: Canada and the U.S.* Ottawa: Statistics Canada.

Freeman, R. B., and K. Needel. 1991. "Skills Differentials in Canada in an Era of Rising Labor Market Inequality." *National Bureau of Economic Research,* Working Paper, 3827.

Gagné, Gilles. 1992. "Les transformations du droit dans la problématique de la transition à la postmodernité." *Les cahiers de droit* 33, 3: 701–33.

Gardes, François, Patrice Gaubert, and Simon Langlois. 2000. "Pauvreté et convergence des consommations au Canada." *Canadian Review of Sociology and Anthropology* 37, 1: 3–26.

Harvey, Fernand. 1995. "Le Québec et le Canada français: histoire d'une déchirure." In S. Langlois, ed., *Identité et cultures nationales.* Sainte-Foy: Les Presses de l'Université Laval, 49–64.

Hiller, Harry H. 1991. *Canadian Society. A Macro Analysis.* Scarborough: Prentice-Hall Inc.

Ignatieff, Michael. 1993. *Blood and Belonging. Journeys into the New Nationalism.* Toronto: Viking.

– "Québec: la société distincte, jusqu'où?" In Jacques Rupnik, dir., *Le déchirement des nations.* Paris: Seuil, 139–56.

Kymlicka, Will. 1995. *Multicultural Citizenship. A Liberal Theory of Minority Rights.* New York: Oxford University Press.

Laforest, Guy. 1992. *Trudeau et la fin d'un rêve canadien.* Québec: Septentrion.

– 1995. *De l'urgence. Textes politiques 1994–1995.* Montréal: Boréal.

Langlois, Simon. 1999. "Canadian Identity: A Francophone view." In Paul Robert Magosci (ed.) *Encyclopedia of Canada's Peoples.* Toronto: University of Toronto Press, 323–9.

Langlois, Simon (dir.). 1995. *Identité et cultures nationales. L'Amérique française en mutation.* Sainte-Foy: Presses de l'Université Laval.

LaSelva, Samuel V. 1996. *The Moral Foundations of Canadian Federalism.* Montréal: McGill-Queen's University Press.

Latouche, Daniel. 1995. *Playdoyer pour le Québec.* Montréal: Boréal.

Lemieux, Denise. 1994. "La violence conjugale." In F. Dumont, S. Langlois, and Y. Martin (dirs). *Traité des problèmes sociaux:* 337–62.

Lenihan, Donald, G., Gordon Robertson, and Roger Tassé. 1995. *Le Canada: la voie médiane.* Montréal: Editions Québec-Amerique.

Létourneau, Jocelyn. 1996. *Les années sans guide.* Montréal: Boréal.

Li, Peter S. 1996. *The Making of Post-War Canada.* Toronto: Oxford University Press.

Lipset, Seymour Martin. 1989. *Continental Divide: Values and Institutions of the United States and Canada.* Toronto: C.D. Howe Institute.

Loney, Martin. 1998. *The Pursuit of Division. Race, Gender, and Preferential Hiring in Canada.* Montreal: McGill-Queen's University Press.

Mackey, Eva. 1999. *The House of Difference: Cultural Politics and National Identity in Canada.* New York: Routledge.

McRoberts, Kenneth. 1991. *English Canada and Quebec. Avoiding the Issue.* Toronto: York University, Robarts Center for Canadian Studies Lecture Series.

– *Misconceiving Canada. The Struggle for National Unity.* 1997. Toronto: Oxford University Press.

Morissette, René. 1995. *Pourquoi l'inégalité des gains hebdomadaires a-t-elle augmenté au Canada ?* Ottawa: Statistique Canada, coll. Documents de recherches no 80.

Morissette, René, John Myles, and Garnett Picot. 1994. *L'inégalité des gains au Canada : le point sur la situation.* Ottawa: Statistique Canada, coll. Documents de recherches no 60.

Morton, Desmond. 1994. "Entrevue accordée à La Presse," 2 juillet, Cahier B-1.

Murphy, K. M., and F. Welch. 1992. "The structure of wages." *Quarterly Journal of Economics* 107, 1: 284–326.

O'Keefe, Michael. 1998. *Minorités francophones : assimilation et vitalité des communautés.* Ottawa: Patrimoine Canada.

Ouimet, Marc. 1994. "Les tendances de la criminalité apparente et de la réaction judiciaire au Québec de 1962 à 1991." In D. Szabo et Marc LeBlanc, eds., *Traité de criminologie empirique.* Montréal: Presses de l'Université de Montréal: 15–47.

Resnick, Philip. 1995. *Thinking English Canada.* Toronto: Stoddard.

Riddell, W. C. 1993. "Unionization in Canada and the United States: A Tale of Two Countries," in David Card and Richard B. Freeman, eds., *Small Differences That Matter: Labor Markets and Income Maintenance in Canada and the United States.* Chicago: The University of Chicago Press.

Robertson, Gordon. 1991. *Does Canada Matter?* Toronto: Institute of Intergovernmental Relations, Reflection Paper 7.

Smith, Donald. 1997. *D'une nation à l'autre. Des deux solitudes à la cohabitation.* Montréal: Stanké.

Taylor, Charles. 1992. *Rapprocher les solitudes. Ecrits sur le fédéralisme et le nationalisme au Canada.* Sainte-Foy: Les Presses de l'Université Laval.

– 1986. "Shared and Divergent Values." In R.L. Watts and D.M. Brown, *Options for a New Canada.* Toronto: Toronto University Press.

Tully, James. 1995. *Strange Multiplicity. Constitution in an Age of Diversity.* Cambridge: Cambridge University Press.

Webber, Jeremy. 1994. *Reimagining Canada: Language, Culture, Community, and the Canadian Constitution.* Montreal: McGill-Queen's University Press.

Wolfson, Michael C., and Brian B. Murphy. 1998. "New Views on Inequality Trends in Canada and the United States." *Monthly Labor Review,* April, 3–23.

The Bulgarian State
at the Turn of the Century

NIKOLAI GENOV

1 INTRODUCTION

How to reduce the state-centered over-integration of societies in
Eastern Europe without substantially damaging their political integration? The question does not have a regional relevance alone. It refers
to the world-wide problem of balancing government and governance.
The development of the Bulgarian state during the nineties vividly
illustrates the complexity of the problem. First, the administrative
framework of the national state was weakened to the extent that it
became unable to perform its major integrative functions. Second, the
rise of crime in the nineties demonstrated the inability of the state to
secure legal justice for its citizens. Third, this is one of the major
reasons why the citizens do not perceive the state as being able to
provide them with tranquility. Fourth, the same applies to the capacity
of the impoverished state to provide for the national defense in a
region which is notorious for its instability. Fifth, the transformation
abolished an ineffective welfare state but the current result is a substantial decline of general welfare. Sixth, as a result of these developments the announced liberties of individuals turned into new forms of
deprivation. Therefore, the current transformation challenges the
very idea of the modern democratic state and its practices. The
prospects for reaching and maintaining a balance between government and governance in the country are open.

The transformations in Eastern Europe raise profound challenges
to social science and to politics alike. Most of them concern the his-

torical background, current problems and future prospects of the state. What were the major deficiencies of the state-centred over-integration of the former state socialist societies? Did the changes after 1989 bring about an efficient new organization? What are the prospects of the state in countries still undergoing profound economic, political and cultural transformations?

Some tentative answers to these questions will be sought within the Bulgarian national context. It bears the major common features of the Eastern European transformations during the nineties. Moreover, in the current changes of the Bulgarian state one may recognize problems and trends of government and governance all over the globalizing world. Thus, the national case under scrutiny provokes general questions about social justice and organizational efficiency, path dependency and social innovations, national specifics and universal trends. There can be no simple, easy and definitive answers to such complex questions. The real task is to reflect on the dynamic relationships between state and society. For theoretically guided, empirically well-based and socially sensitive reflection on the performance of the state is the only hope for efficient and humane politics.

2 HISTORICAL BACKGROUND

After five centuries of Ottoman rule the third Bulgarian state was established in 1878 as a result of a Russian-Turkish war. The same year the new state was divided into three parts by the then great powers. The unification of the Northern and the Southern parts and the Serbian-Bulgarian war followed in 1885. Coups-d'état and authoritarian regimes marked the wave of modernization until 1912. This was the year of the first Balkan war, which evolved into the second Balkan war among the former allies in 1913. Between 1915 and 1918 Bulgaria actively participated in the First World War on the side of the Central Powers. The peace treaty of Neuilly (1919) imposed territorial losses and heavy reparations on the defeated country. Internal clashes led to a bloody military coup-d'état and to a civil war in 1923. The democratization accompanying the recovery from the economic devastations of the Great Depression was interrupted by another military coup-d'état in 1934. The country reached relative stability at the very end of the thirties but it was short-lived. In 1940 Bulgaria joined the Axis. After the Soviet Army entered the country in 1944, Bulgarian forces participated in the war against Germany. Nevertheless, reparations had to be paid to neighboring countries.

A glance at this turbulent national development shows why the period between 1944 and 1989 should not be judged in a simplistic way.

Undoubtedly, state socialism turned out to be a blind alley in historical development. But this was exactly the period of the all-embracing modernization of Bulgarian society. In 1939, 82 percent of Bulgarians made their living mainly in agriculture. By the mid-eighties more than 60 percent of the Bulgarian exports were industrial goods. In the crucial period after the Second World War the state-centered over-integration of Bulgarian society was able to concentrate rather limited national resources on solving strategic tasks. The transition to an urbanized industrial society was accomplished (Shishmanova, 1995: 22).

The major agency of these changes in territorial, economic and social structures was the state. More precisely, it was the state merged with the ruling party. Party-state bodies drafted five year plans for industrialization and for the mechanization of agriculture. State intervention fostered a rapid rise in the educational level of large segments of Bulgarian society. Social security and health care were directly financed from the state budget. They helped Bulgaria to approach some of the achievements of advanced societies. State support of cultural institutions secured a high degree of cultural integration. Bulgarian society looked homogeneous and capable of the organized pursuit of national goals.

However, the potential of the state-centered model of modernization exhausts quickly. The fairly high rate of growth of the Bulgarian economy during the sixties and the seventies gradually declined. This was the case throughout Eastern Europe (Berend, 1997: 12). The over-centralized state could not develop the conditions for sustainable social, economic and environmental development. One of the many pieces of evidence was the country's foreign debt, which amounted to 10.9 billion US dollars in 1990. It had a rather unfavorable structure of short-term loans from private banks.

The crucial problem of this development was the limitation imposed on creativity in economics, politics and culture by over-centralized authorities. Decentralization, liberalization and micro-social initiatives were urgently needed as early as the late sixties. Potentially, some strategic changes might have been introduced into Bulgarian economy, politics and culture around the historical year of 1968. In fact, there were signs of readiness for change at that time. However, the international setting was shaped by the Yalta agreements of 1943. There were no prospects for an autonomous path of reform in Bulgaria. The differentiation of the state from the economy and the culture was put on ice after the suppression of the Prague spring. The Eastern European societies missed the best historical moment for introducing changes in an organized way. The core of the regional power was not ready to recognize and master the challenge. Attempts to reduce political over-centralization during the second half of the 1980s came too late. Radical changes could only start in 1989.

Thus, the modernization of Bulgarian society was marked by discontinuities and by a series of radically new starts (Genov, 1999a). It is not surprising that the national state has experienced diverging definitions in four Constitutions in a period of slightly more than a century. The first was passed in 1879. For that time, it was quite liberal, resembling the constitutional provisions of the Belgian monarchy. Openly or indirectly, it was suspended several times until 1944. Then the Constitution of 1947 copied the provisions of the Soviet constitution of 1936. The completion of the state socialist transformation was signaled by the Constitution of 1971. Both state socialist constitutions laid the stress on the common good, mainly in the form of state owned enterprises. Nevertheless, the individualization accompanying the rapid industrialization and urbanization had to be constitutionally incorporated as well. The Constitution of 1971 clearly defined individual rights and liberties in the way that is typical for modernized states. This did not mean that the constitutional provisions were observed in administrative practice. Nevertheless, the right to work and entitlement to a state pension, the right to receive education and medical care free of charge, etc., were respected as a rule, although the financial capacity of the Bulgarian state to provide them was rather limited.

It was the new Constitution of July 1991 which opened opportunities for personal development and self-realization. The major provisions stressed individual rights and duties (Ch.2), private economic initiative (Art. 19) and competitive politics (Art. 8) became the key issues. They were expected to offer the framework for new forms of social integration.

Now having experienced a decade of transformation we can draw some conclusions about the functioning of the state under the new conditions. Throughout Central and Eastern Europe everyday life is full of economic deprivation, administrative inefficiency and cultural disintegration (Glatzer, 1996). Fundamental questions arise especially in the case of the Bulgarian transformation which was typically described as a failure in the mid-nineties (Economic Survey of Europe, 1997: 57f.): What were the major mistakes committed in its course? What are the consequences for man and society? What can be done to correct the mistakes, or, at least, to avoid their repetition?

Reforms and Social Integration

Contrary to the typical expectations of the early 1990s for a fast, smooth and painless transition, the transformation of Bulgarian society turned out to be a complicated, protracted and painful process. Social integration was badly weakened. The destructive effects of this development are most visible in the economy.

How did this economic collapse become possible? The question is legitimate since Bulgaria has basically followed global trends. By copying the experience of the advanced countries, in just a few years the country joined the world market. Working relations were established with international financial institutions. Prices, foreign trade, and the currency regime were liberalized. Markets for goods, services and labor now function in the country. The major economic actors have a high level of autonomy despite the fact that state ownership of productive assets is still substantial. Privatization of state property advanced at a speed not much different from that in countries similar to Bulgaria (From Plan to Market, 1996: 15).

In the field of politics, the legislative, executive and judicial powers were divided. Free and fair democratic elections were held regularly. More than 200 political parties and 5000 organizations and associations of civil society were registered. As to the structure and functioning of political institutions, Bulgaria has hardly any peculiar feature distinguishing it from other Central and Eastern European countries.

Nevertheless, the national economy has periodically fallen into unmanageability. In the mid-nineties, the volume of industrial production was barely half of the volume achieved in 1989 and it continued to decline thereafter. The wheat harvest of 1870 kilograms per hectare in 1996 was an example of how fast the organizational conditions for modern agriculture could be destroyed. The negative trends in the Bulgarian economy are strong and persistent. The recovery will take long. High levels of unemployment and low incomes marked the period of stabilization after the introduction of the Currency Board in July 1997. The social problems were further aggravated by the increasing inequality of household income. It doubled in the period after 1989 reaching a ratio of 6.8:1 between of the incomes of the highest quintile of households and that of the lowest.

The major risk factors facing the national society are adequately perceived by public opinion. Except for the ethnic tensions which gradually lost intensity after the difficult years of 1989 and 1990, all other types of risks retain a high level of intensity, especially the risk of deepening economic stratification.

In the course of the current transformation governments are wearing out fast. The time horizon of their planning and action has been rather short. Since 1989 they have changed nearly every year. This leads to the permanent instability of political institutions and to their low efficiency. Consequently, trust in the major institutions of the state has plummeted dramatically.

Besides the economic decline and political instability during the 1990s, the nation had substantial difficulty in defining common values. Public opinion involves contradictory and mutually exclusive views on the desirable state of society. In November 1996, 75 percent of respondents in a national survey said that they agree with the statement "The laws should provide full freedom for private initiative." This is clear support for the market oriented economic reforms. However, 80 percent of respondents favored a strong redistributive intervention by the state. They wanted heavy taxation on high incomes in order to help people on low incomes. This agreement on mutually exclusive value-normative and practical orientations is no agreement at all. Rather, it is an expression of disorientation, a mixture of modern liberalism with traditional egalitarianism and statism.

The economic, political and cultural characteristics of present-day Bulgarian society show that it has remained in a condition of social disintegration far too long. How did it become possible? What went wrong?

One has to search for answers in connection with the reforms that were carried out. They destabilized all aspects of the society, starting with the state, which had tremendous potential to concentrate and use resources for achieving social integration. However, the state was not able to perform this function efficiently.

In Bulgaria, domestic and international circumstances in the early 1990s led to chaos. The most visible tendency was the abandonment by state institutions of responsibilities that are major state priorities in advanced countries. Thus the problems facing Bulgarian society in the mid-nineties were paradoxical. The abandonment of the state's domination of society turned into the abandonment of the state's integration of society. Major technological and economic relations were disturbed and new relations were established that did not function effectively. The state's capacity to govern was substantially reduced. The financial sector developed its autonomy to such an extent that state control of credit operations became difficult or impossible. Following legal decisions for a return to family farming and their implementation by state agencies, agriculture was paralyzed. All this made the country a risky place for domestic and foreign investors.

The starting point of this trend was the rapid liberalization of prices and trade at the beginning of the 1990s. The reform was guided by the neo-liberal assumption that market forces would bring about the conditions for their own integration in a spontaneous, fast and efficient manner. It was further assumed that market integration would become the basis for a qualitatively new integration of politics, culture and of the entire social system. This conceptual model has a long history. It promises social integration by means of a market-based co-ordination of interests. It was forgotten that after the experience of Keynesianism in Western Europe and the post-World-War II experience of Central and Eastern Europe. The problem of social integration cannot be meaningfully dealt with without taking the role of the state into account.

In the course of the economic reforms it became obvious that the state enterprises did not possess the minimum free capital to function as real market actors. It also became clear that the protected Eastern European market space had disappeared and that everywhere else the markets were occupied. The hope that this was only temporary was disappointed. In addition, the legal framework of the various markets was yet to be elaborated (Mrachkov, 1995). Managers had to learn from scratch the skills to work under conditions of domestic competition and open international markets.

The results were soon apparent. In order to slow down the increase of unemployment, large state owned enterprises were not adopted hard budgets. With a weakened state, they managed to transfer their economic inefficiency to the state budget via the mechanism of bad loans. This made the collapse of the uncontrolled banking system in 1996 unavoidable. On its part, the social security system was not prepared to cope with the demands of mass unemployment and mass impoverishment.

The Performance of the Bulgarian State
in the Nineties

There are a number of dominant issues in a society undergoing a profound transformation. These issues cannot be analyzed adequately by using conceptual schemes drawn from societies which have experienced decades of relatively stable development. Nevertheless, one may focus on the topics of union, justice, tranquility, defense, welfare and liberty which were systematically introduced first in the American Constitution and later in other democratic constitutions.

3   UNION

The problem of national integration has two major dimensions in Bulgaria, administrative and ethnic. Traditionally, the Bulgarian state was highly centralized. From its re-establishment in 1878 until 1989, national ministries held tight control over finance, education, health care, etc., not to speak of domestic security and defense. To perform its functions in this way, the state administration had a clear hierarchical structure. The relationship between the national government and local governments was typically characterized by the predominance of the national government. Centralism was strengthened to an extreme during the decades after the Second World War, although several administrative reforms during the sixties, seventies and eighties put stress on local initiative and responsibility.

The strong presence of the Turkish ethnic group in two major areas notwithstanding, the unitary character of the national state has never been put into question. In the mid-eighties the party-state launched a campaign to forceably integrate the Turkish ethnic group into the Bulgarian majority. There were several motives. The major one was the fear that the deepening demographic imbalances would bring about autonomist claims and potentially lead to territorial aspirations on the part of Turkey (Genov, 1997: 49f).

Two major tasks faced the administrative and political reformers after 1989. First, decentralization had to give real substance to democratization. Second, the re-establishment of the rights and liberties of the Bulgarian Muslims had to bring about ethnic reconciliation.

The administrative reforms were dominated by hasty decisions. Some of them were not sufficiently attuned to institutional traditions. For instance, in order to overcome the excessive centralization that was typical of previous decades, departments of the Ministry of Interior were given a high level of autonomy at the beginning of the 1990s. The territorial divisions of the Ministry also became much more autonomous than they used to be. In this way, the threat of centralist abuse of power on politically sensitive issues was reduced. However, the efficiency of the Ministry was reduced as well. Ironically, this became a burning issue in 1997 when liberal political forces won the elections and took over the governing responsibility. It became clear that the promise to reduce crime could not be fulfilled if the Ministry of Interior continued to function under excessive decentralization. All the new legal regulations introduced thereafter laid the stress on the recentralization of its departments and territorial divisions.

The Law on Local Self-Government and Local Administration passed in 1991 similarly tried to correct the excessive centralization of the previous decades by going to the opposite extreme. Municipalities received great autonomy in matters of construction, education, health care, etc. This decentralization would have been more meaningful, however, if the municipalities were relatively affluent. In reality, two thirds of them are in very poor financial condition (Genov, 1996: 47f).

They depend on subsidies from the national budget in order to cover more than the half of their expenditures. Political preferences in subsidizing municipalities have disintegrating effects. In fact, the most critical assessment of the European Union in its "Agenda 2000" concerns the problems of the Bulgarian state in general and local administration in particular.

On the surface, the trends in ethnic integration are rather positive. There is clearly a decline in the intensity of ethnic tensions in Bulgarian society. This perception corresponds to reality – in the short-term perspective at least. However, due to the weakening of state institutions the strategic measures for ethnic integration have been put on hold for a long period. This concerns tobacco production primarily. It is the major source of income for large numbers of Bulgarian Turks and Bulgarian Muslims who together comprise about ten percent of the national population. Both groups inhabit regions which have been hard hit by long-term unemployment and decreasing incomes. Thus, the alienation of this population from the national state will probably continue for economic reasons. This might become another source of undesirable developments in the southeast corner of the European continent. This region is notorious for ethnic tensions and conflicts, especially in cases in which an ethnic group can rely on the patronage of a neighboring country.

The last point does not apply to the Roma/Gypsy population. This is the major reason why the situation of this ethnic group rarely become the subject of serious political debate. According to official data from the census of 1992, Gypsies make up 4 percent of the population. This is only an estimate since census data rely on ethnic self-identification. Whatever the real size of this ethnic group, it is clear that the Gypsies suffer badly from the loss of the affirmative policies which were in force in earlier decades. Unemployment and school dropouts are very high among them (Genov, 1997a: 46f.). The economic, educational and value differences between the Gypsies and the majority population have been deepening. There are many reasons for this situation. But the major reason is the incapacity of the state to provide the organizational conditions for ethnic integration. Thus, the performance of the Bulgarian state on the criterion of union during the nineties cannot be rated high.

4 JUSTICE

The start of the transformation in 1989 launched two trends in the Bulgarian system of justice. First, the country witnessed an explosion of crime. In a single year from 1990–1991, the number of registered crimes nearly tripled and then stabilized at a level higher than before (Genov, 1995: 73). Second, the institutions dealing with the prosecution and punishment of crime turned out to be dramatically unprepared for coping with this surge. This is obvious from the widening gap between registered crimes and convictions. Both trends are not exceptional. They can be observed in other Eastern European countries as well (Human Development Report for CEE, 1999: 24).

The situation is more depressing than the above numbers indicate since a large number of committed crimes remain unregistered. Victims do not report crimes. Some crimes, like bribery, invite concealment (Genov, 1997: 24f.).

Hence, the transition period has been marked by a rise of crime unheard of in the national history. The perception of crime as a risk facing the national society is very high. The efficiency of the system of justice has substantially declined during the nineties. Trust in courts and prosecutors is rather low.

Besides the problem of crime, a specific cluster of issues put the system of justice in Bulgaria to a test which it was not able to fully meet. When the government decided not to pay the interest on its huge foreign debt in 1990, the national state was bankrupt. By the end of the same year the economic situation of households became unbearable. The feeling was widespread that the people who were responsible for this situation should be put on trial.

There were also cases of abuses of human rights during the previous decades that needed legal clarification. First, there was the internment of political opponents in camps between 1944 and 1962. Second, during the forceful integration of the Muslim segment of the population in 1984–1985, the basic rights of individuals were disrespected. Third, the Chernobyl disaster had a specific echo in Bulgaria since identifiable persons misinformed the public about the hazards of the nuclear pollution.

Thus, there was enough substance for revolutionary justice in the course of the velvet revolution Bulgarian style. However, because of the weakening of the state in general and the unstable situation of the justice system in particular, the trials and their effects belong to the most unhappy part of the history of justice in the country. The trials of Todor Zhivkov, who was party leader and head of state for 35 years, and of Georgi Atanassov, the last prime-minister before the changes, focused on minor issues. Zhivkov was sentenced to a seven year term on charges like the irregular distribution of apartments. This type of charge against an authoritarian head of state could provoke only disenchantment. The trial on the internment camps reached people who were the least important in a huge hierarchical machine. The case of the forceful change of Turkish-Arabic names in 1984–1985 was not tried at all. The two people sentenced for misinforming Bulgarian society about the hazards of the Chernobyl disasters were among the last links in a chain of misinformation which started far away in the Soviet Union.

All in all, the processes against officials of the "old regime" turned out to be rather ineffective in both legal and moral terms. They left the impression of politically ordered spectacles. In Zhivkov's case they even turned out to be counterproductive, since he acquired the image of an unlawfully treated person. Together with the decline of living standards from the time of his rule to the mid-nineties, this additionally undermined the moral ground of the effort to transform Bulgarian society.

Two other cases exemplify the shaky foundation of Bulgarian justice during the nineties. They mark a trend which may become important for the future of the country's democratic institutions.

In August 1990 the former Party House in Sofia was looted and set on fire. The people who instigated the crowd and the individuals who did the crime are known. They were interviewed by journalists, filmed on the spot, identified and interrogated by the police. Nevertheless, nobody was arrested. Nobody was even seriously accused, let alone sentenced. Whatever the tactical calculations of the political parties, administrators and representatives of the justice system, this capitulation was one of the least admirable chapters of justice in the modern history of the Bulgarian state.

The case of the fire in August 1990 and the legal fiasco in its aftermath might be at least partly explained by the general turmoil at the early stage of the transformation. The storming of the Parliament in January, 1997 cannot be simplified in this way. Whatever the reasons for outrage of the people who gathered in the front of the House of Parliament on the night of January 10th, the police in a stable democracy should have had the organizational and technical capacity to tame the emotions of the crowd. This was not done. The House of Parliament was violently stormed and the lives of parliamentarians were threatened. At a given point in time the democratic state capitulated to political violence. It projected the worst possible image of the country abroad. Although the actors were identified, the police investigation of the case stopped half way. The legal system did not react according to its rules. The debate was not focused on the issue of whether the people who stormed the Parliament were guilty. The issue became whether the police had the right to prevent people from attacking the House of Parliament and parliamentarians. After the clarification that the police had not received any order to proceed violently against the rally, the whole issue was put on hold.

Although we have only briefly discussed cases of bad performance by the justice system, it cannot be graded positively.

5   TRANQUILITY

Prevention of Riots and Insurrections.   The above mentioned riots demonstrated the state's inability to secure the rule of law. In general, however, the transformation of Bulgarian society proceeds without open violence. This is hardly due to the efficient functioning of the state. In reality, Bulgarians are not inclined to participate in riots and insurrections.

Safety of Persons and Property.   While Bulgarians are basically disinclined to participate in open rioting, the experience of the 1990s shows that the weakening of the state might cause a crime wave of unprecedented scale. To make the point clear, in practically all types of crime the country still lags far behind the crime rates of the advanced countries of Western Europe and North America. But there was a tremendous increase in crime during the nineties when compared with the low crime rate of previous decades. The effect is a higher level of personal insecurity. The perception of threat to all kinds of property is also very high, especially the threat to personal property.

The Extent to Which Private and Public Transactions Are Conducted with Civility.   The political tradition of the Balkans is not particularly marked by civic virtues. The mixture of the rationalized politics of Western European style and the Byzantine style of intriguing leads to divisions and mutual accusations. Clientilism fosters mediocracy and destructive forms of political competition. The language used at political rallies and even in parliamentary debates shows a low level of respect for opponents. Thus, in a crucial period of national development the cultural model of reaching consensus on important issues was blocked. This negative experience may be gradually overcome in the future, but it will most probably mark the functioning of the state for years to come.

Mutual Respect Among Citizens.   During the decades before 1989, community life was exalted by the dominant collectivist ideology. Below the surface, however, destructive trends of alienation and mutual hostility made their way. The sudden collapse of former patterns of community life after 1989 showed that the erosion of social solidarity had gone far under the previous regime. The introduction of contractual relations was expected to bring about a new pattern of social integration and mutual respect. The expectation proved wrong. The deepening economic crisis and the lasting political instability stimulated alienation. The widespread corruption of state officers helped to change alienation among citizens into alienation from the state. The sentiment of being improperly treated both by fellow citizens and by state officials is widespread. The reestablishment of mutual respect and trust has been ineffectively promoted by the state.

6 DEFENSE

Modern defense has three major components: armament, logistics and morale. In all three, the Bulgarian state is vulnerable. In the unstable geo-strategic situation of the southeast European region, this is a dangerous condition. In the neighboring territory of the former Yugoslavia, real wars were waged during the 1990s. Practically all of the neighboring countries have border or ethnic problems. Moreover, due to its negative demographic growth, Bulgaria is increasingly vulnerable because of the deficit of human resources.

As to its armament, Bulgaria is clearly worse than its neighbors, except for Macedonia which is still developing its armed forces. During the eighties and nineties, Turkey and Greece received large quantities of heavy armaments as a result of the reduction of armaments in Central Europe. Both countries also received direct financial support from the United States, which they used for renovation of their military technology. Both Yugoslavia and Romania have large armies that are relatively well equipped.

Against this background the outdated armament of the Bulgarian army would not be a serious barrier to a foreign invasion. There is no real prospect that the impoverished state could find the resources to update its military technology. Bulgaria formerly had sophisticated military production specialized for export. The revenues secured the modernization of its own military equipment. When its markets in Eastern Europe and in the Middle East collapsed, this led to a halt in its own military modernization.

The logistical side of defense has suffered from the lack of consensus on major issues of national security. A possible affiliation with NATO is under discussion. In these unclear geo-strategic circumstances the Bulgarian army must be structurally reformed, and its manpower reduced. The morale of the officer corps was severely tried during the 1990s by political uncertainty. Thousands of officers left the armed forces. Those who remained suffered a substantial cut in income like all groups dependent on the state budget. The lack of resources reduces the provision for soldiers' food. Because of the economic constraints, officers and soldiers cannot receive proper training or keep their training intact. Under these conditions, military morale is not high. It is only due to the professionalism of some officers as well as their patriotism that the armed forces still have some defensive capacities.

7 WELFARE

During the seventies and the eighties the Bulgarian population enjoyed a level of welfare that was basically comparable to the level of welfare in other Central European countries. But since the beginning of the nineties, GDP per capita has declined by a third. The incomes of Bulgarian households also declined because of large foreign debt payments and ruined industrial and agricultural production (Genov, 1997: 86). The very high proportion of income spent on food (51 percent for the average household in 1996) is a clear indication that the nation is going through a period of dramatic impoverishment. It makes the structure of expenditures of the Bulgarian population similar to that in Third World countries (Genov, 1997: 92). The tremendous fall in incomes and the unfavorable structure of household expenditure show the incapacity of the Bulgarian state to manage the challenge of transformation. The situation regarding health care, education, pension funds, and unemployment benefits is no better. For welfare, the Bulgarian state clearly does not deserve a positive mark.

8 LIBERTY

The situation of the Bulgarian state and the Bulgarian nation during the 1990s was marked by normlessness. Ironically, this might be interpreted as excessive liberty. It might include the liberty of tax evasion without any threat of punishment. Putting such excesses aside, there is no doubt that the basic freedoms of religion, association, speech, movement, economic initiative, etc., are legally guaranteed and observed in practice. In principle, this means a substantial broadening of the space for personal development and self-realization, well attuned to the global trend of individualization.

On the other hand, the transformation revealed some reluctance to individualize. The reliance on the state in the major spheres of social life remains rather strong while private initiatives are weak.

The mistrust of state institutions that are not believed to manage anything effectively goes hand in hand with the hope of efficient state control.

Against the background of the risks facing Bulgarians in their everyday life, the lowering of aspirations is of prime importance. In the context of continuing crisis, aspirations are minimized. An important factor is the availability of more opportunities for personal initiative in the large cities and especially in the capital. Age also influences life strategies: aspirations are lower in rural areas because of their ageing population. Despite such differences, stable constraints on aspirations reflect limited opportunities.

Of no less concern is the time-scale of personal strategies. The predominant personal strategies in surmounting the problems of the crisis are short-term. In the critical years of 1996 and 1997 every second Bulgarian followed a day-to-day survival strategy, often accompanied by disorientation and helplessness.

Instead of the desired rapid expansion of opportunities for individual choice, opportunities declined for the majority of Bulgarians. Instead of the desired increase in material standards, everyday life is dominated by deprivations. Instead of satisfaction with democratic political institutions, large sectors of the population are suffering from destabilization. Instead of conditions for better personal development, we have the degradation and destruction of the nation's human capital. There is abundant support here for the point that "rights, which impose demands on community members, are effectively upheld only as long as the basic needs of those community members are attended to" (Etzioni, 1996: 8). It is widely acknowledged that national developments which throw a substantial part of the population into poverty have detrimental effects on the nation's competitive capacity (Brock, 1994: 71).

9 TRANSFORMATION MANAGEMENT BY THE STATE

The picture of organizational failures and deficiencies outlined above raises many questions as to the role of the state in the transformation. The hasty retreat of the state from managing the transformation undoubtedly reduced its efficiency. At first glance, this implies a paradox. The major goal of the ongoing transformation is the emancipation of the economy, of civic initiatives and of culture from the close state supervision, which was typical in earlier decades. The paradox is only apparent. The point is the necessity of a transformation of the state itself. In other words, the correction of the state centered over-integration of society can only be achieved by the state itself.

That is why strengthening the state is the key to the gradual resolution of the accumulated economic, political and social tensions. It is the key to the sustainable development of Bulgarian and Eastern European society. It is the means for overcoming the deep disenchantment caused by the current transformation. The task is difficult not only because of the lack of economic resources. That very disenchantment impedes the mobilization of political will. The accumulated dissatisfaction pushes towards extremes of apathy, aggression and doubt. The failure of the reforms sustains the continuing legitimacy crisis of the state and disenchantment with the workings of democracy all across Eastern Europe. Given Bulgaria's experience, it is not surprising that the disenchantment is most intense here (Central and Eastern Eurobarometer, 1998).

In the mid-nineties there was hope that the Bulgarian economy might be liberated from the "big" state, from the all-permeating state interventionism. The transition to a "small" but efficient state was in sight. Some advances were registered. Reality moved in a different trajectory. High inflation led to an interest rate of 300 percent on bank credits in the autumn of 1996. The national currency depreciated dramatically at the beginning of 1997. These events signaled the need for greater involvement of the state in the economy. The alternative paths for overcoming the crisis were not numerous. The most promising seemed to be the introduction of a Currency Board in mid 1997 in order to restore financial discipline. But this measure, which proved to be quite successful, clearly revealed the incapacity of the Bulgarian state to manage the transformation since the mechanism of the Currency Board transferred strategic decisions to the International Monetary fund. Some measures for effective privatization of productive assets and for the painful stabilization of the banking system are still needed. Economic recovery requires the closing of ineffective enterprises, which will increase unemployment. The unavoidable budget restrictions have the same effect. Thus, coping with new waves of unemployment is the most urgent task. Persistent efforts are needed to obtain international financial support for restructuring the national economy and refinancing the foreign debt. All these difficult and unpopular measures will have to be taken despite a low level of confidence in state institutions.

A new economic, political and cultural integration of Bulgarian society will require organizational innovations. Whatever they may be, the nation will experience a severe test of its vitality. Given its strong statist tradition, expectations are again directed towards the state. In spite of the strong disenchantment, public opinion favors an active state.

Some of the current expectations are unrealistic. However, even they might become starting points for the stabilization of the state and such an effort might attempt:

- To foster the dialogue among state institutions and between state institutions and the public about the nation's priorities, especially with a view to the ongoing European integration;
- To focus the legislature on the legal regulation of domestic and international relations;
- To reduce the intensity of political confrontations ;
- To mobilize the executive for an efficient solution of pressing economic issues, including financial stabilization, support for the poor, privatization, the renewal of production and export, and international financial support;
- To undertake all feasible measures to fight crime and corruption.

What are the prospects for resolving these challenging tasks?

Bearing in mind the experience from the current transformation, this program calls for the efficient management of high intensity risks as it is still the case all over Eastern Europe (Genov, 1999b). The alternatives are: either the integration of Bulgarian society by the state or the long-term undermining of the state.

It is clear by now that no spontaneous development of market mechanisms can break the vicious circles that threaten Bulgarian society with a persistent anomie. The insistence on a "small" state freed from its previous responsibility for managing the economy and culture, but well organized and efficient, is more relevant than ever before (The World Bank, 1997). If this type of state materializes, Bulgarian society has a historical chance. If not, the chance may be lost for a long time.

The experience of badly implemented measures for managing the transformation supports this point. The necessary liberalization of the economy was compromised by the unrealistic expectation of a self-regulating balance between the productive and the financial sectors, between prices and incomes, between revenues and expenditures. The right moment was missed to set priorities in technology, production, markets, etc. Such priorities should have guided the privatization. In the event, privatization became a purpose in itself, further hampered by the economic depression, political instability and a backward administrative culture. But state inefficiency was also encouraged by selfish interests. For important pressure groups, it was more convenient to preserve the "big" state, with large scale economic responsibilities that it was not able to meet. Against this background, discipline in managing the state budget is the crucial precondition for stabilizing production and exports.

The window of opportunity for handling the situation is narrow. The current Bulgarian state has demonstrated that self-discipline is not its strongest point. Among the few promising strategies, the Currency Board scheme was chosen. In practice, this means that consumption is restricted while subsidies to losing enterprises and inefficient public expenses are cut. These are the normal requirements of a stable modern state.

This task requires a certain level of political and cultural integration, which would permit a consensus about the need to apply urgent and radical measures for financial stabilization. They need substantial political backing because they are risky. The open question is whether the governing elite will have the will to achieve this consensus. It is difficult for groups enjoying illegitimate privileges to give them up. The fact that the introduction of the Currency Board was postponed several times reflects the latent opposition against financial transparency and discipline.

There is no guarantee that the consensus will hold in the long term. There is still the threat that some sectors of the state administration will bow to the interests of pressure groups. Under the present condition of decentralized decision-making, ineffective control and widespread corruption, that outcome is entirely possible.

Even the operational success of the Currency Board is not making social integration easy to manage. It would still have to be seen whether rapid economic differentiation would continue. The current rise in unemployment is another hazard. The handling of these and other burning issues will determine the efficacy of the stabilization measures. The social reserves are minimal. Many sectors of society have no reserves. To impose new restrictions on their purchasing power may bring them to starvation. The reactions of such threatened groups might evolve into destructive conflicts. The nation can hardly bear more improvisations.

The Bulgarian state owes its citizens more clarity about the direction, content and timing of further transformation, and about its management, given the wide dissatisfaction with previous reforms and the perennial need to start them anew. The most challenging question at the present moment is: Can the state reestablish social integration as was expected at the beginning of the reforms? The question is no less appropriate now than then. We can only hope that the ongoing processes will move the nation closer to a positive outcome.

10 "GOVERNMENT" AND "GOVERNANCE": THE CHALLENGE OF GROWING COMPLEXITY

The tremendous problems facing Bulgarian society and the Bulgarian state are not unique. They are a painful adaptation to global trends like individualization, the rationalization of organizational structures and the universalization of values. Since all present day societies have to cope with the same challenges, there are striking similarities in the problems of state institutions all over the world. There are clear parallels, for example, between Central and Eastern Europe, on the one hand, and Latin America on the other. (Genov, 1998; Governing Globalization, 1998).

The key element in these changes is the growing complexity of the tasks facing state institutions. Traditional hierarchical government must be replaced by new modes of governance engaging multiple actors from the public and private sectors. One aspect of the current transformations in Central and Eastern Europe is the decentralization of government accompanied by stronger governance, stemming from privatization and the expansion of civil society.

Promising as they may be, these processes have many shadows on them. New patterns of governance can turn into new social pathologies. Indeed, many of the problems in the current transformation in Central and Eastern Europe can be ascribed to the haste of the transition from government to governance.

The increasingly complex problems facing society and the state must be handled by the co-ordinated efforts of a growing number of actors and decision-makers which implies a higher level of social integration than is present either in Central and Eastern Europe in general or Bulgaria in particular. The preliminary effect has been not a reduction but an increase in complexity. The roles of particular actors are often unclear. Under these conditions, predictability decreases and failures increase. That is what happened in Bulgaria during the 1990s (see also Stoker, 1998).

The Bulgarian experience supports the principle that government and governance must go hand in hand. If the balance is disturbed, stabilization should have priority. But stabilization in whose favor? In Bulgaria and other countries in Central and Eastern Europe, the current transformation has so far favored rather tiny sectors of society. Instead of dispersing power in polyarchic structures, it has created a new concentration of power in rather limited structures.

These developments put new strains on the Bulgarian state. It must re-define itself under the new circumstances. The adaptation will take decades. Given the difficult economic situation, the process will probably be marked by uncertainties, tensions and conflicts. The experience of the weakened and inefficient state guided by neo-liberal strategies calls for alternative models of development. There is an urgent need to assess the economic, political and ideological aspects of the neo-liberal developmental strategies imposed on Eastern European societies by powerful international financial institutions. A careful analysis is needed of the unintended and undesirable effects of these strategies. They range from the global environmental crisis to the deepening economic differentiation among nations and regions. These trends undermine optimistic visions of the future and stimulate the search for alternatives to the currently predominant neo-liberalism (Anderson, 1992: 279f).

Whatever the specific alternatives, they will have to involve a combination of strategic goals and tactical measures. At the center of debates about organizational rationality and social justice stands the state. The goal of favoring the common good over particularistic interests by using state institutions cannot be achieved once for all. It is a permanent task. Another permanent task is to keep democracy alive by fostering political participation and by removing obstacles to citizen involvement in political decisions. The requirements of a functioning democracy are closely related to the maintenance of an efficient balance between the concentration and the decentralization of power.

The contradictions and pathologies of Bulgarian political life illustrate the difficulties of democratization in Eastern Europe and in the broader global context. This national case exemplifies the open-ended project of balancing government and governance, the urgent project of socially responsible actors in the decades to come.

REFERENCES

Anderson, Perry. 1992. *A Zone of Engagement*. London and New York: Verso.

The Balkan Security. 1996. *Political and Military Problems*. Sofia: Hristo Botev (in Bulgarian).

Berend, Ivan T., ed. 1997. *Long-Term Structural Changes in Transforming Central and Eastern Europe (The 1990s)*. München: Südosteuropa-Gesellschaft.

Brock, Dietmar. 1994. "Rückkehr der Klassengesellschaft? Die neuen sozialen Gräben in einer materiellen Kultur," in Ulrich Beck and Elisabeth Beck-Gernsheim, eds., *Riskante Freiheiten*. Frankfurt am Main: Suhrkamp, 61–88.

Central and Eastern Eurobarometer. 1998. *Public Opinion and the European Union* (20 country survey). Brussels: European Commission, March.

Constitution of the Republic of Bulgaria. 1991. Sofia (in Bulgarian).

Economic Survey of Europe in 1996–1997. 1997. New York and Geneva: UN Economic Commission for Europe.

Etzioni, Amitai. 1996. "The Reponsive Community: A Communitarian Perspective." *American Sociological Review* 61, N1, February: 1–11.

Genov, Nikolai, ed. 1995. *Bulgaria 1995.* Human Development Report. Sofia: National and Global Development.

– 1996a "Transformation Risks: Structure and Dynamics," in Heinrich Best, Ulrike Becker, and Arnaud Marks, eds. *Social Sciences in Transition. Social Science Information Needs and Provision in a Changing Europe.* Bonn: Informationszentrum Sozialwissenschaften, 1996, 39–54.

– 1996b Bulgaria 1996. Human Development Report. Sofia: UNDP.

– 1997 Bulgaria 1997. Human Development Report. Sofia: UNDP.

– 1998 Central and Eastern Europe: Continuing Transformation. Paris and Sofia: UNESCO-MOST and Friedrich Ebert Foundation.

– 1999a "Bulgarian Society 1960–1995: The Challenge of Two Transformations." In Nikolai Genov and Anna Krasteva, eds, *Bulgaria 1960–1995. Trends of Social Development.* Sofia: National and Global Development, 1–35.

– 1999b) *Managing Transformations in Eastern Europe.* Paris and Sofia: UNESCO-MOST and Regional and Global Development.

Glatzer, Wolfgang, ed. 1996. *Lebensverhältnisse in Osteuropa. Prekäre Entwicklungen und neue Konturen.* Frankfurt am Main: Campus.

Human Development Report for Central and Eastern Europe and the CIS 1999. New York: UNDP.

Mirachkov, Vassil. 1995. *Bulgaria.* Deventer and Boston: Kluwer Law and Taxation Publishers.

Montesinas, Jorge Nieto, ed. 1998. *Governing Globalization. The Policy of Inclusion: Changing Over to Shared Responsibility.* Mexico City: Demos Edition.

Shishmanova, Maria. 1995. *Trends and Problems in the Development of the Structure of Settlements in the Republic of Bulgaria.* Sofia: National Centre for Territorial Development and Housing Policy (in Bulgarian).

Statistical Handbook. 1998. Sofia: National Statistical Institute (in Bulgarian).

Stoker, Gerry. 1998. "Governance as Theory: Five Propositions," *International Social Science Journal* 155, March, 17–28.

The World Bank. 1997. *The State in a Changing Society. World Development Report 1997.* Washington, DC: The World Bank.

World Development Report 1996. *From Plan to Market.* Washington, DC: The World Bank.

Grading the French Leviathan

HENRI MENDRAS

1 INTRODUCTION

Two centuries later, what remains for us of the Great Revolution? Are we definitely through with the Ancien Régime? Has the extraordinary mutation that France has undergone in the past thirty years, and that I have qualified elsewhere as the Second Revolution[1] because it seemed so profound and decisive, destroyed the industrial and bourgeois society that sprang from the first?

If I were to respond in the most lapidary way to these questions, I would say that yes indeed the social structures that emerged from the Revolution have definitively crumbled. But on the other hand, its ideals have finally penetrated into the deepest layers of the fabric of our society. By way of a curious backlash, the result of all this has been a "democratization" of social structures accompanied by an "aristocratization" of its mores. Let us argue these points in what follows. "Liberty, Equality, Fraternity" is more than ever the ideal of the French citizen.

2 SOCIAL STRUCTURE

The first Revolution replaced the orders of the Ancien Régime with the industrial society's classes, while affirming the equality of all individuals before the law. Today, those major social classes that Marx defined and analyzed have all disappeared. With this almost everyone agrees, except for a few unrepentant orthodox Marxists. The end of the peasantry, which I pointed out as early as 1965 to the indignation of many, is today a fait accompli.[2] The million or so agricultural producers who feed us no longer have anything in common with the peasants of a century ago, who managed to survive until just after the Second World War thanks to constantly favorable policies on the part of all governments.

In much the same way, the bourgeoisie, which controlled the most significant part of the national wealth, has been slowly ruined. Let us remember that the French bourgeoisie depended more for its livelihood on stable rent and interest income than on entrepreneurial risk. Some had small businesses, but it was their offices, their leased real estate, and the interest they earned on stocks and bonds that provided most of them with their living. Before 1914, French capitalism, when compared with that of England or Germany, was more financial than industrial. To be a bourgeois meant to have acquired property, mostly through inheritance, and to live off it. World War I, the end of the gold-standard franc, the crash of 1929, World War II, and inflation finally got the better of it. Today, almost no one lives exclusively on the revenue generated by property, and the famous cry "I am ruined. Now I am going to have to work," often heard in boulevard comedies of the past, now seems incomprehensible.

The middle class of shopkeepers and small retailers has been significantly reduced and transformed. Their last champion was Pierre Poujade, a small shopkeeper himself and the ultraconservative leader of the Union et fraternité françaises party, which received 11 percent of the votes in the legislative elections of 1956. The "small independents" who made a living off their modest shops, businesses, or country farms were the stuff from which the Parti radical sprang. They fed on an egalitarian ideology that defended the "little guys" against the "big guys," and poujadisme was quickly associated with narrowminded unionism and opposition to economic and social progress.

Formed rather late in France, the working class associated with heavy industry has been on the decline since 1975. The steel industry was born in Lorraine and next to the old coal mines at Le Creusot, thanks to the wealth of the Wendel and Schneider families, only at the very end of the nineteenth century. At the turn of the century, Renault was the first industrialist to build mass-production factories inspired by Frederick W. Taylor's scientific management model. And 1936 was the year that marked the triumph of this "traditional" working class that had recently come into being. For twenty years now the number of industrial workers has been declining. Their positions and the tasks they perform are no longer those of their fathers. They are paid monthly rather than weekly, and though their job of overseeing machines remains difficult, it can in no way be compared to the physical effort required of manual labor in the past. The attaché case and blue jeans have replaced the haversack, used for carrying one's lunch, and the worker's cap.

In 1945, the "independent" households living off a small business, a farm, or inherited wealth still comprised virtually half of all families in France. Today 85 percent of the French population are wage earners. The world of Balzac and Zola has completely disappeared.

3 SYMBOLIC INSTITUTIONS AND CONFLICTS

At the same time, the large national institutions have lost their symbolic power and are no longer the butt of major conflicts, which used to animate the ideological and political life of the country. The legitimacy of the Republic is no longer contested from the Right or from the Left. A call for a huge demonstration in defense of republican institutions, its participants marching from the Place de la République to the Place de la Nation, which occurred several times until only a generation ago, would today fail on deaf ears. The existence of the military is now accepted as a national necessity: no pacifism, insubordination, or antimilitarism worth noting challenges the legitimacy of the armed forces and of their function. The Communist Party, which in 1945 presented itself as the party of the people and of the resistance against the Nazi oppressor, numbered a million members and used to capture almost 30 percent of the ballot in the days following World War II. Today, the discrediting of Marxism has all but wiped out the ideology around which it rallied. Its peasant and labor rank and file has been substantially reduced, and the party is only a shadow of its former self with less than 10 percent of the vote – rapidly dwindling – and fewer than 100,000 members.

The Catholic church has given up being the church of France in order to become that of believers: the 10 percent of regular church-goers and the 20 to 25 percent who still recognize Catholicism as their religion. The staunch nonbelievers represent about 15 percent of the population. There are almost a million Protestants. Islam and Judaism have acquired legitimacy and now are officially acknowledged as churches in their own right. France, which was for a long time considered to be completely Catholic, since almost all of the French used to be baptized, has now rather abruptly become a pluridenominational nation. As a result, there is no longer any basis for anticlericalism. For half of the French people, the veneration of the dead is the only ostensible manifestation of religion.

Finally, the battle over schools has lost much of its impassioned fervor. Swept up in the energy of a crowd of a million militants demonstrating in June 1984, the cardinal archbishop of Paris proclaimed himself a defender of a fundamental freedom, that of families to freely choose their children's schools. Seventy-five percent of the French supported his position. That was the death knell for a republican school system whose self-appointed mission had been to "liberate." Through a curious reversal of position, the church seems to garner better support when it defends a public freedom than when it preaches about private morality. According to various polls, half of the Catholics who claim to be regular churchgoers refuse to allow the pope to lecture them about sexual morality, which is a matter to be left entirely up to one's free will, in their collective estimation.

In 1983, the socialist prime minister abandoned his economic policy to resume that of his predecessor, Raymond Barre. This had the effect of affirming that the economic mechanisms of capitalism were the more powerful and that it had finally become necessary for the socialists to throw in the anticapitalist sponge. It meant that France was officially reconciling itself to such notions as profit and free enterprise when in fact, deep down, whether on the right or on the left of the political spectrum, the French people had all along kept the precapitalist convictions of their elders, the peasants, the shopkeepers, the moneyed bourgeois, and the civil servants. Polls immediately registered this abrupt ideological turnabout: earning money and making a profit were now positive values, and the head of a successful business was viewed as prestigious.

Two nineteenth-century icons were thus disappearing at the same time: republican schools and anticapitalism. After some delay, France was finally coming to grips with the values of the modern world. All the old conflicts were beginning to lose their foundation.

In the past, republicans and antirepublicans, Catholics and anticlericals, patriots and pacifists, Marxists and free-market advocates, schools run by the nuns and schools run by the Republic, used to confront each other in ideological conflicts that swept the entire nation, from the Parliament to the smallest and most remote village. Oddly enough, these conflicts linked together "irreconcilable" adversaries in a struggle that had the effect of reinforcing national unity. The apparent instability of the political system along with street demonstrations made civil war a permanent threat for the French people and conveyed to other nations the image of a fragile country, always ripe for anarchy. In reality the social structure built on the ruins of the Ancien Régime after 1789 proved to be remarkably solid, since it unfailingly endured for so long. Until recent years, that is. All of a sudden, in less than a generation, it has collapsed. The saber, the aspergillum, the flag must now be stored in the national museum alongside the schoolmaster's book. The primary-school teacher, the bourgeois, the peasant, and the worker of 1936 are by now nothing but historical figures.

4 THE SOVEREIGNTY OF THE NATION

The French citizen has a profound relationship with the Republic and the state, made up of mixed feelings of trust and mistrust; a relationship that contributes to the construction of his or her very personality. Since Henri IV and Richelieu, the history of France is no more than a long illustration of the sovereign power of the nation. Louis XIV, Napoleon, Clemenceau, and de Gaulle represent and incarnate this continuity and reinforce the French pupil's trust in the strength of his or her nation, a process that begins as early as primary school. It is because the state is strong that the French citizen himself or herself feels strong. The strong state ensures her liberty and protects him from all dangers, both those within and those without; from foreign armies and fanatic terrorists, from criminals and disease.

We need only think of the celebrated French texts. *La Déclaration des droits de l'homme et du citoyen* states: "The principle of all sovereignty resides by essence in the Nation; no body or individual can exercise any authority that does not issue expressly from the Nation" (Article 3). The Constitution of 1791 specifies: "Sovereignty is one, indivisible, and inalienable" (Title III, Article 1). And the Constitution of 1958 adds: "National sovereignty belongs to the people, who exercise it through their representatives or the referendum process" (Article 3).

The sovereignty at issue here is that defined in the sixteenth century by Jean Bodin (1520–1596) in his major work, *La République*, which remains a founding work of political science. A magistrate and successor to the royal jurists, Bodin developed the doctrine of absolute monarchy with the purpose of freeing the Kings of France, François I and his successors, from all allegiance to the Holy Roman Emperor and the Pope, and of affirming the king's authority over Protestants and the nobility. At the time, this was brandishing an ideological weapon in the service of one's king. The political scientist and international relations specialist Bertrand Badie (1999)[3] has judiciously reminded us that in the eyes of History, sovereignty was as much demanded by the King of France in the sixteenth century as by nationalities in 1848 and by the former colonized countries today, so badly carved out by the colonizers. Indeed, sovereignty, by its very abstractness, functions symbolically as the ruler's instrument of identity and power.

That which was a demand in the sixteenth century became an absolute doctrine in France. An inviolable principle, first for the monarchy over a period of two centuries, then, starting in 1791, for successive French Constitutions. This principle was a legal fiction, an abstraction first incarnated in the King, an absolute monarch; the Republic took over when the king was no more. Every French citizen has learned, in primary school first of all, about the glory of Louis XIV and Napoleon, the majesty of the single and indivisible Republic. In the internal order, state sovereignty is "unlimited and the foundation upon which all else rests." This means that the state is the unique incarnation of sovereignty for the citizens, and recourse to force is justified to ensure respect for that sovereignty. In order for this legitimacy not to be contested by any other form of legitimacy, the people's religion had to be that of the Prince: *cuius regio eius religio,* for there was no true sovereign but God. In the external order, sovereignty signified that nothing could be imposed on the state without its consent, that every international rule was produced through the consent of states. The only limit against which this sovereignty came up was, of course, other states: recourse to force was legitimate if a state wanted to impose its will on another. This was the world installed on the ruins of the Germanic Holy Roman Empire by the Treaty of Westphalia (1648).

This notion of sovereignty presupposes a territory within which sovereignty is exercised and borders beyond which it does not apply. The inviolable, sacred border that the people in arms hurried to defend is both a Roman and peasant heritage; it is characteristic of Western European civilization, as I have explained in my book about Europe.[4]

Since 1945, the traditional protective state has also become a welfare state. Every French citizen is deeply attached to the universal health care coverage system (the Sécurité Sociale) and many demonstrated for its continuance in November 1995, after the government of the time proposed radical changes to it. The state also provides free education to all its citizens, and highways and railways. The principles of eighteenth-century political philosophy have finally been realized: the government is expected to ensure its citizens' happiness.

Unfortunately, we have little descriptive data with which to analyze the fundamental tie between the French people and the Nation, between citizen and state. In effect, since this has not been made a subject of open debate, no survey has ever been ordered by the media and no researcher has investigated the question. Still, a few scattered results make it possible to identify certain developments, and differences among categories of French people.

Contrary to a widespread idea, *patrie* (fatherland) is not a value on the decline. Quite the contrary, it is on the rise, even among young people. In two SOFRES studies, spaced 12 years apart, young people aged 15 to 24 were asked if certain words "represent something very important, fairly important, not very important, and not important at all." For "patrie" the proportion of positive responses (very or fairly important) went from 38 percent to 53 percent between 1984 and 1996. ("Patrie" was, however, far behind "friendship," "family," "love," all on the rise.) To the statement, "If necessary, I would be ready to fight to defend my country," 59 percent of young men responded "yes" in 1996.

On these questions, young people's responses varied little from those of the nation taken as a whole. This is surprising; we might have expected young people to be less patriotic and less ready to defend their country than preceding generations. Positive responses to patriotic symbols, on the other hand, such as the Marseillaise (French national anthem), the French flag, and Bastille Day, have gone down sharply (34 percent to 26 percent from 1976 to 1983) and the sense of their relevance does vary with age: 42 percent of young people deemed them" outmoded" against 14 percent for the over-60. Curiously, however, these symbols do not seem to have declined in value when associated with athletic feasts: athletes step onto the awards podium to the sound of the Marseillaise and the raising of the French flag. These indicators show an unexpected consistency of opinion about the nation among the French people.

5   THE REPUBLIC

Another way of looking at national sentiment is to compare it to feelings about Europe. A survey conducted by the *Centre d'Etude de la Vie Politique Française* (CEVIPOF) asked the following question: "Do you, personally, feel only French, more French than European, or equally European and French?" The responses hardly reflect generational difference, except for "May '68ers," slightly more divided between France and Europe. Education level, specifically the distinction between people with university education and those without, is the only variable that makes a clear difference. That difference is sharpest between, on the one hand, upper managers and teachers, with the strongest feelings of being European (53% and 66% respectively), and blue-collar workers and unemployed women, who feel the least European.

The contrast could not be sharper between blue-collar workers who vote for Le Pen's extreme right National Front party and teachers aged 50–59, the "May '68ers." On the one hand, a political philosophy that valorizes the Republic, the French incarnation of the nation-state; on the other a clear renunciation of that doctrine and an opening up to Europe and the world, combined with a return to local and regional identity and a readily aroused humanitarian sensibility. Springing from contradictory doctrinal roots, these two conceptions of the *patrie* cut across the right/left dichotomy.

"*La France aux Français*" (France for the French), one of Le Pen's rallying cries, may be understood in two ways. The first, crude interpretation is that France should be exclusively populated by people of French origin; the intruders must be gotten rid of. The second, more profound, understanding implies that the French should govern themselves, be the masters in their own land. In this form, Le Pen's slogan resonates in all sectors of public opinion. There must, therefore, be open debate on this issue in France; Le Pen must be answered rather than diabolized. These feelings, shared more or less openly by nearly half of the French people, are surely not absent from the deepest folds of consciousness among our fellow citizens, who experience the loss of French sovereignty as an attack on their personal security and the integrity of their personalities. Le Pen's racism is only a symptom of this suffering, of a deeper pain.

In fact, what does the French citizen see when he or she turns on the television? All the images over the past twenty years have shown the "kingly" privileges of the state being violated every day and their very foundations contested. Sovereignty is being chipped away – this is what the citizen observes and reads about day after day. Let us consider in succession the major areas in which the sovereignty of the Republic has been demolished.

6 THE MILITARY

The army, instrument and power of the sovereign, is no longer at his complete disposal nor capable of accomplishing on its own the tasks assigned it. The impotence of the "forces" France sends to Africa and other regions of the world became manifest in Bosnia and Kosovo. The President of the French Republic, commander-in-chief of military forces, can no longer legitimately command his troops at will but must instead wait for approval from various international organizations – NATO, the UN, the EU – before giving his orders, and usually he cannot act without the logistic support of the American army. In fact, the only sovereign who has remained sovereign is the Emperor in Washington, who can start a war in Iraq without the UN Security Council pronouncing an opinion and without any assistance, except from his vassal, the United Kingdom.

Since 1993 more and more French people have come to be in favor of a professional army; by 1997 this was the majority opinion.

The data clearly underscores the two political cultures and corresponding conceptions of the nation and the Republic analyzed above. Moreover, on this specific point, age is highly discriminating: 24 percent of young people disapprove of the elimination of military service, while for seniors the figure is 53 percent. The progression is continuous, with the "May '68ers" getting back into line.

France's lost military sovereignty can now only be recovered at the European level. For a young Frenchman, defending his country no longer means what it did for his grandfather, who performed his military service and learned how to wield a bayonet or machine gun. At a time of missile and zero-casualty warfare, the young Frenchman has difficulty imagining what his contribution to the defense of his country could consist of. He will never be called up to defend its borders.

7 THE LAW, THE JUDICIARY AND ENFORCEMENT

Ever since the French Conseil d'Etat, in 1989, established the superiority of treaties signed by the Republic over laws voted by the Parliament, the people's representatives have not been able to legislate with full independence and legitimacy. From one legal quibble to the next, we eventually reached the Treaty of Amsterdam, ratification of which required a makeshift reworking of the French constitution – makeshift in that clearly we have gone back on the principle of Article 3, together with the article from the *Déclaration des droits de l'homme et du citoyen* of 1789, which remains the reference for determining whether a law is constitutional. Here the very principle of Democracy has been infringed upon.

What is happening in the area of law-making is also happening to the justice system. French citizens can now appeal judgments handed down by French courts by taking their case to the Luxemburg court – not to mention the Court for Human Rights in Strasbourg. Few have done this so far, and these cases are not much publicized by the media, but an attentive citizen will certainly be aware of this possibility. The development of a specifically European jurisprudence is having a major effect on everyday practice in national courts: in delicate cases that might be appealed, judges have begun asking the European Court for a preliminary opinion before making their own rulings.

After the *Acte Unique* and the Schengen Accords, national borders no longer prevent the circulation of persons and goods but continue to limit the jurisdiction of judges and police. This contradiction seems very strange to the French people, who have always conceived of the border as a rampart protecting them from external dangers. Instead, what the citizen sees on television almost every day are drugs arriving from Holland and Albanian, Kurdish, and gypsy refugees crossing through Italy to come here. The police and even the judges find their ability to intervene limited by a border that no longer stops delinquents from entering.

8 THE ECONOMY

Not to coin money any longer clearly means renouncing a fundamental privilege of sovereignty as defined by Jean Bodin. The realization of Euroland is the last step in a policy that has been pursued with perseverance by all French governments, whether right- or left-wing, for the past twenty years. The French have known for a long time that French economic policy is decided at least as much in Frankfurt and Brussels as in Paris. French farmers were the first to realize this, and they have been benefiting from it: European farming policy has ensured them markets, minimum prices, and subsidies for their products. In 1992, when the franc was attacked on the currency markets, the Bundesbank supported it and devaluation was avoided; when the pound came under attack it was not supported by the Bundesbank, and the Bank of England was forced to float it.

Moreover, everyone knows that business enterprises no longer bother themselves with national borders; they are plurinational in terms of their markets, if not their production. Nonetheless, through a strange contradiction, even the most internationalized of such firms remain national: Air Liquide, Saint-Gobain, Michelin, and many other companies are clearly French, while IBM is American, Sony Japanese, and Siemens German. But in what way do these great champions remain national when 40–45 percent of their share capital on the Paris stock exchange is held by foreigners? The British are selling their most prestigious companies to the Germans, Japanese, or Dutch as they might sell the Crown Jewels, whereas the French have the feeling that their common patrimony is imperiled if a foreigner takes control of a French firm. The peasant mentality is still alive.

For a French person, economic sovereignty can hardly be better incarnated than by public service companies that enjoy a monopoly on the national territory. That the great national companies should be the property of the nation, of the people as a whole, is a doctrinal principle that the socialists themselves have now abandoned, after invoking it in 1981 to justify a series of nationalizations. Clearly this principle is incompatible with internationalized capitalism. But the French man or woman may consider that water, electricity, transportation by rail or air, and the post are services to which they have a right as citizens; postal, railway, and electricity workers may consider themselves quasi-functionaries, similar to teachers and policemen in the service they render to the citizens.

When a national or municipal public service is privatized the user's status changes from citizen to client. Advocates of privatization argue that the client is better and more economically served than the citizen, who may feel disarmed when face to face with the state functionary. But as a client, the citizen thinks, rightly or wrongly, he or she loses the status that ensured him or her of the right to be served, whatever his or her social condition or income. Competition is supposed to ensure lower prices, but clients of Vivendi or the Lyonnaise des Eaux management companies have seen their water bills go up. On the market the client can negotiate if he or she is in a strong position; but consumers up against the strong supplier feel weak, whereas before they could put pressure on the mayor by refusing to support him or her in the next election.

9 GOVERNANCE AND SUBSIDIARITY

The sovereign state's function is to protect citizens from external and internal dangers, ensuring their fundamental safety and security. To be free from fear[5] is the first condition of the people's happiness, and any good government should assign itself this objective. Finally, the nation-state provides each citizen with an essential instrument of self-identification by means of which he or she constructs his or her person and identity. That identity presupposes the feeling of being able to master one's destiny and have a say in the decisions that affect one, thanks to the democratic process by which citizens elects their governors. The concept of citizenship has become an object of reflection today; we now speak of economic and social citizenship.[6]

In contemporary Europe, these objectives can no longer be attained, or even pursued, within state borders. This is obvious for small countries but it is also true for the four great powers, with their larger territories and populations; the difference between Denmark and Germany is now a quantitative rather than qualitative one. Military protection against possible aggression, protection against ecological dangers and epidemics, organized crime and terrorism, monetary fluctuations and unfair economic competition can no longer be ensured within each nation. It is hoped such protection will be more effectively provided by the European Union.

But the public good is surely better managed through close proximity to the citizens, and hence, for the great nations, at the international level. The devolution of new powers to Scotland and Wales, the breaking up of Belgium between Walloons and Flemish, and the autonomy of Catalonia give the French matter for reflection. The great French regional capitals have become places of political decision-making in the broad sense of the term. Transportation, public health, economic development, and cultural promotion are so many areas in which that level of government has attained a kind of autonomy, one that has certain attributes of sovereignty. The proof is that though the prefect remains present as a representative of the sovereign state, the Président du Conseil Général became head of the executive at the department level in 1982 (*Loi de décentralisation*). The citizen may then wonder who incarnates sovereignty. The second piece of proof is that many French regions (the administrative unit above the department) have "embassies" in Brussels to defend their interests at the supranational level.

Political scientists, who, blithely ignoring the issue of sovereignty, directly analyze power and decision-making relations between the national state and the supra- and international levels, have invented a theory of this kind of governance; that is, "this vast range of institutions, networks, directives, regulations, norms, and usages, political and administrative, public or private, written or unwritten, that contributes as much to the stability, orientation, and ability to govern a political regime as to its aptitude to provide services and – this is essential – to ensure its own legitimacy."[7] But legitimacy does not mean sovereignty, and such analyses explain the developing reality without resolving its fundamental contradictions.

10 "THE STATE IS NOT DEAD"

This vision of sovereignty enables us to understand why, despite appearances, the state is not being pauperized, and why despite what many have hastily and frivolously announced, it is, of course, not dead.[8] State sovereignty has lost its symbolic absoluteness, but the state's effective powers, though now shared, continue to grow. It will readily be recalled that in Western Europe, the state absorbs half of the national wealth, and that, despite attacks on it, the welfare state has never been in better condition. In this respect the state is ever more at the service of the citizens whose protection it ensures; that protection is of course far from perfect, but it has been increasing and progressing over the long term. Though the nation-state is losing ground to external sovereignty, it would seem to be gaining internal sovereignty by being more and more attentive to its citizens' well-being. More exactly, what it loses in the way of symbolic power does not bring about a loss in effective power. Often, curiously, the reverse is true.

The emergence of infranational and supranational powers seems to be to the detriment of state powers. Nonetheless, the state still has a decisive say at both these levels. Nothing can be done in Brussels or the regional capitals without the support of the state. The triadic game among these powers makes them indissociable partners; they back each other up, sometimes even to the point of projecting their particular responsibilites onto one another so as to dodge public criticism.

In the economic field, the privatization of companies and public services and the progressive internationalization of markets give people the feeling that the state is withdrawing. But governments continue to subsidize their industries at enormous rates – 50 billion euros, according to The Economist. (Company bosses who sing the praises of liberalism should not forget this.) Moreover, close analysis of decision-making shows that the sale of the Crédit Lyonnais bank was negotiated between the French Minister of Finance and the competent office in Brussels, a fact that has scandalized the citizens, who know that it is they who will have to pay the bill. In Great Britain, the privatization of electricity, water, gas, and telecommunications has led to the creation of regulating agencies which ensure a kind of state control; they are surely more interventionist than the former sub-ministries. France followed this example when it created the Agence de régulation des télécommunications.

Each state has obtained guarantees that Brussels will take charge of and pursue policies of primary importance to it: competition and privatization are largely British priorities and the British have a leading role in formulating those policies; monetary policy is largely formulated by the Germans; agricultural policy by the French, and so forth. And as mentioned, every Brussels policy is heavily influenced by the affected professional sectors. Farmers were the noisy pioneers in this pressure game; other professions are more discreet but also more effective.

Contrary to appearances, the creation of the euro has not brought about a loss of power for the state. As the economist Jean-Paul Fitoussi has expressed it:

The euro means that governments will have much more control over the destiny of our societies than in the past. The almost daily game of the markets has made it necessary for literally everyone to pay excessive attention to the short term: what investment project, either personal or business, can really resist the unpredictable fluctuations of interest and exchange rates? The return of the political is thus also that of the long term.... The paradox is that the return of the political made possible by the single currency has occurred in the context of a dominant ideology which affirms that it is the market that connects all forms of dynamism and all powers.[9]

We see that governments can no longer formulate policy and give orders absolutely independently; they have to reach decisions through negotiation with Brussels and with national and regional interest groups. Everything has become more complicated, but the state is still present at the center of the mechanisms. The role of politicians is to convince the citizens that though they are losing a symbolic type of sovereignty, sovereignty *à la Française*, the state is still present, protective, concerned for their well-being – in a word, the state still incarnates their identity.

11   LIBERTY, EQUALITY, FRATERNITY

By a strange paradox, the social classes and institutions resulting from the Revolution of 1789 were in fact obstacles to the penetration of revolutionary principles into the fabric of the French society.

Liberty, equality, and fraternity were proclaimed by the Revolution and affirmed as the essential ideology of the Republic. But in the past this trilogy remained largely confined to the ideological realm. Economic institutions, class antagonism and the texture of daily sociability successfully resisted the application of democratic principles for a long time. It was not until the breakdown of social classes and the weakening of traditionally dominant national institutions that the way was finally cleared for these values to blossom. The revolution of May 1968 had no other meaning than this, and its leaders were right in identifying not only with the philosophy of the Enlightenment but with that of socialist utopias from the previous century. Society could at last begin to accept them, although piecemeal.

Freedom is inconceivable without equality, and both, along with fraternity, are rooted in a common principle: individualism. Individualism has been making headway from as early as the Reformation, and it was proclaimed as fundamental to the Enlightenment philosophy. But it had barely been integrated into French society over the course of two centuries. For twenty years now, it has spread with lightning speed into all sectors of our society. The family unit, which constituted the last bastion of resistance, has begun to yield: today it has to serve the cause of the individual, and not the other way around, as in the past. Each of us seems to expect our family to answer to our needs and one does not feel that one is a member of a lineage to which one owes allegiance. All want to be themselves and construct their identities in their own way. This is much easier to do today than in times past. The happiness of ordinary citizens is becoming more and more the goal that political and social institutions set for themselves, just as the philosophers of the eighteenth century wanted.

The much-vaunted value of equality made barely any progress during the XIXth century. It was only with great difficulty that a few peasant children, overwhelmingly male scholarship recipients, were able to make their way into positions predominantly held by the bourgeois, for the latter kept for themselves and accumulated all the distinctive stripes. Every lowly soldier was said to have his own field marshal's baton stuffed away somewhere in his knapsack pouch. But from 1870 on, the recruitment of officers became increasingly less open to commoners. The military embodied a hierarchical vision of society that also served as a model for management; every factory or company owner thought of himself as the equivalent of a colonel, leader and father of the regiment. Finally, in spite of the Ralliement, through which a number of monarchists had made their peace with the Republic at the urging of the pope in 1892, the church continued to cling to an Ancien Régime conception of society.

Class struggle was evident. It was not only experienced firsthand by striking workers who hoped for the great social upheaval that would forever change their destiny, but it was also felt deeply by the bourgeois, who lived in the constant fear of their wealth being confiscated and themselves being hanged from a streetlight. In those days, the worker obeyed the supervisor only out of fear of being laid off, which meant misery, sickness, and an early death. Likewise, the sharecropper obeyed the landowner for fear of being thrown out and reduced to nothing more than a migrant worker. Both were forced to be submissive in order to hold on to jobs that gave them enough to eat.

With the collapse of these structures, today freedom has been able to make significant inroads into our daily life. Signs of excessive deference seem to be outdated, and we all feel a little less constrained by hierarchal relationships. France is no longer an authoritarian land, with the notable exception of its civil service. The enrichment we have enjoyed as a result of the *Trente Glorieuses*,[10] along with the relaxing of social relationships, have authorized each of us to be less obsequious to our direct superiors. And the latter know full well that they will have to obtain the consent of their subordinates if they want to be followed (we no longer dare say "obeyed"). Fear and violence, formerly the primary mechanisms of social relationships, have effectively disappeared, except in the more marginal sectors of society, particularly in the "galley ship" existence of unemployed youth in large metropolitan suburbs who harbor a rage against society for not creating a decent place for them to live and work. But although overall freedom may have taken two centuries to work its way into the framework of French society, it has probably done so better than in any other nation.

According to one of Tocqueville's laws, the more equality progresses, the more inequalities become intolerable. Certainly, discrepancies in income are less pronounced today, but they change slowly and invariably reappear in other forms, as in the way we choose to live, as well as in our access to limited goods. Today, the same school system welcomes children from all social categories starting at a very young age[11] and inculcates in every one of them the rudiments of the same culture. But by and large it unfortunately continues to return these children right back into the same social positions as their parents.[12] We have learned with great dismay that the democratization of education does not translate into an equality of opportunity for all our children. So it appears that the enrichment of the French people did not occur without creating a new category of poverty, which is scandalous in such an opulent society as ours.

If our society is still far from being a fraternal one, brotherhood and solidarity have become nevertheless its major ideals. This is expressed in diverse ways, in support of the Rights of Man or against racial discrimination. Still as prompt to rally behind a cause, today's youth no longer respond to political rabble-rousing but do react vigorously each time the brotherhood of humankind is imperiled, whether in France or anywhere else on the planet. The widely popular slogan "Don't lay a finger on my buddy" applies as well in defense of children of North African immigrants in Paris, Lyon, or Marseille as in the fight for human rights worldwide. Indeed, the youth of today want a society in which all men and women are brothers and sisters, and through such a notion, they recapture the ideal of 1789.

With the church now playing a minor role, the fundamental principle that derived the authority of the state from religion no longer carries any meaning. The bishop no longer speaks alone in defining what is good or evil, true or false, in the name of God. The rabbi, the mullah, the Protestant Bible, and the sole reasoning faculties of the unbeliever speak as well. Each must learn to respect the other, and no arbitrator can come between them. The tolerance of others and of their values is becoming more and more the foundation of all life in our society. This is a radical innovation for the French people, who were accustomed to a guiding authority that was accepted by some and against which others rebelled.

To judge a society properly, a sociologist must pay close attention to the values of that society as they manifest themselves concretely. With this in mind, it appears indisputable that in recent years, our society has reduced the gap between the values it proclaims and the ways in which people live them. I defy anyone to prove the opposite. And it seems that the Revolution has made more progress in these past twenty years than it had in the previous two centuries.

If the society stemming from the events of 1789 has disappeared, clearing the way for the creation of a more favorable climate in which revolutionary values can flourish, what kind of society is going to emerge from the ruins that surround us today? The best model for understanding the new structures beginning to take place seems to be the aristocratic society of the eighteenth century. And this is no paradox. Let me be clear: I am speaking here about mores, relationships, and social practices, a system of standards and values, and not about the model of one's working life, nor the functioning of a productive system, nor about the power of the state.

The aristocratic model has always been an ideal for the French. Virtually from the beginning, as they accumulated wealth, the bourgeoisie and the peasantry have been driven by the goal to buy land and to become part of the nobility. Even the most reclusive and most frugal members of the bourgeoisie in the previous century dreamed of heroic deeds. They did not have the means to live like the nobility and therefore had to be content with adopting as their model Cyrano, that poor, poetic, and utopian soul. Miserly and thrifty, they rounded out their nest eggs, all the while nurturing extravagant dreams in which money was lavishly spent. The colonial Empire offered to its sons a way of escaping the mediocrity of the bourgeois and provincial life of their parents.[5] It offered an arena wherein they could realize their dreams while providing at the same time a place of destitution and sacrifice for its missionaries. Father Charles de Foucault and Captain Henri de Bournazel became the symbolic embodiments of this double ideal of a noble life that could not be realized in the bourgeois France of that period. To the youth of today, the Third World offers an opportunity to live out an ideal by fighting hunger, misery, and injustice. Yet this ideal no longer has much in common with that of their ancestors, as they go off to serve the less fortunate and not to civilize them.

Athletic prowess is now ritualized and exalted far beyond all measure. Outdoing oneself through some gratuitous act remains one of the foremost ambitions of our young, whether achieved vicariously through watching a broadcast of the Olympic Games or astride a powerful, shiny motorcycle. Nowadays these ambitions are not the privilege of young bourgeois, but extend to all categories of young people. For a period of about ten years, they enjoy a transition into adult life that is filled for most of them with sports, cultural activities, and travel, and for a minority with unemployment and delinquency.

New lifestyles are being elaborated and becoming more acceptable. They will be far more various in the future, leading to a broad diversification throughout the whole of society. But all will have in common the effect of restoring to the place of honor those clusters of values that had been abandoned because of the impoverishment of society in the period between the two world wars, and as a result of the exclusive emphasis on work and economic success during the *Trente Glorieuses*. The return of the whole society to aesthetic values, gratuitousness, idleness is going to take place through the conduit of its senior citizens and its youth.

There is reason to believe that from now on, technology and economics will no longer be the principal factors structuring French society. Ideology, values and mores, lifestyles and savoir-vivre will be the elements shaping society and providing its dynamic. Only a short while ago, each of us received behavioral models from our social position and then endeavored to conform to them. From now on, the multiplicity of these models will give to each and every one of us the opportunity to design our own way of living according to the value system we have each fashioned for ourselves. Shaped further by trends as well as by other fundamental markers such as national and world events, manufactured or natural, this multiplicity of choices bequeaths a new kind of fluidity to a society in which groups of cultural innovators happen to come together and bring about major change. In this sense, we can say that our society is becoming once again aristocratic, with all of us searching for means to "distinguish" ourselves by refining our own ways of being who we are.

NOTES

1 See Henri Mendras, *La Seconde Révolution française: 1965–1984*, with Laurence Duboys Fresney (Paris: Gallimard, 1988). For the English translation of an extensively revised version, see *Social Change in the Fifth Republic: Towards a Cultural Anthropology of Modern France*, with Alistair Cole (New York: Cambridge University Press; Paris: Maison des Sciences de l'Homme, 1991).

2 See Henri Mendras, *La Fin des paysans: Suivi d'une réflexion sur La Fin des paysans vingt ans après* (Le Méjan, Arles, Actes Sud; Bruxelles: Labor; Lausanne: L'Aire, 1992). For the English translation of the first edition, see

The Vanishing Peasant: Innovation and Change in French Agriculture, trans. Jean Lerner (Cambridge: MIT Press, 1970).

3 Bertrand Badie, *Un monde sans souveraineté: les Etats entre ruse et responsabilité* (Paris: Fayard, 1999).

4 Henri Mendras, *L'Europe des Européens. Sociologie de l'Europe occidentale* (Paris: Gallimard, "Folio" collection, 1997).

5 See Gian Franco Poggi, "La nature changeante de l'état," in Wright and Cassese, eds., *La recomposition de l'état en Europe* (Paris: La Découverte, 1996), 19–35.

6 Dominique Schnapper, *La communauté des citoyens* (Paris: Gallimard, 1994).

7 Wright and Casesse, eds, *La recomposition de l'état en Europe*.

8 Vincent Wright, "L'Etat n'est pas mort," in D. Jacques-Jouvenot, ed., L'Oeil du sociologue (Besançon: Presses du Centre Unesco de Besançon, 1998).

9 Jean-Paul Fitoussi, ed., *Rapport sur l'état de l'union européenne 1999* (Paris: Fayard and the Presses de Sciences-Po, 1999).

10 See Jean Fourastié, *Les Trente Glorieuses: Ou la révolution invisible de 1946 à 1975* (Paris: Fayard, [1980] c. 1979). Thanks to this extremely insightful book, "Les Trente Glorieuses" is now an expression commonly used among French historians to designate the formidable economic expansion and resulting social mutations that took place in France during the thirty years preceding the oil crisis of the mid '70s.

11 More than 95 percent of all children living in France begin public preschool at age three.

12 It must be noted that, for the longest time, when women experienced the "opportunities" offered by the Empire, it was as spouses or companions of colonial administrators, soldiers, or merchants.

Concluding Remarks

THEODORE CAPLOW

We seven authors speak with different voices and concerns and our judgments are fallible. Two of us have presumed to give letter grades to the performance of our respective Leviathans in meeting their essential responsibilities. Like any evaluation of a complex performance such as figure-skating or governing, these grades are partly objective and partly subjective. The other authors in this collection have refrained from the presumption of letter grades but they too have rendered judgments that are not completely objective but are nevertheless grounded on close observation and quantities of data. The subjectivity that matters has more to do with differences of perspective than with matters of fact. Karl-Otto Hondrich makes this explicit when he describes the prevailing conception of justice in contemporary Germany and shows how little it resembles the prevailing conception of justice in the United States.

Six of these states belong to the set of technologically advanced, economically developed western democracies. (The seventh, Bulgaria, aspires to join that set.) Among their common features are very low rates of infant mortality, low fertility, universal literacy, very high rates of home, automobile and appliance ownership, fringes of great wealth and stark poverty, and a gamut of rights and restrictions, including universal adult suffrage; freedom of speech and press and of occupational and residential choice; due process; legal protections for women and children and for ethnic and religious minorities; old-age, disability and unemployment pensions; the controlled distribution of drugs and intoxicants; the licensing of professionals; the regulation of business, banking and markets; the maintenance of an elaborate infrastructure for transportation and communication; the regulation of fisheries, mines and forests; and other functions too numerous to specify.

These states embody the latest and most humane variant of an organizational pattern that has been evolving in Europe since the Peace of Westphalia and has now spread to the rest of the inhabited world so that nearly all of our six billion neighbors live under the flag of a national state that strikes coins, prints postage stamps, grants citizenship, issues passports, receives ambassadors, enacts laws, tries lawbreakers, levies taxes, defends its frontiers and causes its national anthem to be played on suitable occasions.

With trifling exceptions, these national states were created by war or armed rebellion and for a long time they valued themselves and were respected by others according to their success in war. The services they provided for their people were generally intended to enhance the military assets of the sovereign; the happiness of the recipients was a secondary consideration.

At the beginning of the twentieth century and through its first half, the world was effectively administered by half a dozen great powers, assisted by a score of secondary powers, all heavily armed and eager for territorial aggrandizement. No effective challenge had yet been raised to the centuries-old theory (by Hobbes and Bodin among others) whereby sovereigns were unfettered in dealing with their own subjects and recognized no external constraints except the armed forces of other sovereigns. Right up to 1940, many European heads of state customarily appeared at peacetime ceremonies in military or naval uniforms with swords at their sides. Hitler and Stalin omitted the sword but kept the uniform.

Seven great powers entered World War II – Britain, France, Germany, Italy, Japan, the Soviet Union and the United States. The fortunes of war ordained that the latter two emerged with enormous military assets while Germany, Italy and Japan were demilitarized and Britain and France reduced to relative military insignificance. Throughout the Cold War the two superpowers, although agreeing on little else, cooperated in speeding the dissolution of the British, French and Dutch colonial empires on the premise that colonies were unsuitable for states that had no serious war-making capacity. Most of the new independent states that emerged from the ruined empires promptly furnished themselves with the largest military forces they could afford and turned to the U.S. or the Soviet Union, or to both, for additional military aid. Only a few of those forces were seriously intended for warfighting but they were useful against domestic opponents.

The invention of nuclear weapons limited the opportunities for successful war-making in ways that only became clear over the ensuing decades. The Cold War between the U. S. and the Soviet Union raged, in a manner of speaking, for more than forty years while each side prepared for an imminent attack by the other although it was clear almost from the beginning that the initiation of such an attack would constitute national suicide. During all those years, two great armies, mobilized and ready, confronted each other in eastern Germany and never fired a shot in anger. But the scenario by which the Cold War was conducted compelled West Germany, Italy, France and some of the smaller western European states to seek the shelter of American power, embodied in NATO, lest they find themselves alone in no-man's land. That affiliation not only conferred immunity from a Soviet invasion; it allowed these erstwhile powers to reduce their military expenditures and use the savings for economic and social development.

Of the seven states discussed in this book, only the United States and Bulgaria can be properly evaluated today on the criterion of Defense. The United States, with a preponderance of the world's military power and an enormous nuclear arsenal, faces vague threats from Russia, China, a possible Muslim federation and two or three "rogue states" but has no really plausible enemy. Bulgaria, with inadequate armed forces, faces a number of potential adversaries in the only European region where conventional war is still an option.

The five other states covered in this volume – all members of NATO – have no independent war-making capacities and therefore represent a new variety of the national state as an institutional form. They have been abandoning conscription in favor of small professional forces designed for peacekeeping and humanitarian missions of a type originated by Canada in the 1950s. Many of their troops already serve in binational or multi-national units. None of them has a significant navy or an important air force. France and Britain have nuclear arsenals whose strategic purpose is no longer clear.

The European Union, now comparable to the United States in demographic and economic weight, has not so far succeeded in developing a separate military role. It remains militarily subordinate to NATO, which is firmly under American control.

The transformation of these formerly bellicose states to permanently peaceable ones has far-reaching implications. Their ancient responsibility to protect their territories and people from invasion has been cheerfully discarded. They now look to the United States, whether acting independently or in the name of NATO or of the United Nations, to do it for them.

Since the five non-bellicose states in our set are, at least for the time being, completely insulated from threats of invasion or conquest, it should now be more difficult for them to satisfy the criterion of Union than it was when they still provided their own defense.

In each of our five essentially demilitarized states, there has been a massive devolution of functions from the central government to provincial authorities. The details are different in each case but the effects are the same – a shift of power from the national state to its geographic components together with the reinforcement of provincial attachments and a corresponding modification of patriotic sentiments.

Meanwhile, the four states in our set that belong to the European Union have been ceding other prerogatives of sovereignty to that supranational entity, which is not itself a state. They can not even decide who may enter their territories and use their public services.

This double erosion of the national state – upward to supranational authorities and downward to provincial authorities – has not occurred in the United States or in Bulgaria, the two states in our set that retain an independent war-making capacity. Despite much talk of devolution, the sovereignty of the fifty states that compose the United States has become entirely fictive. Even in those areas – such as the reformed welfare system – where they are allowed a small degree of autonomy, the exercise of that autonomy is closely supervised by federal agencies and monitored by the federal courts. Bulgaria is even less inclined to bestow new powers on its administrative subdivisions.

The actual fracture of the national state is seriously proposed in Canada and might involve not only self-government by Quebec but the secession of other provinces. Meanwhile, the native peoples of Canada have achieved something close to independence within the existing federation. The possibility of partition between North and South is seriously discussed in Italy. Two distinct forms of disunion compete in Germany – the continuing rift between the former West Germany and the former East Germany and the rising importance of the old imperial provinces. Spain is already fractured beyond the previous experience of any other modern state. Its multiple "autonomies" challenge the national state in day-to-day administration and compete with it for the hearts and minds of the people. France has been somewhat more successful in resisting regional and linguistic separatism but has initiated an extensive decentralization of political and economic power.

It is impossible to know at this point whether the European Union will eventually become a national state by acquiring an independent war-making capacity and evoking a European patriotism or whether the present American hegemony and the existing thicket of international organizations will evolve into a de facto world government. And it is supremely difficult to judge the adequcy of the existing institutional arrangements for the prevention of a nuclear war.

On the criterion of Justice, the results from our small set of national states are remarkably complex. Justice, it turns out, means two different things to our contributors. Ordinary justice protects citizens from each other. Social justice provides for the equitable distribution of social rewards.

In Germany and Canada today, the state concentrates on the achievement of social justice, giving special attention to the grievances of such minorities as Amerindians in Canada and Turkish immigrants in Germany. In both of those countries, the criminal justice system has been permissive in the face of rising crime rates, creating what Hondrich calls "liberal injustice," whereby the punishments meted out to offenders are too light to satisfy the collective conscience.

In Italy and Spain, social justice is a live issue but has not been incorporated into public policy to the same extent. The complaints of disadvantaged regions and ethnic groups remain, for the most part, unsatisfied. In both countries, the criminal justice system is characterized by ineffectiveness, delay and corruption. Objectively, Italy has much more crime than Spain but public confidence in the system is low in both countries.

In Bulgaria, the criminal justice system been unable to cope with a soaring crime rate. In the aftermath of decommunization, the number of registered crimes rose to an unprecedented level while the number of arrests and convictions declined. There is also a social justice issue in Bulgaria – the inability of the state to punish human rights violations that occurred under the previous regime.

In the United States, the concern for social justice is expressed by an elaborate and unpopular system of ethnic and gender preferences. Meanwhile, the ordinary justice system has become extraordinarily punitive and less and less responsive to ethical considerations, with the unintended result that the criminal justice system has become an instrument of ethnic oppression.

Insuring domestic tranquility is another of Leviathan's tasks. Indeed, Hobbes saw it as fundamental. Tranquility implies the safety of the people from mutual molestation, the prevention of armed conflict among them and the conduct of private and public transactions with civility. Riots, insurrections, and terrorism disturb a nation's tranquility as do those labor-management disputes, ideological controversies and ethnic antagonisms that escalate to violence.

218 Leviathan Transformed

Each of these national societies has experienced a brief surge in violent crime at some time during the past three decades and a higher level thereafter. The principal offenders in every case were the young males of disadvantaged groups – ethnic minorities and recent migrants. In absolute terms, there are extraordinary differences. Most large U.S. cities have more homicides annually than all of Spain. Bulgaria, whose critics deplore the total collapse of law and order, has far lower crime rates than France, where crime is not regarded as an especially pressing problem.

Although U.S. crime rates have declined sharply in recent years, the penalties for all sorts of crime, and especially for non-violent drug offenses, are still being steadily ratcheted up. American prisons and jails now hold more prisoners, mostly black or Hispanic, than all of the other advanced nations combined. Each of our specimen states has experienced at least one surge of violent crime in recent decades, although not synchronized. In Spain, Germany, Italy and Bulgaria, the criminal justice systems are regarded as excessively lenient, and most crimes go unpunished. Only France and Canada seem to have reached some sort of equilibrium in this respect.

Riots, mob actions and terrorist acts are unevenly distributed in time and space. Each of the seven countries has minorities who have been either victims or aggressors or both in mob actions – North Africans in France, East Germans and Turks in Germany, Albanians and Sicilians in Italy, Catalans and Basques in Spain, Amerindians in Canada, gypsies in Bulgaria, blacks and Hispanics in the United States.

Terrorism is a low-grade but chronic threat in each of these countries and the counter-terrorism measures installed in airports, public buildings and around the persons of political leaders are costly and restrictive. But only in Spain is terrorism a political as well as a police problem.

Despite these difficulties, Leviathan – in democratic states with market economies – has never been more secure. For the time being, there are no serious challenges to the political order from the left or the right. None of these states faces a serious revolutionary threat. Communism is a spent force in Italy and France. The Red Brigades are long gone from Germany. Basque separatism is effectively resisted by the Spanish State. Quebec separatism expresses itself at the ballot box. No one is preparing to overthrow the unpopular government of Bulgaria. The only challenges to the American political system come from a tiny fringe of unpopular fanatics.

During most of the past two centuries, these seven states were continually confronted with "the social question," i.e. the conflict between capitalists and workers over the conditions of industrial work and the distribution of its fruits. That conflict expressed itself in insurrections, civil wars, coups d'état, invasions, massacres; in innumerable enactments of the class struggle.

Then, by imperceptible degrees in western Europe and North America and by a sudden convulsion in eastern Europe, the social question shrank to insignificance. The revolutionary parties of the left and the right disappeared or changed their colors. Strikes and lockouts became rare. Although the distribution of wealth and income is still exceedingly unequal in each of the seven countries, and becoming steadily more unequal in the U.S. and Bulgaria, Leviathan's attention has been diverted to issues – immigration, education, family policy, foreign trade, health care, pollution – that divide the body politic along other lines and obscure the old fissure between capital and labor.

For all seven of these states the promotion of the general welfare has become Leviathan's principal task. The term welfare, as used here, covers much more than its current usage in the U.S. where it denotes government aid to indigent female-headed families. It also covers much more than it did in the eighteenth century, when it was only an expressionof vague goodwill. The welfare function in today's democratic states includes both the overall management of the national economy and the direct provision of services by government. The usual goals of economic management are continuous rises in gross domestic product and in average earnings, low inflation, low unemployment, favorable trade balances, the abolition of poverty and the reduction of income inequality. The welfare functions for which Leviathan is now responsible include both the basic human services of education, health care, child care, pensions, and public assistance to the indigent and handicapped and also the maintenance of the national infrastructure – transportation and communication facilities, environmental protection, policing, product safety, the regulation of markets and so forth.

Any attempt to compare states with respect to their performance of these complex functions must take account of differences of purpose as well as of results. Not all welfare goals are mutually compatible and the balances struck among them vary greatly from one country to another. The American condition of low job security and increasing inequality would not be acceptable in Spain, but an unemployment rate as high as Spain's would be considered catastrophic in the U.S.

It is also essential to distinguish those elements of the general welfare attributable to the policies of the state from those that have other causes. Discussing welfare, Alberto Martinelli concludes that,

"The overall performance of Italian society is good. The functioning of the welfare state is much less satisfactory." The same might be said of the United States.

Once again, the United States and Bulgaria are outliers – Bulgaria because of its abject poverty, the U.S. because of its unprecedented wealth. Bulgaria's transition to a market economy has reduced its GDP to the point where the median family must spend half its income on food. The American transition to a stock market economy has created millions of millionaires. In both of these dissimilar cases, there have been sharp increases in economic inequality and a steady deterioration of public services.

The five other states in our set have concentrated on the reduction of inequality and the elimination of poverty. All five provide universal health care and free or almost free education. But the reduction of regional inequality has proved more difficult for them than the elimination of poverty. Between the east and west in Germany, the north and south in Italy, the autonomous regions of Spain, francophone, anglophone and Amerindian Canada, between the Parisian region and the rest of France, large disparities of wealth and income persist. But for the most part, these can not be ascribed to actions of the state.

With respect to unemployment, the U.S. and Canada make the best current showing, Bulgaria the worst. In the two North American nations, unemployment has ceased to be a political problem. The right of employers to hire and fire at will permits very rapid adjustments in labor supply and demand. The four western European countries, which give workers much greater job security, now suffer from chronically high unemployment. The impact is cushioned by generous, long-term assistance to the unemployed.

It used to be taken for granted that increases in per capita national wealth would be accompanied by the increasing equality of income and wealth. That was clearly the trend in the U.S. for most of the twentieth century. But since 1980, the trend has reversed. The distribution of income and wealth in the U.S. is now much less equal than in any of the other countries in the set. Inequality has recently been increasing in Canada also, but much more slowly.

Meanwhile, the gradual progress of equality continues in France, Spain and Italy, and seems to be stalled, perhaps temporarily, in Germany. In all four of these democratic nations, there is a vast gulf between the rich and the poor, but the poor are not in abject need and the rich are not shamefully profligate, as in the United States.

All seven of these states now offer their citizens, free and open elections; freedom of speech, press and assembly; freedom of movement;

freedom of religion; freedom of marital and occupational choice; a large measure of free enterprise, and a fair degree of protection from abusive actions by agents of the state.

These traditional liberties protect the citizen far better from arbitrary exercises of state power than in the recent past. They are designed to prevent the recurrence of the hard tyrannies endured by the five European nations in our set at various times in the twentieth century and the not infrequent abuses of state power in the U.S. and Canada.

But the concept of liberty (or freedom) has been widened in all of these countries to include group rights and social goals that require the active intervention of the state in every aspect of collective life.

Thus, for example, in the U.S. since 1970, the federal government has extended its jurisdiction into all of the areas formerly reserved to the several states and into many areas that had been outside the purview of government at any level. The federal role is paramount in public education, criminal justice, scientific research, family policy, occupational safety, environmental protection, product advertising, medical care, abortion, gambling, automotive design, infant nutrition, the membership policies of private clubs, farm management, historic preservation and almost every other organized activity. The claims of ethnic minorities, of women, and of handicapped persons for preferential treatment in employment, housing, education, contracting, borrowing, are enforced by the federal government against private organizations as well as public agencies.

There are similar trends in all of the other countries in our set. In Canada and France, the government ordains which languages may be used in particular contexts. Bulgaria oscillates between the small state that its people prefer and the large state which might be capable of transforming the national society. The German state struggles with the challenging assignment of equalizing the social conditions of east and west Germans. In France, Italy, Quebec and Spain, the declining role of the Catholic church leads inexorably to the assumption of additional responsibilities by the state.

As each of these states more and more closely supervises the relationships between parents and children, employers and workers, priests and parishioners, teachers and students, neighbor and neighbor, man and nature, private authority of every kind decays. The state becomes responsible not only for building roads and bridges but for reviewing parental competence, suppressing flirtation in the workplace, setting the menu of school lunches, prescribing the proper care of pet animals, overseeing the grading practices of school teachers, changing the smoking habits of the population, supervising the sale of used cars, and performing innumerable other functions for which it was not originally designed.

The resulting soft tyranny puts every citizen under the direct control of the state in the activities of daily life This soft tyranny is much easier to bear than the harsh tyrannies of other eras. But it is also much harder to resist.